BLACK LIVES AND
SPATIAL MATTERS

A Volume in the Series
Police/Worlds: Studies in Security, Crime, and Governance
Edited by Kevin Karpiak, Sameena Mulla,
William Garriott, and Ilana Feldman

A list of titles in this series is available at cornellpress.cornell.edu.

BLACK LIVES AND SPATIAL MATTERS

Policing Blackness and Practicing
Freedom in Suburban St. Louis

Jodi Rios

CORNELL UNIVERSITY PRESS   ITHACA AND LONDON

First published 2020 by Cornell University Press

Library of Congress Cataloging-in-Publication Data

Names: Rios, Jodi, 1967– author.
Title: Black lives and spatial matters : policing blackness and practicing freedom in suburban St. Louis / Jodi Rios.
Description: Ithaca [New York] : Cornell University Press, 2020. | Series: Police/worlds | Includes bibliographical references and index.
Identifiers: LCCN 2019058749 (print) | LCCN 2019058750 (ebook) | ISBN 9781501750465 (hardcover) | ISBN 9781501750472 (paperback) | ISBN 9781501750489 (epub) | ISBN 9781501750496 (pdf)
Subjects: LCSH: Blacks—Race identity—United States. | Blacks—Race identity—Missouri—Saint Louis Suburban Area. | Race—Social aspects—United States. | Space—Social aspects. | Discrimination in criminal justice administration—Missouri—Saint Louis Suburban Area. | Sociology, Urban—Missouri—Saint Louis Suburban Area.
Classification: LCC HT1581 .R56 2020 (print) | LCC HT1581 (ebook) | DDC 305.896/073077865—dc23
LC record available at https://lccn.loc.gov/2019058749
LC ebook record available at https://lccn.loc.gov/2019058750

*This book is dedicated to those who struggle in St. Louis,
past, present, and future.*

This system is not broken; it is doing exactly what it was designed to do. There's nothing broken about it. We will have to show you that your perfect system doesn't work for us.

—Mama Cat

Contents

A Note on Figures

I made a methodological decision early on in this project not to carry a camera or take photos by phone at any point in this research because the act of photography inherently alters the relationship between the photographer and the "subject." For this reason, the photographs included in this book were taken by photojournalists or posted on social media and reprinted with permission.

Acknowledgments

This book has been almost twenty years in the making and has benefitted from the influence, insight, and support of so many people that it is not possible to name them all. Foremost are the many people of North St. Louis County who prompted me to begin asking questions in the first place and who generously shared their stories over the years, always challenging me to "get it right." Determinations of whether or not I have succeeded in getting it right will, I am sure, vary across readers, and I could have spent several more years in the attempt. Nevertheless, the rudder that set the course for this work was always steered by the people and voices of this place. Additionally, the individuals who told their stories from the perspective of Ferguson resistance and entrusted them to this book were constantly on my mind as I wrote the final draft. It is my sincere hope that I've honored those stories.

There are a few specific people whom I want to thank up front, who greatly and explicitly contributed to this research. Angel Carter's work, her ability as an interviewer, and her insight into the issues facing Black people in this region, and particularly Black women, were unequivocally essential to this book. Without her help it would be so much less than it is. The assistance of Brandice Carpenter, Anuradha Samarajiva, Daniel Sachs, and Adrian Smith was also critical, and I am deeply indebted to them.

At Cornell University Press, the backing and encouragement of Jim Lance and the meticulous attention to detail by the editorial staff made the publishing process remarkably easy. I greatly appreciate their persistent belief in the book and commitment to making it the best that it could be. I cannot say enough about the efforts of the coeditors of the Police/Worlds series, Kevin Karpiak, Sameena Mulla, William Garriott, and Ilana Feldman. Their hard work and support were absolutely essential. Sameena Mulla, in particular, went above and beyond the call of duty with her tireless reading and rereading of chapters and with her dependably productive comments and suggestions—I am grateful for her dedication.

I began the research for this book while on the faculty of architecture and urban design at Washington University, and many colleagues influenced and supported this work. The geneses of my "undisciplining" approach to research occurred when Tom Thomson, upon retirement, entrusted me with the cross-disciplinary, cross-institutional course he had helped to develop over many years, and I am grateful for his faith in me. Several people involved in that course, including John Ammann, Peter Salsich, and Mary Domahidy, all of St. Louis University, shared their extensive experience of working with, rather than in, communities, and it was through the Urban Issues Symposium that I began working with residents of North St. Louis County. I could not have carried out the early phases of this project without the support of the two deans of architecture and urban design I worked under during my time at Washington University. Cynthia Weese allowed me the flexibility to explore emergent issues through my courses, and Bruce Lindsey enthusiastically supported and expanded the scope and reach of the work upon his arrival at the school. My colleague and friend Bob Hansman exemplifies what it means to teach, and live, the change one desires, and his mentorship profoundly impacted my approach to teaching and research. I am additionally thankful to Carl Safe, Gay Lorberbaum, Lindsey Stouffer, Stephen Leet, Zeuler Lima, Paula Lupkin, Peter MacKeith, Barbara Levine, Carmon Colangelo, Sandy Cooper, the late Sandy Brennan, Patty Heyda, Don Koster, Derek Hoeferlin, Ian Fraser, and Heather Woofter, who supported me in various ways during those years. I am, however, most indebted to the many students who taught me so much and greatly contributed to this work through their insights in class and participation with communities.

This book was significantly informed by the research carried out by the team of faculty, students, and community members for the health impact assessment in Pagedale, of which I was part. The assessment was supported by the Robert Wood Johnson Foundation, Washington University's Institute for Public Health and Center for Social Development, and the Missouri Foundation for Health, and revealed many of the issues taken up by this book. I am particularly thankful for my collaboration with Christine Hoehner, whose high bar regarding the integrity of research became the test I would employ in my subsequent work. I am also grateful to Faye Millett and to Chris Krehmeyer for sharing so much of their knowledge with me and for their dedication to this area.

Many people read early drafts and chapters and their critical insights improved this book greatly. My consistent engagements with Stephen Small and Ula Taylor, who supported and encouraged me toward pushing the limits of my methodological approach, were absolutely critical to the conceptual development of the book. I could not have written part II without the help of Nadia Ellis, whose laser-sharp critiques brought clarity and depth to my analyses. Likewise, there are several chapters in part I that were significantly advanced with the focused reading of Michelle Wilde Anderson. I am deeply grateful for the countless hours Donald Moore spent in conversation with me and his unrelenting insistence on clarifying and fine-tuning the fundamental concepts that undergird the overall work. George Lipsitz, whose shared interest in the St. Louis region made him an early mentor and interlocutor, never turned down a request to read chapters. His unwavering belief in me and the importance of this project made a huge difference when the road appeared very long. Kim Hester Williams enthusiastically read the entire manuscript at several stages, and her willingness to hold me accountable when needed was so appreciated.

Many more people lent support by graciously reading chapters, talking through conceptual roadblocks, affirming and challenging ideas, or simply sharing their wisdom. My heartfelt appreciation goes out to each of them. Listed in terms of space and time, these include Carolyn Finney, Loïc Wacquant, Paul Rabinow, James Holston, Margaret Crawford, Paul Groth, Michael Johns, Jill Stoner, Rosemary Joyce, the late Maggie Garb, Milton Reynolds, Manolo Callahan, Sunny Lim, Yoel Haile, Bruce Haynes, Jesus Hernandez, Christen Lee, Rosa Linda Fregoso, Juan Herrera, Marcia McNally, Tarecq Amer, Ines Schaber, Mathias Heyden, Tony Platt, John Archer, Colin Gordon, Thomas Harvey, Angela Harris, Walter Johnson, Arturo Escobar, Vicki Swyers, Joan Solomon, Terry Jones, Lee Smith, Tayé Foster Bradshaw, DeAndrea Nichols, and the late Bassem Masri. I am also thankful to the anonymous readers for Cornell University Press, who thoroughly engaged the work, calling attention to the weak links while affirming that which must not be lost in revisions.

I cannot adequately express what this book and I myself owe to Michael Rios. Beyond the intellectual insight and critical discussions that directly impact almost every page, his everyday encouragement and practical support were unmeasurable in terms of simply completing this project. Our children, who collectively make up the quilt we call family, do not remember a time when I was not doing this work, and my presence was often sacrificed for its sake. Thank you to Sam, Maria, Zach, Olivia, Mateo, and Julia for that sacrifice and for inspiring me each day to try to live up to the claims that I make.

Chapter 3 was published, in a different form, in "Racial States of Municipal Governance: Policing Bodies and Space for Revenue in North St. Louis County, MO," *Law and Inequality: A Journal of Theory and Practice* 37, no. 2 (2019): 235–308. Some material found in chapters 4 and 5 was published in "Everyday Racialization: Contesting Space and Identity in Suburban St. Louis," in *Making Suburbia: New Histories of Everyday America*, edited by John Archer, Paul J. P. Sandul, and Kate Solomonson (Minneapolis: University of Minnesota Press, 2015), 185–207. I first explored a few of the themes presented in chapters 6 and 7 in "Flesh in the Street," *Kalfou: Journal of Comparative and Relational Ethnic Studies* 3, no. 1 (2016): 63–78.

List of Abbreviations

ACTION Action Council to Improve Opportunities Now
MORE   Missourians Organizing for Reform and Empowerment
NSD   Normandy School District
OBS   Organization for Black Struggle
SLU   St. Louis University
TIF   tax increment financing

Voices

Most of the residents and activists quoted and named in this book were interviewed by the author or by a trained research assistant with ties to North St. Louis County and/or the protest community. Interviews were conducted and recorded according to protocols approved by Washington University or University of California, Berkeley. Respondents were asked whether they wished to have their first names used and cited in the research. Although the majority of respondents requested to be named and cited, the identifying information for several people was not reliable. In the case of those who wished to remain anonymous or whose information was insufficient to use, pseudonyms were randomly assigned using pseudonym software.

The people who provided extensive interviews and whose voices and insight appear throughout the chapters that follow include: Alexis, Alisha, Angel, Antwan, Brianna, Brittany, Cameron (pseudonym), Cassandra (pseudonym), Cathy/Mama Cat, Cheyenne, Chuck, Darwin (pseudonym), Diamond, E. J., Estell (pseudonym), Evelyn, Gloria (pseudonym), "Haiku Unsung," Ivy (pseudonym), Jamell, Jonathan, Ms. Jones, Kathryn (pseudonym), Kelly, Kiera, Kristina (pseudonym), Marlene, Mary (pseudonym), Mitchell, Mr. Moff, Nell (pseudonym), Patrice, "Sixela Yoccm," Tia (pseudonym), Valerie (pseudonym), Vanessa (pseudonym), William.

BLACK LIVES AND SPATIAL MATTERS

DANCING WITH DEATH

We talk about the people who are dead a lot but we don't talk about the people who are alive and living this every day; because they don't value our lives.

—Kiera (pseudonym), resident of Pagedale, Missouri

In the suburbs of North St. Louis County, city governments discipline and police Black residents as a source of steady revenue.[1] The same city governments that fine residents simultaneously fail to provide many basic services to the community, except for an ever-expanding police force. To put it in the way many residents do, municipalities view poor Black residents as "ATM machines," to which they return time and again through multiple forms of predatory policing, juridical practices, and legalized violence. As part of this system and to hold on to the coveted yet hollow prize of local autonomy, Black leaders invest mightily in the white spatial imaginary of the suburbs by adopting a rhetoric of producing good citizens, promoting safety, protecting private property, and upholding norms of respectability.[2] Narrated through questions of rights and *suburban citizenship*, the double bind of living as Black in North St. Louis County means that Black residents both suffer from, and pay for, the loss of economic and political viability that occurs when they simply occupy space.

Risk

The systems that create and profit from this double bind rely on tropes of Black deviance, honed over the course of centuries; the illegibility of Black suffering; and questions concerning Black personhood. These systems confirm new and old claims that racialism, which is rooted in antiblack logics of thought and policy, is ever-changing yet no less with us now than ever. Ironically, the quest for Black political empowerment in North St. Louis County utilizes and perpetuates the same attachments of risk, precarity, and fungibility that followed Black families into the suburbs and left tiny cities—that quickly became majority Black—with few options for remaining economically solvent.[3]

In addition to experiencing traffic stops for every possible vehicular and driving infraction, residents throughout North St. Louis County are policed for the number of people around their barbecues, the types of music they listen to, the coordination of their curtains, the way they wear their pants, where they play basketball, how they paint their back doors, where their children leave their toys, who spends the night at their houses, who parks a car in their driveways, and how they use their front porches.[4] Although these low-level infractions may appear trivial relative to the scope of mass incarceration in the United States, they follow a similar pattern of catastrophically entangling residents in the legal system for decades. Since many residents cannot pay the high fines and fees for the inordinate number of citations handed out across this geography, tens of thousands of residents face warrants for their arrest and jail time, which impose even more fines and fees, not to mention numerous other impacts on their lives and livelihoods.[5] In some municipalities, residents justifiably fear the city will take their property and demolish their homes if they are unable to fix aesthetic yet non-safety-related issues with their dwellings.[6] Cumulatively, this has led to what many residents express as a lifetime of indebtedness and fear, and a feeling of being trapped in a place they do not have the means to leave.

The policing of minor infractions occurs in municipalities across the United States and is a primary method used by the broken-windows policing policy made famous in New York City and developed by the then police commissioner Bill Bratton in 1994.[7] However, the specific and extreme forms of cultural and spatial politics used to implement policing practices at an intimate scale in North St. Louis County occur at the intersection of discursively produced *urban* (Black) residents in historically produced *suburban* (white) space. And, while broken-windows policing is also known to target nonwhite people across the United States, the implementation of practices in this area keenly demonstrates the interdependencies between race and space and the powerful role spatial imaginaries play in producing racialized bodies in and through space—how bodies code/de-code space and how space codes/de-codes bodies.

This case also illustrates how metropolitan space and local governance are critical instruments in the remaking of the modern racial state and processes of subject-making (and subject-unmaking).[8] Municipal officials have become the authors and administrators of urban austerity policies and increasingly act as gatekeepers of citizens' rights in what Neil Brenner and Nik Theodore describe as geographies of "actually existing neoliberalism."⁹ Borrowing from well-developed discourses of propriety, risk, and property rights perfected by much larger cities, administrators of tiny majority-Black municipalities in North St. Louis County write, pass, interpret, and justify laws and policies that discipline residents and extract revenue through formal and informal policing and real and perceived forms of oversight and surveillance that appear rational and routine.¹⁰

Racialized policing and governing practices in North St. Louis County shocked many people who live elsewhere when these practices were exposed in 2014 by people protesting the killing of Michael Brown Jr. in the city of Ferguson (which sits in this geography). This book, however, documents how cities across this area have been carrying out similar practices for decades—practices that were unnoticed or ignored by all except those who experience them daily.¹¹ As modes and motivations of policing were made public, revealing that some cities fund as much as 48 percent of their municipal budgets through fines and court fees, residents and outside observers alike accused Black leaders of coveting power, mismanaging city funds and budgets, and practicing what some understood as Uncle Tom politics—using the "tools of the master" to gain political clout and oppress other Black people.¹² At first glance, there is evidence to support some of these claims. However, none of these public assertions considers how or why these cities and their leaders were put in the position of relying on predatory policing in the first place, nor do they recognize the obstacles that many leaders, especially Black women, have consistently overcome in order to reach and hold on to leadership positions. Taking an expanded view of these factors brings a much more complicated story to light.

When Black women, who today hold the majority of elected offices in North St. Louis County, began to win hard-fought municipal elections in the 1970s, the risk historically attached to them and their Black constituents was already driving investment and resources out of their historically white jurisdictions. This trend, described later in this book, accelerated quickly as more and more Black families moved to this area of suburbs from the City of St. Louis throughout the 1980s. As a result, public and private investment declined, redlining practices and Home Owners' Loan Corporation guidelines blocked lending in many neighborhoods, blockbusting tactics and racial steering by real estate agents lowered property values and sent white families to outer suburbs, and growing majority-white municipalities on the metropolitan periphery poached resources (such as state, federal, and private development dollars and amenities such as groceries stores) out of cities left behind. Nevertheless, elected officials across North St. Louis County needed to keep municipal budgets solvent and provide basic services to residents or face disincorporation. Driven by a fierce desire to hold on to real and perceived political gains made in the 1960s, Black leaders turned to what were already well-established practices of using suburban norms to police residents, and further capitalized on perceptions of Black criminality and social deviance in order to fill increasing gaps in city budgets. The same historical forces that drained resources out of North St. Louis County—through the linking of Black people to risk—proved highly effective for generating new "legitimate" sources of funding to maintain political autonomy, albeit as a hollow prize symbolically awarded to Black enfranchisement.[13]

The complex and often paradoxical motivations behind Black leaders' seeming propensity for preying on poor Black residents are also evidenced in various forms of respectability politics used both by and against Black women who hold leadership positions in North St. Louis County. The Black women in elected office I spoke with throughout this study vehemently denied that a need for revenue drives policing practices. On the basis of these interviews, it appears that most Black women in leadership truly believe they are simply claiming their right to live in an aesthetically pleasing, safe, and economically viable environment where people care about their property and abide by basic codes of conduct— a right that they also recognize as providing a much-needed funding source. Leaders additionally claim that policing residents is not an issue of race or class. As one leader put it, "we're all Black and we're all poor," although degrees of poverty between leaders and some residents could be argued. Complicating the narrative of predatory governance, it became clear in speaking with these women that they have for decades pushed back against racialized, gendered, and sexualized stereotypes specifically attached to visible Black women and have overcome a multitude of oppressions waged against them. Interviews with residents, however, revealed that these same leaders utilize racialized and gendered tropes of Black male masculinity and female promiscuity, in addition to perceptions of urban incivility, to implement and justify policing practices that in turn fund city services. Thus, Black women in both formal and informal leadership roles in this area simultaneously embrace and resist practices that are deeply rooted in constructions of blackness, class, gender, sexuality, and suburban space. Black women are in fact central to the two critical stories told by this book—the story of extreme practices of policing and the story of radical practices of freedom.

Freedom

Although Black residents across the St. Louis region have resisted oppressive and antiblack practices for centuries, this resistance recently became visible to a world audience when protestors, especially young Black women and Black queer individuals, used their "out-of-place" and "in-the-way" bodies to disrupt racialized, heteronormative, and gender-compliant constructions of regional power. This book argues that although it was not specifically named by Ferguson protesters, the history and contemporary use of suburban respectability rooted in risk to police residents for profit in this area, as well as particular histories of racialization in St. Louis, heightened the degrees of performance, visibility, and efficacy of blackness, and the imaginative capacity of embodied Black resistance. Ferguson resistance resonated with people suffering multiple forms of violence and unfreedom across continents and did much to launch a sustained critique of antiblackness at local, national, and global scales. What came to be known as the Ferguson Protest Movement revealed how the same visibility that registers death—the image of Michael Brown's slain body lying on the hot blacktop for hours on a hot summer day as his parents pleaded with officials—can also expose the unique capacity of blackness to embody freedom in the face of death and to imagine other worlds, other futures. This type of embodied freedom, what I call *an ethics of lived blackness*, or blackness-as-freedom, not only holds the potential to liberate those suffering the legacies and realities of physical, emotional, and economic bondage (colonial pasts and presents) but also offers hope to a larger society that is unaware of its own condition of unfreedom: a world that currently faces a shared lack of a future.

In North St. Louis County, dynamics of place and people specific to the experience of this region converged to shape a social movement that leveraged and connected particular histories and experiences of blackness while simultaneously drawing from a shared diasporic belonging and struggle. This reckoning with the intimacy of alterity, as Nadia Ellis observes, is part of Black experience found in different modes of diasporic belonging, all of which are haunted by ghosts of the historical past and present.[14] The body of Michael Brown lying in a street in North St. Louis County released another form of "flesh in the street" that, unlike Brown's victimized flesh, demanded the reconfiguration of how blackness is understood, claimed the right to live without fear, and revealed the radical futuring work of Black people, particularly those who also identify as women, queer, and trans, in the advancement of liberatory projects. Although this movement emanated from the specificity of this geography, it required a deterritorialization of gendered bodies and a forced reckoning with the risk associated with the same racialized, gendered—dehumanized—bodies that keep municipal governments across North St. Louis County economically desperate and financially solvent.

The ephemeral space of violence that displayed Brown's desecrated body and the space of resistance that was opened up by a very different form of visibility in the suburbs of St. Louis became worldwide symbols of how both profane and sacred spaces can paradoxically exist within the same place. The bodies that *appeared* in North St. Louis County connected diaspora subjects in both horrific and beautiful terms, linking Black experience, Black people, indeed blackness, across time and space—what Ellis describes as a "territory of the soul."[15] According to authorities in Ferguson, racist or racialized policing practices, formal or otherwise, did not lead to Michael Brown's death. The bodies that continued to show up night after night, month after month, however, haunted these claims like specters and ultimately connected practices of extreme violence, which residents across this region had lived with for decades, to historical violence that seeks to order Black (gendered) bodies. In this way, haunting moved beyond trauma and practical interventions such as body cameras on police officers, and into the realm of a something-to-be-done that imagines, and thus demands, alternative futures.[16]

What followed in the days after August 9, 2014, revealed a rupture in the status quo. Blackness—as an intentional praxis, rather than a conferred identity—was reconfigured as a register of freedom *in this space*, and it held, even if for a moment, the possibility to shift defuturing paradigms. For those able to see these ghosts, the short stretch of Canfield Drive where Brown died may just as well have been the hold of a ship traveling the Middle Passage. The tree that hung over Brown's body in the street could easily have been the tree where a Black body hung just a few decades prior. The visibility of the body on that particular day had distinctive resonance in a place where violence, as an act of control, exploitation, and desperation is not exceptional but mundane—violence that many deemed necessary in order to compensate for the outcomes of risk that follow blackness through time and space.

Producing and policing "disposable life" in and through space are what make violence for profit in North St. Louis County, or anywhere else, possible and invisible. This is an extension of biopolitics, the politics of life, and what Achille Mbembe calls "necropolitics," a racialized politics of death.[17] These practices rely on expectations of what can or should happen to populations that are racially differentiated by establishing who should live fully (those intended to flourish), and who could die (those who are disposable). These practices also rely on racialized and differentiated space—protected spaces where suffering is never tolerated and spaces of abjection where suffering is not only tolerated *but expected*.

Space

North St. Louis County was originally developed and promoted as a space for people who "should live fully." It is a mix of turn-of-the-century garden suburbs where elite white families spent summers, and of post–World War II working-class suburbs where many European immigrants staked their claim to the American

Dream and became unarguably white. The space where people should live fully, however, became occupied (or "infiltrated," as policy briefs often described it) by people who could not, no matter where they lived, become white. Black families moved to the suburbs to participate in the American Dream but claiming or gaining the full benefits of suburban citizenship remained out of reach. Rather, they found that the space was recoded as urban because imaginations of sub-urban space precluded the presence of risky urban (Black) people. For reasons explained in chapter 2, the demographic inversion (from majority-white to majority-Black) in North St. Louis County was swift. The spatial dissonance that resulted from the intersection of opposing spatial meanings—space that requires protection and space where suffering is expected—produced the double bind of living as Black in the historically white suburbs of St. Louis County.

The historical and perpetual tolerance of Black suffering and acceptance of premature Black death create the spaces where suffering is expected and where death is considered routine. The space of the "ghetto," understood today as Black urban space or the inner city in the United States, represents, and is, a place where suffering is normalized and life is viewed by those on the outside as having com-paratively little value. The mythical space of the suburbs was and is imagined and produced in contradistinction to, and is necessarily dependent on, imaginations of dark urban space, even though suburban space has always had levels of diver-sity. This is a biopolitical dialectic whereby the white spatial imaginary of *making live* in the suburbs is dependent on the very real possibility of *letting die* in the inner city. Of course in reality the suburbs are not a panacea, for reasons many people have identified. A collective imagination of space, however, is a powerful thing. As described later in this book, North St. Louis County is rhetorically rep-resented as *suburban* when referring to its white past and definitely described as *urban* when confronting its Black present. Throughout North St. Louis County, Black residents themselves simultaneously embrace and reject representations and identities of urban and suburban people, and their contingent and often contradictory expectations and definitions of urban or suburban space reflect their experience of feeling both in and out of place.

Hortense Spillers conceptualizes the expectation of suffering as the basis of exploitation of gendered Black bodies, which she describes as "pornotrop-ing."[18] The pornotrope is that which is exploited on the basis of the expectation, normalization, and tolerance of sustained suffering. For Spillers, the gendered Black body, like the object of pornographic desire, occupies a unique position between subjectification and objectification, between revulsion and desire, in ways that perpetuate perceptions of deviance and the less than human, yet also create unspoken and forbidden desire and intrigue through processes of objec-tification. The representational humanity, freedom, and protected life of the "selected" white male subject was critically dependent on the dysselected slave object understood as subhuman, unfree, and necessarily exposed to death. These mutually dependent binaries—human/subhuman, free subject/bound object, life/death—construct whiteness in contrast to blackness in all subsequent iterations of racialization, what Saidiya Hartman describes as the afterlife of slavery.[19] These same binaries construct the imaginations and, in many cases, the realities of urban and suburban space. In the same way Black people are dehumanized, subjugated, denied, and rendered deviant, yet consumed through othering and objectification, porno*topologies* represent deviant and risky space where suffering is expected and illicit desire is fetishized, commodified, and consumed by popular culture (i.e., in clothing, music, dance, visual arts, and other representations associated with "ghetto" and urban space).[20] North St. Louis County is a libidinal geography where "the virtual absence of prohibitions or limitations in the determination of socially tolerable and necessary violence sets the stage for the indiscriminate use of the body for pleasure, profit, and punishment."[21]

Pornotroping is integral to the perpetual tolerance of Black suffering and the acceptance of premature Black death. Likewise, pornotopologies are spaces where it is not just acceptable but expected that the indiscriminate policing of residents for revenue occurs and where events like the "justified" death of an unarmed Black teenager and the prolonged terror inflicted by the public desecration of the corpse are considered routine. Hartman asks, "What does the exposure of the violated body yield? Proof of black sentience or the inhumanity of the 'peculiar institution'? Or does the pain of the other merely provide us with the opportunity for self-reflection?"[22] For those who do not live in North St. Louis County, self-reflection can provide an opportunity to be glad one has the means to live elsewhere. But in these historically white suburbs the exposure of the violated Black body also poses a problem in that it provides proof of suffering where suffering was not tolerated, proof of a peculiar institution in a society that claims such things are over and done with. A particular visibility of the violated body in a place of extreme violence, and the subsequent work of sentient bodies—as an embodied blackness—gave rise to a movement that forces a different type of self-reflection. A reflection that asks, "Where does inhumanity lie relative to this peculiar institution?"[23] Whether or not we are moved to reflect differently remains to be seen.

The pornotopology is an important conceptual framework used in this book to understand space where thresholds of the intolerable are constantly in flux and where subjectivities and identities of oppressor and oppressed collide and become blurred. The pornotopology is the space produced and controlled through the repetition of justified violence, seen and unseen. It is a container of risk attached to dark gendered bodies, but it is also fetishized as a place where opportunity and freedom are said to exist for all yet are available to a few. North St. Louis County is not the ghetto or Black urban space. Nor can it be understood as the suburbs, or even a simple relocation of the ghetto to the suburban context. Rather, it is a pornotopology where life is consistently and ruthlessly mediated through the signifiers of protected suburban space and precarious urban bodies. Importantly, it highlights how differentiated rights and differentiated expectations of life and death are produced and maintained in and through space.

A Note on Methods

Long before Michael Brown's body lay on a street in North St. Louis County and before most people had heard of a place called Ferguson, I began the research that would become this book. In 2002, as a faculty member at Washington University, I set out to develop a pedagogical approach to teaching and research that would challenge conventional service-learning models by tying all components to two overarching questions: How can place-based teaching and research shift the assumptions of future decision makers regarding places and people? And how can engagement facilitate community-driven outcomes? Having seen and been involved in service-learning teaching that expected time and energy from communities and offered nothing in return, I did not want to replicate that approach. Consequently, I pursued a relationship with a nonprofit agency that worked in North St. Louis County and was willing to be a partner in efforts and help find funding for projects. Eventually the initiative evolved into a series of interdisciplinary graduate seminars, symposia, design-build studios, and funded research projects I oversaw and cotaught between 2002 and 2010.[24]

As I spent more and more time in North St. Louis County, I became aware of vast discrepancies between the stories told by residents regarding this area and those told by elected officials. Resident after resident relayed various versions of the same story: of seemingly unimaginable harassment and exploitation carried out by municipal police, inspectors, administrators, and judges in the form of traffic and nontraffic violations and associated fines and fees. As residents described it, these low-level infractions, such as "failure to secure a trash can lid," often led to increased economic hardships and jail time, and they almost always led to deep feelings of resentment and hopelessness. The everyday experiences of fear and loss associated with economic exploitation, physical harassment, confinement, and even death seemed to permeate residents' lives, and people often made connections to slavery, indentured servitude, and intimately lived experiences of segregation and second-class citizenship. Most residents I spoke to believed that the types of harassment and exploitation they experienced occurred because the neighborhoods in which they lived were majority Black and, for the same reason, regional decision makers either did not notice or did not care about what was going on. Many longtime residents who moved to what were then the white suburbs of North St. Louis County in the 1970s and 1980s explained that predatory policing was not new; however, they, as Black citizens, felt increasingly targeted as time went on.

The municipal leaders I spoke with told a very different story. Administrators and judges alike downplayed policing practices and blamed nonconforming residents when asked about residents' claims regarding high numbers of traffic and property violations and warrants issued across this area. Leaders consistently brought up the rights of the city to create "a nice environment," whereas the rights of residents were framed as conditional and tied to one's ability to "live as suburban." Leaders from the nonprofit agency with which the university was partnering repeated narratives that focused on personal responsibility and property maintenance, citing things like community asset building, neighborhood pride, and broken-windows policing to justify city practices. This was confusing to me because the agency was doing much to help poor residents secure housing and resources they needed to stabilize their everyday lives, but it also appeared to be straddling a line that separated the "undeserving" poor from those who could succeed in their programs.

Throughout the first two years of working with residents and leaders, I was struck by what appeared to be a locally scaled yet fully functioning police state justified and naturalized by Black municipal leaders using a cultural politics rooted in well-honed tropes of suburban respectability, white spatial logics, and Black deviance. Unlike people caught in what is conceptualized as "the prison pipeline," which ties disproportionate incarceration rates of nonwhite men and women to systems designed to permanently remove people from society, it appeared that residents in North St. Louis County were caught in a "catch-and-release" policing strategy that depended on the ability to derive a steady stream of revenue from the same people over and over again.

By 2005, my research turned toward exploring the specific histories and conditions that led to extreme forms of predatory policing. I was particularly interested in the work that culture, race, and space seemed to perform as means to enact and justify practices that appeared legal and allowed cities to differentiate and exploit residents in the name of the public good. Between 2006 and 2009, I actively worked at applying design-thinking—the way I was trained to see the world—to my research in North St. Louis County. This approach intentionally expands rather than limits variables and it blurs disciplinary boundaries, what Arturo Escobar has since called the accommodation of "radical relationalities."[25] It meant that next steps in the process were always determined in response to deeper forms of knowledge and emergent questions stemming from interactions with people and place; it required me to broaden the spectrum of scholarship and disciplinary fields by engaging with discourses outside of design and urban studies. As I continued to work in and with communities, I expanded the interdisciplinary initiative by coleading several funded community-focused research projects examining relationships between health (broadly defined) and spatial equity. During this time, I became increasingly aware of the inherent limitations of my faculty position in architecture and urban design, which included explicit roles and presumed ways of approaching education and practice. As the multiyear research project—a health impact assessment of a proposed development in North St. Louis County for which I was a principal investigator—began to wind to a close, the university's commitment to place-based teaching also seemed to be at a crossroads. For me to see this project through to its most ambitious conclusion, a change was needed.

In 2010, I made the difficult decision to leave my position at Washington University, uproot my family, and enter a doctoral program at University of California, Berkeley with the specific purpose of completing my study of North St. Louis County. Beginning the doctoral work in architectural history, I quickly transferred to the little-known interdisciplinary PhD program designed for projects that do not fit within any disciplinary home. Through this program, I worked between five departments and several more fields, including anthropology, geography, African American studies, law, history, sociology, English, ethnic studies, architecture, and city and regional planning. While North St. Louis County was the location of embodied research through which I encountered people, places, and events, this period provided the intellectual space and time to look deeply at the data and determine additional routes of historical research and conceptual frameworks needed to see underlying forces and relationships. Working outside of a department allowed me freedom to pursue mentors, interlocutors, and perspectives across many disciplines at critical points in the project. I was fortunate to work with a committee of distinguished scholars, each coming from a different disciplinary background, who supported my ethical commitment to an undisciplining methodological approach, while holding me to the highest standards of research. This strategic undisciplining of the work is evident throughout the book and does not mean that I do not deeply engage with disciplinary frameworks and perspectives; however, the overall project and this subsequent book do not follow singular disciplinary norms.

I was well into the writing phase of this project when the previously anonymous geography I had long struggled to explain to anyone outside St. Louis exploded onto the front pages of newspapers around the world. Sitting in California, I initially watched events in Ferguson unfold from a distance and saw the response of people with whom I was intimately connected. Many people advised me that a good social scientist keeps writing, ignores the noise, and regroups later. While I did not relish extending the time or the boundaries of the project, I was too deeply committed to a methodological process that foregrounds people, places, and events to ignore what was happening. I returned to North St. Louis County in September of 2014 for another six months of ethnographic research. As a result of that decision, this book took a completely different turn. In addition to adding many more voices, it was necessary to engage entirely new disciplines and bodies of literature in order to consider and contextualize the emerging resistance movement. These new engagements and concerns broadened the dimensions and the scope of the work but further muddied the intellectual waters—something I learned to embrace throughout this process.

As with many ethnographers and researchers, there is a gap between my own subjectivity and experiences, and those of residents and leaders in the communities I work with. Having begun my time in this area as part of a pedagogical praxis designed to challenge the assumptions and identities of my students and myself, as well as challenging accepted paradigms for publicly engaged teaching, I was prepared for some aspects of navigating this gap, though there were still many instances in which I was not well equipped. I had the benefit of having invested much time in the area and had produced tangible work with residents and leaders in the form of reports and policy briefs linking health disparities to policies and the built environment, as well as physical amenities my students had built in several neighborhoods in response to residents' input and requests. As a result, I was able to forge connections through established networks and a record of completing projects with mutual benefit. I found that middle-aged and older residents, regardless of gender or race, were more or less willing to talk to me at length about their experience and assessment of North St. Louis County. Conversations were further facilitated through a program for seniors my students initiated that helped older residents by fixing property-related issues, which resulted in many close relationships between myself, my student researchers, and elders. I also found that children under the age of sixteen routinely volunteered their unfiltered impressions of, and solutions for, their neighborhoods, and my students had worked for several years with after-school programs in order to better understand the experience and views of young people. Human subjects reviews at both Washington University and University of California, Berkeley understandably made the collection and use of data from this particular group challenging, however, which limited what was available from this group for formal analysis.

It was residents between the ages of eighteen and twenty-five who were generally uninterested in speaking to me. Their skepticism of a forty-something white academic who claimed to do research on race and space in North St. Louis

County could not be faulted. In order to include youth perspectives in my project, I relied on three paid research assistants from the area who were young and identified as Black women. These three women, Angel Carter, Adrian Smith, and Brandice Carpenter are deeply rooted in North St. Louis County and the region. All three went through human subjects protection training and were trained to conduct interviews. They were absolutely essential to the reflexive process of checking me and my assumptions regarding observations, analysis, and findings. Their impact and contributions to the project were great.

The reader will notice that throughout the book and particularly in part II, I include many direct quotes from those who shared their stories. These voices are often curated, or choreographed, as groups, some of which take up a page or two. These passages are a very intentional part of my methodology, and I include these voices when what they say does more justice to the emergent arguments than I could ever do. I also do this to include as many of the voices as possible, although there were many important things said that I simply was not able to include because of limited space. Some readers may be tempted to skip over these excepts because of their length, or believing that they are included to support a point that I am making. This would be unfortunate, since there are many things expressed in these excerpts that are not conveyed through my analytical text.

Reading This Book

Many people learned of this area through media coverage of Ferguson unrest in 2014, and this book will likely be categorized with those that directly emerged from those events. As I describe above, however, I began this research long before 2014, and the book would have been written, albeit in a somewhat different form, had Ferguson remained an obscure suburb somewhere in North St. Louis County. Although the forces examined in great detail throughout these chapters are the same forces that led Darren Wilson to stop and kill Michael Brown and also precipitated the events that followed, readers expecting a book about Ferguson will be disappointed. Rather, this book provides a backdrop against which to read events in Ferguson, as well as racialized practices across the globe.

Although it is not about Ferguson, this book does problematize many of the narratives that emerged "post-Ferguson." For example, in the months following the death of Michael Brown, reporters, as well as scholars writing op-ed articles and blog posts, often pointed to the majority-white leadership and police force in majority-Black Ferguson to explain degrees of the sustained unrest that was unfolding. A racial mismatch between those in power and the community, it was said, led to extreme predatory policing practices in this area, which were gaining public attention through the work of protesters.[26] Initial responses called for the election of Black leaders and the hiring of more Black police officers as primary means to remediate oppressive practices said to fuel anger and actions. This position assumed that Black residents in the many majority-Black cities in North St. Louis County with all-Black leadership and a greater percentage of Black police officers experience less predatory policing and racialized exploitation than in cities where Black residents are represented and policed by majority-white administrators and police officers.

The findings presented in the chapters that follow do in fact support the claims that predatory policing led to the circumstances of Michael Brown's death and, I argue, extreme forms of exploitation found in North St. Louis County did produce a particular and sustained form of resistance. The data, however, contradict the assertion that racial imbalances between leadership and residents are at the root of predatory policing practices. Majority-Black cities in this area with all-Black leadership and significantly higher numbers of Black police officers in fact carry out even more extreme predatory policing practices targeting so-called Black behavior than those seen in Ferguson.[27] As these statistics eventually came to light through the efforts of protesters and activist organizations, many people were quick to throw Black leaders under the proverbial bus, depicting them as greedy, power hungry, and incompetent. While it is hard to have empathy for leaders shown to prey on their own citizens, these simplified versions follow a long history of blaming Black leaders for conditions they did not create, attacking the character of Black officials, and categorically ignoring the root causes that place Black communities in catch-22 situations. In fact, as chapter 3 reveals, there is a direct correlation between degrees of resource poaching (out of majority-Black cities and into majority-white areas) and degrees of predatory policing (of residents in majority-Black cities), both of which trend upward as the percentage of Black citizens increases. As the data clearly show, poaching and predatory policing are not dependent upon the race or gender of elected officials. They do however rely on the logics of antiblackness, and in the case of North St. Louis County, these practices are contingent upon the percentage of Black people that occupy historically white space. Ultimately, these practices are both cause and consequence of the risk attached to Black residents.

At its core, this book is about two powerful sets of practices—the cultural politics of race and space that attaches risk to Black people and Black space, and the politics of possibility that reaffirms blackness as a unique site of imagination and freedom. My methodological approach was iteratively determined through encounters with people, places, and events over a fifteen-year period, and the organization of the book directly reflects this process, in that each chapter represents a different path taken and different disciplinary orientation.

By including what could be considered disparate studies within the same book, it is my hope that readers will see relationships and draw conclusions beyond those presented—in light of their own experiences, backgrounds, and perspectives.

The chapters are organized into two parts with a break in between. Part I provides the intellectual, historical, and experiential context for understanding the place of North St. Louis County, and it focuses specifically on how risk is attached to blackness and the outcomes produced through these processes. Part II shifts in both style and emphasis to look at the radical imaginaries deployed by people who became visible in North St. Louis County and who demonstrate practices of freedom embedded in blackness itself. The change that mobilized radical imaginaries of what could be in the face of what is in North St. Louis County was dependent upon the visibility of Black and nonconforming bodies, and it resonated because of the implausibility of the modern state's representational claims. In this case, it was the implausibility that the liberal state would deliver justice (for specifically Black individuals) under and through the law. Set between these two parts in the form of an interlude is a brief recounting of August 9, 2014, which represents a theoretical shift in the book and a practical shift in space and time.

Chapter 1 traces the ways by which culture is used to produce, police, study, and represent blackness specifically in conjunction with racialized metropolitan space in the United States; the cultural politics of race and space. This chapter is particularly intended for readers who may be unfamiliar with how contemporary urban policies and practices are rooted in the long arc of history that conflates culture, race, and space. Cultural politics is the scaffold for modes of informal disciplining, and it establishes the conditions of possibility for formal policing. When Darren Wilson said during questioning that Michael Brown looked like the Hulk because of his size and his face looked like a demon, adding that the community in which he was killed was a hostile community where nobody wanted to go, he deployed the cultural politics of race and space and did not need to explain what he meant. Chapter 1 outlines some of the contours of the cultural politics of race and space that are important for understanding the practices and phenomena in North St. Louis County. Because scholarship produces powerful discourses that reveal, obscure, and sanction violence in and through space, chapter 1 also considers the ways in which culture, race, and space have been historically conflated in different spaces of scholarship.

In chapter 2, I highlight some of the moments and patterns that are illustrative of the particularities and peculiarities of this region and are therefore important for understanding North St. Louis County. In many ways, the history of St. Louis in the latter part of the twentieth century closely follows the histories of most cities in the rust belt of the United States—in terms of de jure and de facto segregation in housing, education, and the labor force, as well as histories of suburbanization, discriminatory lending, and white flight. Chapter 2 pays particular attention to entanglements of race, space, and culture, and to the social, political, and geographic fragmentation that are unique to experiences in this region. In Hartman's words, "a history of the present strives to illuminate the intimacy of our experience with the lives of the dead, to write our now as it is interrupted by this past, and to imagine a free state, not as the time before captivity or slavery, but rather as the anticipated future of this writing."[28] Chapter 2 lays the groundwork for understanding how risk is attached to the lives of the dead and intimately connected to the lives of the living.

Much of the time I spent researching this book was focused on documenting the means, motivations, and extreme experiences of predatory policing practices in North St. Louis County. Chapter 3 brings this research together and provides a vivid account of the racialized methods that are used in North St. Louis County to extract money and resources from citizens. Foregrounded are the specific impacts these practices have on residents. By juxtaposing the stories of residents and leaders with statistical evidence of racialized municipal practices, I argue that many cities in this geography operate as localized racial states where one's access to rights and the ability to live freely are determined at the most intimate scale of governance. This chapter provides extensive evidence that the predatory policing of Black citizens is not tied to the race of leadership, as has been suggested. Rather, these practices are directly relational to the perceived risk and illegible suffering attached to the blackness of constituents. Adding an important layer of complexity to the larger story, the chapter goes on to consider how racialized regional practices and codifications of space led to circumstances that left municipal leaders with seemingly few options for remaining incorporated. From this standpoint, the book raises critical ethical questions regarding how these practices are framed in debates, where responsibility lies, and what rights tiny majority-Black cities have with regard to economic viability, beyond policing their own residents for revenue.

Looking at the detailed evidence of policing practices in North St. Louis County led me to study what makes these practices possible and invisible. Chapter 4 examines the discursive regimes—the making and unmaking of truth—upon which cultural politics in North St. Louis County relies. The cultural politics of space deploys culture as a regulatory discourse to produce spatial imaginaries and social meanings that explain disparity as a "natural consequence" of inferior Black culture. Using a discursively produced cultural politics of suburban citizenship and capitalizing on expectations of suffering in spaces qualified as urban, leaders, administrators, and judges police residents. This policing has cultural, spatial, economic, and embodied iterations, and is often neither measured nor checked. Additionally, contradictory identities (suburban and urban) that result from powerful spatial imaginaries are both claimed and deployed by leaders, residents, and law enforcement, sometimes interchangeably, in and about North St. Louis County, depending on the work these identities perform, the polities they mobilize, and the distinctions they are intended to make. This results in complex and nuanced relationships of race, space, and power that cannot be reduced to simplified readings of economic rationalism, identity politics, or racial imbalances in the police force.

Chapter 5 looks specifically at the City of Pagedale, which is an extreme example of how the white spatial imaginary of suburbia is deployed. This small municipality aggressively passes and enforces "quality of life" and "nuisance property" ordinances targeting circumstances of poverty and so-called Black behavior by criminalizing such things as hanging mismatched curtains, installing a basketball hoop, and wearing sagging pants. Pagedale, which made history as the first municipality in the United States to elect an all-Black, all-woman leadership in 1982, troubles many of the popular explanations for the "Ferguson uprisings" and complicates the idea that predatory policing by Black leadership is simply a result of power, greed, or corruption. As this chapter details, the Black women leaders who came into power in the 1980s used visibility to push back against the limits placed on their bodies—as Black and female—yet worked within the terms that had been set by previous administrations and the historical structures of racism and sexism that construct blackness-as-risk.

Part II makes an important shift toward the modes of resistance that arose in response to everyday policing after the exceptional yet routine event of Michael Brown's death. As the first chapter in part II, chapter 6 uses a framework of queer theory to argue that the particular aesthetic and affect of resistance in North St. Louis County made visible the extreme violence of the state in addition to exposing the inherent contradictions within masculine and heteronormative spaces of Black struggle. This is a critical component of queer of color critique. Similar to an Afro-pessimistic perspective of blackness, which locates Black life as a site of ontological death, this chapter argues that "the problem posed by blackness" is an antagonism rooted in the historically naturalized logics of society, including physical space, and is not a conflict that can be rectified through legal means. Through a more optimistic lens, this chapter also highlights the various ways Black women and gender nonconforming individuals practiced a choreopolitics—of bodies in space—that demanded the terms of visibility be set by those "in view."[29] This particular practice of visibility and an insistence on simply *living* as an act of protest illustrate the capacity and power that Black lives and life hold in revealing the truth (of who and what are actually inhuman) and thus reconfiguring the metrics of living as fully human.

Chapter 7 details the conflicts that arose between Ferguson protesters and local and national activist organizations, as well as the misrecognitions concerning relationships to, and alliances with, the Black Lives Matter organization and subsequent movements. These contestations of meaning, belonging, and territory, as well as concerns regarding who may speak for whom, reveal the multivalent and fluid conditions and constructions of blackness and gender. The Black diasporic subject (or nonsubject, as Frank B. Wilderson, III argues) is fundamentally shaped by shared loss, displacement, trauma, and forms of political death. But the ways individuals and groups generatively (and differently) practice sociality and antagonize beliefs about "civil society" are creative acts that draw from particularized experiences across space and time. In this way, blackness is "the irreparable disturbance of ontology's time and space."[30] The resistance that emerged in Ferguson interrogated the boundaries of Black intelligibility and exposed the tensions and contradictions that simultaneously exist within what Cedric Robinson called the ontological totality of Black struggle.[31] This chapter looks at some of those tensions in order to foreground the complexity and contradictions of an ontological blackness, which could also be understood as all that celebrates a location outside, or beyond, the world as we know it.

Taken together, the chapters that follow are a call to reconsider the epistemic violence that is committed when scholars, policy makers, and the general public frame Black precarity as just another racial, cultural, or ethnic conflict that can be solved through legal, political, or economic means. The historical and material production of blackness-as-risk is foundational to the historical and material construction of modern society and, as a critical component of antiblackness, it provides fundamental systems that order contemporary metropolitan space. Although the logics of antiblackness transfer across spectrums—of gender, ethnicity, class, sexual orientation—to create difference in relationship to power, these logics of differentiation absolutely rely on the historically contingent fungibility of the Black dispossessed person.[32] The positionality of blackness, as Wilderson (following Franz Fanon) has argued, is critical to understanding and intervening in processes of subjugation. Wilderson succinctly makes this point when he states, "Blackness cannot become one of civil society's many junior partners: Black citizenship, or Black civic obligation, are oxymorons."[33] The propensity of liberal politics and even radical social movements to misunderstand intersectional oppressions and represent Black abjection as but one problem facing civil society "cannot be called the outright handmaidens of white supremacy," but "their rhetorical structures and political desires are underwritten by a supplemental anti-Blackness."[34] The failure to understand blackness as violently, necessarily, and generatively located beyond the map of our current world forecloses the potential insight and access that an unmappable blackness may provide for imagining different worlds.

An ethics of lived blackness—living fully and visibly in the face of forces intended to dehumanize and erase—recognizes its location outside privileged positions of power, but it also recognizes this position as a powerful counterpoint to the current logics that order bodies and space. This embodied and emplaced praxis of blackness-as-freedom is an enduring response to places and systems built on the expectation and tolerance of Black suffering and premature death. While I do not argue for abandoning pursuits of legal, political, and economic solutions to vastly uneven distributions of resources across the globe, we will continue to reproduce structural and physical violence if we do not recognize how the logics of antiblackness undergirds every mode of injustice we seek to remediate. Likewise, efforts to fight against the many manifestations of unfreedom will be limited in their efficacy if we do not learn from the embodied and emplaced practices that reorient blackness as a fundamental location of freedom. As Wilderson also argues, "we must admit that the 'Negro' has been inviting whites, as well as civil society's junior partners [the nonblack worker, the immigrant, the woman], to the dance of social death for hundreds of years, but few have wanted to learn the steps. . . . This is not to say that all oppositional political desire is pro-white, but it is usually antiblack, meaning that it will not dance with death"[35]—the death (social, political, physical) that is conferred on Black life.

The ethics of lived blackness relies on the claimed visibility and location of Black life (as outside). It is lived through bodies that span physical, psychic, representative, and temporal identifications within and through blackness yet share in the ability to haunt historico-racial constructions of systems and spaces of gendered white heteronormativity. If ethics is, as Michel Foucault insisted, *the practice of freedom*,[36] then the persistent visibility of unapologetic blackness in the form of fully lived, fully desiring, fully outside Black flesh in the historically and violently constructed white gendered space of suburban St. Louis was and is a futuring dance of freedom in the midst of a defuturing world. Those who wish to learn the steps toward alternative futures must first be willing to dance with death.

Part I
BLACKNESS AS RISK

RACE AND SPACE

We knew we couldn't make it illegal to be either against the war
or black, but by getting the public to associate the hippies with
marijuana and blacks with heroin, and then criminalizing both heavily,
we could disrupt those communities . . . arrest their leaders, raid
their homes, break up their meetings, and vilify them night after night
on the evening news. Did we know we were lying about drugs? Of
course we did.

—John Ehrlichman, adviser to Richard Nixon

A cultural politics of race employs and conflates culture, race, and belonging
across space and time. In the four years it has taken to write this book, the political
rhetoric in the United States has relentlessly illustrated this statement as immigrants and citizens identified as "nonwhite" or Middle Eastern are portrayed
(through cultural signifiers) as threatening to and incompatible with so-called
American ideals. Evolving racial logics disguise racism in cultural references and
follow the routes of people, institutions, and increasingly globalized political cur-
rents. Although these logics manifest differently within the specificity of local
environments and temporal contestations of cultural practice, they rely on the
"persistent production of blackness as abject, threatening, servile, dangerous,
dependent, irrational, and infectious."[1] The state of Black fungibility and its relationship to the ordering of the modern world is theorized and named by Saidya
Hartman and many others across the field of Black Studies. Indeed, Black Studies
is a response to this condition. For the purposes of the arguments made in this
book, I refer to this condition as blackness-as-risk. This phrase acknowledges the
critical work that risk and fear perform within every dimension of subjugation—
social, cultural, physical, spatial, phenomenological.

Part one of this book specifically studies historical and contemporary forms
of cultural politics that produce and rely on blackness-as-risk in the context of
space, specifically the space of metropolitan St. Louis. It is therefore useful to
begin by considering some of the ways culture, race, and space have been discursively conflated and deployed and how cities in the United States directly reflect

and reproduce these legacies. For readers who may be unfamiliar with discourses of race and/or space, it is additionally helpful to review some of the ways scholarship codifies space in relationship to culture and race and how these codifications are used to advance political projects. Because this book is an interdisciplinary project rooted in a design-thinking methodology, this chapter also provides insight into the genealogy of concepts and disciplinary engagements informing the early stages of the research while drawing parallels to what I found in North St. Louis County.

Mapping Race

Although varying constructions of race linked to city-states, tribes, citizenship, and degrees of humanity appear in ancient texts, late seventeenth-century philosophers discursively established an ontological dualism by which reason and civilization were understood as synonymous with European culture, geography, and constructions of race. Simultaneously, unreason and savagery provided a culturally and territorially linked counterpoint *embodied* and *emplaced* in nonwhite populations and locations that were understood as reflective of an unevolved proximity to nature.[2] This is a critical legacy of Enlightenment thinking because it established Europe as the dominant frame of reference in Western philosophy and the arbiter of truth, effectively writing off non-European people and societies. The ontological binary of civilization and nature was the consistent racializing device employed by Enlightenment philosophy to order the world (and bodies) for its own purposes. Degrees of culture and savagery were mapped first to geography and national identity and then to bodies explained through climate. Many discussions sought to reconcile aberrations of skin color, skeletal features, and ingenuity of people originating outside of the "temperate zone" (of Europe) with reference to groups such as Asians, Native Americans, or displaced Africans.

Hegel, in his *Lectures on the Philosophy of World History*, used culture to famously write Africa out of history, linking "civilized" culture to geography and climate.[3] According to Hegel, Europeans, who were conveniently located in the temperate zone, "must furnish the theatre of world history" and had a responsibility, through slavery and colonization, to oversee and civilize supposedly uncultured non-Europeans. Hegel held little hope for the education of Africans, stating, "The condition in which they live is incapable of any development or culture. . . . In the face of the enormous energy of sensuous arbitrariness which dominates their lives, morality has no determinate influence upon them. . . . We shall therefore leave Africa at this point, and it need not be mentioned again."[4]

Intentionally linking European culture to a construction of "the human," Hegel acknowledged philosophically that slavery should not exist within humanity, since "humanity is Freedom," but he used the same logic to argue that the "Negro" must be matured into humanity. Thus he solved the problem slavery posed to the human by using enlightenment culture to locate Africans in a zone of "pending humanity." While indigenous and colonized peoples were mapped to locations said to possess uncivilized savage cultures, blackness, as represented by "the Negro," was conceptualized as lacking the capacity for culture and deterritorialized even from the map of Africa, commodified as labor to be bought, sold, and reproduced with no ties to geography or history. Through this cultural logic linked first to territory and then (very importantly) to deterritorialization, Hegel helped to establish the primary tenets from which contemporary racisms would evolve. These include the following (enduring) beliefs: slavery, unfreedom, or quasifreedom constitute an improved state for Black "beings"; white Europeans have a responsibility to manage "a race" whose humanity is in question; Africans, through no fault of their own, are devoid of culture and possess only a sensuous arbitrariness that lacks a moral capacity; and since Africa is erased from any hierarchy of world order, Black "bodies" no longer belong anywhere. The result is a stateless bare life.[5]

Racial logics that link culture to basic rights and freedoms (or lack thereof) persist today and are clearly seen in North St. Louis County, although manifested differently. For example, many municipal leaders in North St. Louis County argue that any circumstance in their jurisdictions is an improved state from that of the "urban ghetto." Many also argue that they have a responsibility to manage and teach a so-called urban population that does not know how to act in the suburbs, and the cultural inferiorities and uncivilized nature of people they describe as "moving from the projects" are justification for extreme policing practices.[6] As Sylvia Wynter theorizes, the attachment of a discursively constructed civilization to the Enlightenment construct of Man results in the conflations of Man, the human, and the white European in contrast to "the other," "the less than human," and African and nonwhite peoples.[7] In the case of North St. Louis County, the historically white suburbs are imagined as representative of civilized humanity, and the humanity of those moving from the "urban ghettos" is conveniently called into question, citing cultural and moral deficiencies rather than using overtly racist language. The same logics link a so-called cultural inferiority to economistic rationales for policing and harassment—"These folks don't know how to act in the suburbs, and that brings everybody's property values down."[8]

Roughly a century after the beginning of the French Revolution, which many scholars cite as the end of the Enlightenment era, a critical period emerged in the United States in which race, culture, and place were visibly reconfigured in metropolitan space. As the nineteenth century came to a close, the failed Reconstruction era denied benefits of full citizenship and personhood to Black Americans, and white backlash to Reconstruction policy produced new and virulent forms of everyday racisms based on old racial tropes as a means to assert white privilege in a postslavery society.[9] While cities across the globe have always been a location of exclusion and assimilation, the shaping of twentieth-century US cities reveals the specific work that space performs as a tool of racial exclusion, on one hand, and of ethnic assimilation on the other. This relegation of different races and ethnicities to different places developed at a certain moment in history when formal racial codes were threatened and increasing numbers of European immigrants were entering the United States. Working in tandem with frames of culture and fitness for citizenship, metropolitan space and spatial practices sorted populations, separating those that could be safely absorbed into white society and white space, those that posed a threat and must be contained in and through space, and those that occupied the marginal spaces in between. For example, the space of the ghetto, which was originally produced as a space of ethnic containment (most specifically the containment of Jewish residents within European cities) to minimize cultural and biological "contamination," was racialized in the United States according to evolving spatial logics aimed at undermining freedoms granted to Black citizens. In this way the space of the ghetto evolved into the urban container of risk, which was said to be posed by populations of color, with blackness occupying the furthest end of the risk spectrum.[10]

At the same time that racial meanings were shifting within the space of US cities, the boundaries of white citizenship were broadened to encompass ethnic Europeans through the occupation of equally racialized white space—especially within the space and imagination of the suburbs in the late 1800s and into the first half of the twentieth century. The imagined space of the early twentieth-century suburbs was developed in contradistinction to the dark spaces of the city and indeed relied upon this binary. While the ghetto was always viewed as a space of containment—an urban form of incarceration—the suburbs offered protection as a place that could only be penetrated by those who were perceived to pose no threat. The power of spatial imaginaries to link culture, race, and people is easily understood when we consider the layers of racialized meaning attached to simple codifications of metropolitan areas in the United States. Indeed, as the next chapter explains, the suburbs of North St. Louis County were originally marketed to elite St. Louis families as a place to escape the chaos, grime, and questionable humanity of the city between 1880 and 1930, and tracts of smaller single-family homes built after 1940 became a place where European immigrants claimed the full benefits and status of white citizenship. When Black families moved to this area beginning in the 1960s, spatial qualifications were necessary as the area became majority Black, such as the "suburban ghetto" and the "Black suburbs" of North County, indicating that space described as simply suburban is imagined as white and rarely needs qualification.

While culture has been fundamentally part of racialized difference for as long as race has existed as a concept, new forms of cultural politics in the United States were necessary to maintain racial hierarchies when legal policies that relied on inherited markers, such as skin color, were challenged. The fields of sociology and anthropology in the first half of the twentieth century did much of the work to locate racial difference more formally within the fluid realm of culture rather than fixed biological difference, although anthropology was in many ways founded on describing and sorting biologically defined groups. Lee Baker points out that "an obvious division of labor emerged in social sciences in the United States that enabled anthropology to specialize in describing the culture of out-of-the-way indigenous peoples while empowering sociologists to specialize in explaining the culture of the many in-the-way immigrant and black people."[11] Scholars contributing to the early field of cultural anthropology developed a rhetoric of racial apologia, which in turn created new cultural hierarchies linked to race. Franz Boas, for example, categorically dismissed evolutionary hierarchies and argued for a cultural relativism that did not qualify different cultures as necessarily better or worse. Boas, however, managed to provide the intellectual landscape of cultural hierarchy by which Native American culture (mapped to tribal locations) was deemed worthy of preservation while African American culture was reinforced as disposable.[12] Similarly, Boas's student Ruth Benedict, who focused her career on debunking biological racism and showing how race is constructed for the sake of power, used cultural citizenship as a metric, stating in 1940 that "great numbers of negroes were not ready for full citizenship."[13]

Some scholars working on antiracist projects from a sociological perspective also sought to debunk phenotypical markers by shifting discussions to that which could change—culture and rights of citizenship—as opposed to that which was represented as a given—biology. For example, W. E. B. Du Bois used the frame of fitness for citizenship in his early speech "The Conservation of Races," which argues against biological differentiation of "the Negro" while also suggesting that Black people at the turn of the twentieth century were not ready for full citizenship.[14] In this early work, Du Bois is still tied to Enlightenment concepts of civilization as he debates the degree to which the dark race contributed to civilized culture. Following Herder, from the standpoint of culture, nation, and citizenship, he discusses both the extent to which "the Negro" is American and the limits to that identity. Du Bois's conceptualization of double consciousness is important in that it operates at the level of a subjective self versus the objectified other, in addition to theorizing dual national identities—that of the American and, more importantly, the Pan-Negro, which he remaps back to Africa. The emphasis Du Bois places in the second half of the essay on racial uplift and the sociological vices of "the Negro" also responds to popular iconography of cultural degeneracy in the late Victorian era.[15] Similar ideologies that espouse notions of racial uplift and blame supposed cultural inferiorities for racial disparities form the basis for policing individuals and space in North St. Louis County today. In this case, the frames of suburban citizenship and a respectability politics based on the imagined norms of suburban culture are used to police so-called urban residents, justify the denial of basic rights, and extract profit from Black bodies deemed out-of-place.

Du Bois's "The Conservation of Races" closely coincided with his extensive sociological study of Black settlement, space, and experience in Philadelphia. *The Philadelphia Negro*, published in 1899, is one of the earliest sociological studies to formally link race and space and to acknowledge that all Black people in the United States—indeed, even in one city—do not have the same experience.[16] Using multiple datasets including household surveys, neighborhood audits and maps, and census data, Du Bois shows that differing experiences and identities are tied to location, environment, class, education, and family, and he illustrates a multiplicity of social structures across the Black community. As in the work of other Black intellectuals writing and lecturing at the turn of the twentieth century, the idea of racial uplift and moralizations based on class distinctions and behavior are evident throughout, with language concerning the "untutored race in whose hand lay an unfamiliar instrument of civilization."[17] While civilization is a prevailing frame, Du Bois links the problems of "the Negro" to physical and social segregation within *the city*. This precedent would establish the analytical tools for urban sociology several decades later, although Du Bois was not generally credited for this important work, nor were the complexities of Black culture that his work revealed taken up by white scholars at that time.

As culture and civilization continued as dominant reference points in early twentieth-century discourse and analysis of race and space, these frames were becoming increasingly important in the emerging fields of urban studies and urban sociology. The fetishization of Cartesian mapping and quantitative analysis of physical urban space by Enlightenment thinkers intersected with the growing subfield of urban sociology in early twentieth-century scholarship. Clearly using yet not referencing Du Bois's observations and methodology in his study of Philadelphia, scholars began to conceptualize the city as an urban ecology of social interaction, assimilation, and exclusion. Most notably with regard to the early confluence of spatial and social studies, the Chicago school of sociology under the direction of Robert E. Park and Ernest W. Burgess literally mapped race, culture, and ethnicity onto the physical space of Chicago as a way to analyze social relations in the city.[18] This method identified areas where clear physical and cultural boundaries contained distinct racial groups that, because of markers of blackness, "naturally" defied assimilationist logics.[19] Burgess also diagramed areas (figure 1.1) that formed concentric circles around the inner city where more porous boundaries allowed for the passage of ethnic Europeans out of the slums, which he describes as "the purgatory of 'lost souls,'" and toward the "Promised Land" of normative white society and space beyond the city center.[20]

In 1937, the urban historian and sociologist Lewis Mumford published what would become a highly influential essay in the study of metropolitan space and spatial practice titled "What is a City?" Although Mumford was an ardent critic

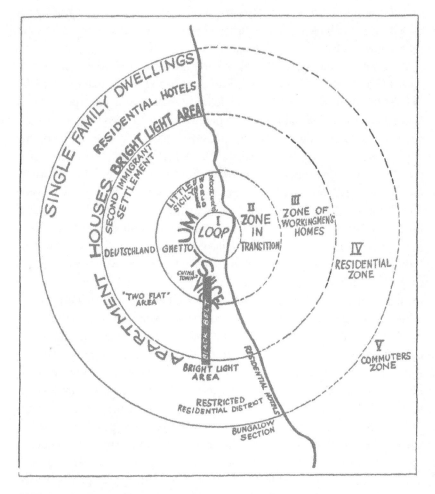

FIGURE 1.1   Ernest W. Burgess, "Chart II. Urban Areas," diagram of Chicago, 1925. Burgess, "Growth of the City," 55.

of modernist design, this piece translated what had become the mantra of modernist architecture, form follows function, into the urban scale.[21] As a critic of modernism, Mumford believed modernist design brought about what he saw as the destruction of cohesive cultures and the dehumanization of urban space, although Mumford's definitions of *culture* and *human* privileged white societal norms and racialized stereotypes. Mumford argued that the form of the city should respond to the social interactions and cultural requirements of its inhabitants. The success of his work and that of others who followed his lead, such as Jane Jacobs, did much to discursively link social space to physical space in urban policy and design. Ironically, however, modernists used such arguments to justify the clearing of nonwhite areas, which they claimed were ridden with pathological behaviors, to make way for infrastructure projects that facilitated suburban expansion and to build segregated urban housing projects that were said to solve urban social problems through design.[22]

A year after Mumford published "What is a City?," the Chicago school sociologist Louis Wirth published another urban critique titled "Urbanism as a Way of Life," in which he argued that space actively produces different types of social interactions and "personalities" within the city. Wirth believed that the modern city encourages individualism, anonymity, superficial relationships, and fictional kinships between people.[23] The analyses of both Mumford and Wirth drew upon the Garden City movement and operated from an urban/rural binary, which tended to judge "good space" as closer to nature, whereas "bad space" existed outside the natural or the human.[24] The discursive power of the suburban spatial imaginary that was developing at the same time used a similar frame and viewed the city as crowded, dirty, chaotic, and filled with questionable humanity. In contrast to the city, the spaces of garden developments and the new suburbs were celebrated for their low population density, their clean air, their orderly space, and the white "humanity" found within them. In all these examples, cultural norms were used to signify race (differentiating those who conformed from those who didn't) and to distinguish between good and bad space, while also reinforcing connections between such spaces and the "more human" or "less human" people who occupied them. Contrary to Enlightenment constructions and contemporary tropes of race, whereby nature was equated with the uncivilized and closer to the "less-than-human" races and cultures, discourses that emerged from the Garden City movement resignified nature as pure and good and theorized suburban space as the "most human" environment, in order to promote settlements outside the urban core.[25] Not surprisingly, these two contradictory frames of nature—as savage on one hand and unadulterated and pristine on the other—existed simultaneously and were deployed according to the work they were intended to do. The same advertisements for developments in North St. Louis County that evoked a lack of civilization and morality in the city utilized romanticized imagery that celebrated proximity to nature as a major selling point to both elite and working-class white families.

In 1939, soon after Mumford and Wirth published essays on the city, E. Franklin Frazier (also a student of the Chicago school) published *The Negro Family in the United States*, which, like Du Bois's *The Philadelphia Negro*, more specifically linked race to space and culture and, unlike the work of Park and Burgess, went beyond viewing Black space in strictly pathological terms.[26] Frazier intended the book as a historical analysis of forces shaping the domestic cultures of Black families migrating from the rural South to northern cities, and he attributed these forces to social rather than racial factors. Contrary to Mumford and Wirth, Frazier did not romanticize rural space; instead, he equated the rural with slave culture, which had in his view made Black migrants from the South less civilized than Black people living in northern US cities. As he saw it, southern "Negroes" were detrimental to culturally advanced urban Black social structures. Like the early writings of Du Bois, Frazier's work embraced the theme of racial uplift while also bringing nuance to understandings of Black identity and culture. Frazier's decoupling of distinct Black experiences was still a needed counterpoint to the tendency by white scholars and Black nationalist activists and scholars to lump blackness and Black identity in the United States within a singular definition.[27] In a similar vein, St. Clair Drake and Horace R. Cayton published an extensive ethnography in 1945, looking at the complex social structures and spaces of Black Chicago. Drake and Cayton looked with particular interest at class distinctions within the Black community, with specific attention to space. Although Frazier, Drake, and Cayton were sympathetic to the larger Black community and intended to add levels of complexity to views of Black culture and identity while holding white society accountable for the plight of Black citizens, these two publications would help establish the grounds on which social pathologies and risk were linked to Black people and Black space by white policy makers twenty years later.

In the same period that Chicago school sociologists were producing detailed descriptions of everyday life in Black communities with an emphasis on social patterns often linked to social pathologies, another student of the Chicago school, Oliver C. Cox, made different observations regarding social dynamics. As a Marxist, Cox argued that racial disparities and antagonisms were caused by the forces of capitalism and by the "peculiar type of economic exploitation characteristic of capitalist society," rather than by social differences, pathologies, or cultural deficiencies.[28] While culture and urban space did not explicitly factor into Cox's work, the *absence of culture* as an explanation for disparity and his focus on economic structures were important yet overlooked contributions to studies of urban space at that point. Around the same time, an older Du Bois approached culture in a much different way from his early work. Forty-three years after his essay on racial uplift, Du Bois shed his Enlightenment skin with respect to "civilization" and returned to the concept of race in 1940, now situated within his own experience and through the prism of the racial narratives of his ancestors.[29] Like other Black scholars, Du Bois theorized a diasporic Pan-Africanism and held that the imaginative capacity of memory and struggle culturally links groups of people to specific geographies across time and space. According to this view, "the fact of race" emerges as a response to racialized struggle and is a product of shared histories, memories, and culture.

Du Bois's theorizing of a Pan-Africanism and embrace of blackness as experience were not dissimilar to the work of other relatively well-known Black scholars. Aimé Césaire's incitement to discourse from an anticolonial perspective conceptualized Negritude as "a violent affirmation" of shared blackness and a culture of freedom.[30] Similarly, Frantz Fanon equated liberation with the emplaced and embodied cultural expression of the liberated—a creative culture of struggle and resistance in contrast to the repressive culture of an oppressor.[31] For Fanon, culture is constituted by the collective practices of a people in order to "describe, justify, and praise the action through which that people has created itself and keeps itself in existence."[32] Cultural practice is therefore rooted in struggle—the struggle for or against freedom. Theorizing a national cultural consciousness, which he clearly stated is not nationalism, Fanon held that culture transforms, and is transformed by, struggle within the context of group domination and subjugation. Understood in this way, racist and antiracist practices do not just employ or deny culture; they are in fact culture itself. For Fanon's project, this meant reconceptualizing what blackness was in relationship to rewritten histories and present and future possibilities for nationhood and collective identity.

Throughout the first half of the twentieth century, a Black radical tradition rooted in memory, emplacement, cultural expression, and activism was nurtured by many scholars, yet the intersections of other oppressions such as gender and sexuality within the space of Black scholarship and activism were primarily identified and theorized by Black women who struggled to be heard and recognized. Many of these women, who are less known than their male counterparts, used the prevalent frame of racial uplift and culture to argue for the inclusion of Black women in the struggle for full citizenship and the recognition that Black women faced greater struggles when it came to individual rights. Anna Julia Cooper, for example, relentlessly confronted Black male scholars, activists, and clergy, demanding that the unique experiences of Black women and poor Black families be equally elevated within critical debates of the time regarding race, rights, and social relations. In her book *A Voice from the South*, published in 1892, Cooper also argued that the North, which claimed a moral authority and prided itself with abolishing slavery, in fact perpetuated southern sentiments toward Black citizens as culturally inferior by capitulating to the South when it came to laws and practices impacting the everyday lives of Black Americans and especially those of Black women.[33]

Within the spaces of journalism and political reform, Charlotta Bass is another Black woman who made critical contributions to the Black freedom struggle, yet the Black men with whom she worked, such as Marcus Garvey and Paul Robeson, were more recognized for similar efforts. Bass understood that space is a critical factor in the struggle for freedom and rights in the United States, and much of her work focused on segregation in the workplace, schools, and housing, including important work targeting racially restrictive housing covenants. Bass also understood the power of discourse and the intersecting nature of oppression. The newspaper she operated, the *California Eagle*, provided alternative representations of African Americans in Los Angeles to those found in the popular white media outlets and helped to promote coalition building between those fighting against minority-targeted oppressions. The women who led Ferguson resistance similarly understood the power of space and discourse to both reinforce and disrupt unjust practices and embraced an understanding of intersecting oppressions. These same women and gender-nonconforming individuals were often overlooked by the media and dismissed by men in the movement.

Amy Jacques Garvey was also marginalized by the attention given to Black men doing the same work. After the death of her husband, Marcus Garvey, Jacques Garvey continued the work of the Pan-African movement, but much of her experience was shaped by the considerable male chauvinism she encountered. Like so many Black women in the first half of the twentieth century, Jacques Garvey occupied the territory of what Ula Taylor describes as "community feminism"—"a territory that allowed her to join feminism and nationalism in a single coherent, consistent framework."[34] This territory allowed Black women the space to exist within male-dominated Black nationalism as well as a platform from which to critique chauvinistic attitudes toward women's intellectual and political capacities. A few decades later, in the 1970s and 1980s, Black women in North St. Louis County found themselves in a similar territory when they began to unseat white men and took over many municipal offices. Seeking political legitimacy in the region, which counted their race and gender against them, while also trying to preserve their communities, these women simultaneously critiqued white gendered norms while working within existing frameworks and normative constructs of suburban governance and respectability. The women and gender-nonconforming individuals leading Ferguson resistance, however, did not concede space to men who demanded higher visibility or recognition for the same or less work, nor did they feel the need to conform to external expectations of respectability or "civilized" conduct. In this way, the site of resistance is not just a physical space of protest but is equally the everyday spaces in which people unapologetically live and act as they choose, thus shifting the landscape in which a cultural politics operates and creating an opening for blackness-as-freedom.

Blackness and War

Daniel Patrick Moynihan did not appear to have much knowledge of the rich work Black radical scholars had produced when he selectively drew from the work of E. Franklin Frazier and adopted the anthropologist Oscar Lewis's 1959 coinage "the culture of poverty" (originally used in reference to Mexican villages) to draft his 1965 report *The Negro Family—The Case for Action*.[35] Written in conjunction with the Johnson administration's "war on poverty," the report illustrated how scholarship that seeks to ameliorate conditions of racial oppression can be strategically reinterpreted to aid and abet policy and rhetoric that absolve the state and blame victims.[36] It also began what would become a long history of policy wars discursively and literally aimed at discrediting and criminalizing blackness and Black citizens *specifically in and through urban space*.

Although the report named slavery as the underlying evil and credited "the Negro" with "not dying out," it framed the Black population rather than the color line for ongoing problems in US society, because of what Moynihan identified as cultural inferiority. Claiming that Black culture inherently deviates from heteronormative family structures, Moynihan placed Black women—in the form of the "Negro matriarch"—at the center of a "tangled pathology" of social deviance.[37] The report emphasized and quoted Frazier's use of disorganization to characterize Black families and Black space: "The impact of hundreds of thousands of rural southern Negroes upon northern metropolitan communities presents a bewildering spectacle. Striking contrasts in levels of civilization and economic well-being among these newcomers to modern civilization seem to baffle any attempt to discover order and direction in their mode of life."[38] Not coincidentally, the report appeared at a time when growing impatience within the Black community was pressuring lawmakers to pass and enforce civil rights legislation, and the growing unpopularity of the Vietnam War was creating difficulties for the administration. Moynihan's re-presentation of Frazier's "disorder" and the conclusions drawn regarding an inherently inferior "Negro culture" were read against a backdrop of media images portraying disorder in the streets of Black neighborhoods, Black people confronting authorities, increasing solidarity with the Black Power movement, and visible public frustration over the war in Vietnam. Jonathan Metzl has pointed out that during this same period, racial anxieties prompted further conflations of mental illness with blackness, spawning countless "pathologies of blackness" that strengthened Moynihan's tangled pathology thesis and delegitimized the aim of protests.[39] Almost fifty years later, similar language was used to single out the failure of Black mothers (matriarchs) and the absence of heteronormative families in Ferguson, Missouri, which also occurred against the backdrop of images depicting angry Black residents "disrupting the peace."

The legislation credited to the Johnson administration's war on poverty prior to 1970 included tangible poverty interventions; however, the discourse promoted by the Moynihan report ushered in, and shored up, two decades of federal and state legislation that subsequently hollowed out new public programs and dealt a substantial blow to prior New Deal–era public policy.[40] Shifting subsidies to the private sector and criminalizing nonconforming individuals and groups, the war on poverty quickly morphed into the war on drugs under the Nixon administration in 1971. As the epigraph to this chapter reveals, the war on drugs targeted the two most visible opponents of the administration, hippies and Black people.[41]

While the criminalization of Black citizens was not new, postemancipation methods in the United States had operated primarily through overtly constructed Jim Crow segregation laws or through accepted forms of violence, such as lynching and intimidation by white mobs and individuals. These forms of criminalization and violence used the fear of contamination (racial mixing) and the fear of violation (of white women) as the primary rhetorical devices to maintain hierarchies. The war on poverty and subsequent war on drugs expanded the threat that blackness posed in the white imagination by framing blackness itself as a threat to US ideals, exceptionalism, and economic success, all of which reinforced an imagined link between the United States and whiteness. Both wars (on poverty and drugs) placed Black citizens, and particularly Black women, outside heteronormative social structures. As many people, including geographer Ruth Wilson Gilmore, have shown, this rhetoric was not motivated merely by personal racist attitudes. It also served as an important political tactic for quelling resistance and bolstering the US economy through prison expansion developed from surpluses of finance capital, labor, land, and state capacity.[42] Areas of cities where Black residents were forced to live because of longstanding racist policies—such as exclusionary zoning, racial covenants, red-lining, lending biases, and real estate practices—were further coded as places where cultures of poverty, drugs, and deviance coalesced and risk was firmly attached to the bodies and spaces of Black people through seemingly rational means resulting in what amounts to a social death.[43]

The war on drugs was picked up in earnest and expanded in 1981 by the Reagan administration, which filled in the gaps to establish a full set of legislative teeth for the criminalization of the Black family. With the help of the Just Say No campaign, spearheaded by the First Lady, Black men, as well as women, were incarcerated at exponentially increasing rates for nonviolent offenses throughout the 1980s and blamed for drug epidemics that hit Black communities especially hard, while a steady flow of illicit drugs made their way to white suburban communities with few consequences. The criminalization of space became an increasingly important factor in the criminalization of citizens of color, a process that went hand in hand with rhetorical representations of space and associations with chaos and dysfunction. At his 1981 address to the International Association of Chiefs of Police, Ronald Reagan invoked the "urban jungle" and "dark impulses" of moral degeneracy, stating that "only our deep moral values and strong institutions can hold back that jungle and restrain the darker impulses of human nature."[44] People in entire areas of a city were associated with crime by virtue of where they lived, while space itself was criminalized (or venerated) according to the predominant race of those who lived there. Zero-tolerance policing policies in urban areas and pressure from local and state politicians to build more prisons meant that the prison industrial complex became a local enterprise.[45] The blocking of syringe access programs in inner-city neighborhoods at the same time coincided with the rapid spread of HIV/AIDS and added gay and nonconforming bodies to those criminalized in and through urban space. Meanwhile, Black women were represented as the bane of the welfare system—accused of refusing to work, milking the system, emasculating their men, and pumping out deviant children in order to increase their status as "welfare queens."[46]

As rationales for diverting federal and state funding away from social programs were honed by local, state, and federal administrators and politicians, federal and state funds to cities—especially areas that were predominantly nonwhite—were substantially cut throughout the 1970s and 1980s. Government spending on affordable housing and community development and tax incentives for urban revitalization were highly contested at both the federal and state levels. Many programs that did exist contained loopholes by which funds were funneled to, and through, private investment or came with significant strings attached, aimed at social conformity. By associating public housing with crime and people of color, while also vastly underfunding basic maintenance of housing projects, it was possible to blame highly publicized failures of subsidized housing on residents. As projects were demolished, President Nixon declared a moratorium on all new construction of public housing in 1973. In spite of continued underfunding of housing policy following the Nixon era, it is important to note that grassroots community initiatives partially filled the housing gap by creatively taking

advantage of policy that encouraged public-private partnerships and by forming nonprofit corporations that took on large-scale projects.[47] One of the iconic
images used to illustrate the failure of public housing programs featured the
demolition of thirty-three high-rise buildings in the Pruitt-Igoe housing project
in St. Louis between 1972 and 1976.[48] The demolitions displaced thousands of
residents, many of whom followed other Black St. Louisans who had begun moving to areas of North St. Louis County adjacent to Black neighborhoods in the
City of St. Louis.

Prior to, and just after, the passage of the Fair Housing Act in 1968, many
people believed that inequalities between white and Black citizens in the United
States could be resolved by breaking down legal barriers preventing African
Americans from accessing the full benefits of middle-class status and, specifically, the resources associated with suburban neighborhoods and ways of life. By
the 1960s, the imagined "authentic" suburbs were almost interchangeable with
an ethos of the American Dream.[49] Civil rights–era logic assumed that Black
families gaining entrance to middle-class suburbs would gain the same advantages that ethnic Europeans found when they left the central cities several decades
before. These included higher standards of living, wealth accumulation through
home ownership, low-interest financing, access to better schools, convenient and
upscale shopping districts, the ability to selectively control land use through zoning, and improved safety. Many discourses around inequality shifted from race
to class to culture, with an emphasis on individual responsibility and moral fortitude. Lacking in these discussions was whether or not areas in which middle-
class Black families settled would maintain the benefits of middle-class status.
Although many Black residents displaced by urban renewal programs did find
their way to the suburbs, the promise of postracial suburban privilege was not,
in fact, the experience of many Black residents moving to the suburbs and certainly not the experience of most Black suburbanites locating in North St. Louis
County.[50] What they experienced instead is described in detail in the chapters
that follow.

Within scholarship focused on race and urban space in the last quarter of
the twentieth century, the culture-of-poverty thesis prevailed, although this
approach was highly critiqued as well. The continued impact of Chicago school
theory on the discipline of sociology, combined with the influence of Marxist
theory, reinforced the shift away from racially based paradigms of antiblackness
toward paradigms focused on class difference and structures of the state. Some
of the work of Black sociologists also linked "pathologies of culture" to class, with
race appearing as secondary.[51] When race *was* discussed in earnest within sociology and proximate fields, the discourse was often framed by the highly influential 1986 publication *Racial Formation in the United States*, by Michael Omi

and Howard Winant.[52] Taking a Gramscian approach to hegemony—defined as the power (of the state) to naturalize the values and norms of a dominant group in order to maintain dominance—Omi and Winant argue that race is a manifestation of specific "racial projects" that use particularized notions—racial formations—of ethnicity, class, and citizenship to reinforce white racial hegemony. While Omi and Winant contribute important conceptual framings regarding the fluidity and political motivations of racial construction, their work has also been problematized as decoupling race from racism and deemphasizing global histories regarding the fungibility of specifically Black life.[53] Critics of racial formation theory argue that, while it explains formations, it does not sufficiently explain why they are formed. Other critiques of a racial formation model include: it problematically deemphasizes the work of whiteness and overemphasizes certain racial projects; it is overdetermined by state politics; it lacks the tools to look at deep foundations rooted in blackness by simplifying the formation process; it fails to address sufficiently the role of white actors; it does not attend to the everydayness of racial experience; and it essentializes identity through a "people of color" framework.[54]

More recently, critiques of racial formation theory have come from Black studies, specifically afro-pessimism and queer of color theory, that argue against the concept of racial democracy embraced by Omi and Winant and insist that race cannot exist independently from blackness.[55] P. Khalil Saucier and Tyron P. Woods point out that "Omi and Winant are racial optimists because they insist on the general progressive trajectory of racial politics, despite evidence to the contrary."[56] Building on the work of Frank B. Wilderson III and Jared Sexton, Saucier and Woods reject the idea that racial formation occurs through similar processes with different inflections for all groups considered nonwhite and insist on the historical recognition of blackness as "*the* originary racial project."[57] This view also rejects the idea that the color line will progressively become less of a problem as society continues to advance its liberal projects. Saucier and Woods in fact use Darren Wilson's (successful) justification for killing Michael Brown which was in essence "I feared his unarmed body because it was a weapon," to illustrate how "the structure and method of fungible blackness exceeds the grasp of racial formation theory."[58]

Throughout the 1980s and 1990s, there was a push to study inequality within the context of a larger global project including factors that are consistently deployed for the purpose of securing non-rights-bearing subjects in the service of production. These studies increasingly focused on the conditions of late capitalism and a growing concern regarding neoliberal policy under Reagan and Thatcher (which eschewed state regulation but required state enforcement).[59] Rigorous Marxist critiques of the links between militarized action, cultural production, and global capitalist markets emerged from this research.[60] Many critiques looked at the policing of urban space in the United States and the United Kingdom and attempted to define the specific characteristics of neoliberal urban policy *in space*.[61] Class was privileged over race in much of this work as an analytic for studying the causes and effects of spatial disparity. An exception is Cedric Robinson's *Black Marxism*, published in 1983, which took Marxist scholars to task for ignoring the fact that *all capitalism is racial capitalism*; Robinson provocatively and effectively rewrote history from the perspective of a Black radical tradition.[62]

Between 1975 and 1995, the fields of literature and cultural anthropology also produced work that drew lines between histories, experiences, and practices of colonial and imperial oppression across time, space, and economies. Much of this work was by non-Western authors and helped expand the discourse to Africa, Asia, and the Middle East.[63] Feminist sociologists took on the male-dominated discipline of sociology and the race/class paradigm by theorizing intersectional oppressions as a sociological concept.[64] In keeping with this shift, new fields emerged, such as gender studies, ethnic studies, and Black studies, which were intended as specific critiques within the larger discourse of postcolonial analysis and often emphasized a Foucauldian understanding of power—as a force reproduced at every scale of public and private life.

Attempts by antiracist projects to shift discussions of culture away from culture-of-poverty critiques and to affirm nonwhite, and specifically Black, cultural production were met with new forms of racist practice. Writing in 1987, Gilroy was among the first to call out the work of race in neoliberal projects in terms of renewed conflations of nation, culture, and belonging in conjunction with the new order of capitalist imperialism. Defined through this prism, multiculturalism works within the context of national identity to *recognize* different cultures so as to actually not have to recognize them at all. David Theo Goldberg later argued that when cultural difference is placed between two poles of celebration and risk, bodies are neutralized, on the one hand, and disciplined, on the other.[65] Recently, João H. Costa Vargas has argued that, similar to multiculturalism, a "people of color" framework denies that antiblackness is fundamental, ubiquitous, and transhistorical to the construction of nonwhite bodies deemed more and less human.[66]

The 1990s saw continued growth in both the military and prison industrial complexes, which directly impacted metropolitan space. Public discourse continued to blame individuals and culture for "unfortunate" outcomes, and cities were increasingly run as private corporations in the business of policing disorderly bodies and space, using military-style tactics to make way for profitable development. Legal theory arguing for public choice described cities as businesses competing for customers in an environment of governmental austerity, further propelling a business model of risk management. Defenders of localism echoed neoliberal arguments that private markets logically sort people and space and operate at the highest level of colorblind and democratic practice.[67] Conversely, proponents of regionalism objected to the idea that localism supports spatial inequality and argued that cities with geographic and economic advantages would poach taxes and resources from areas with fewer advantages, thus funding services for their own citizens on the backs of poorer cities.[68] This is in fact the case in North St. Louis County where municipal poaching practices are at the root of predatory policing practices, both of which use risk attached to Black residents to gain needed resources.

For the past thirty years, government funding to metropolitan areas increasingly has been directed toward policing and surveillance activities that protect private property and facilitate private development. This mirrors global trends toward militarizing public space—increasing surveillance of citizens while suppressing democratic dissent—under a banner of stamping out threats to democratic ideals. As cities were encouraged to compete for resources, the economic consequences of blackness (as risk) posed much anxiety but also many opportunities for mayors, city and county administrators, and urban planners. Using and amplifying an already robust public discourse regarding Black deviance, municipal leaders passed laws and ordinances aimed at policing minor offenses of "disorder" common in poverty-stricken areas. These measures in turn removed peoples who were in the way of development, and routed nonwhite youth and individuals into zero-tolerance court systems that fed the pipeline to incarceration, while simultaneously funding city budgets and private contractors. By the 1990s, policing policies such as the broken-windows approach, enforcement of newly passed nuisance laws aimed at poverty and homelessness, and later stop-and-frisk tactics provided the tools for police to harass and arrest individuals viewed as a threat to private property on any level.[69] Clinton-era legislation that effectively ended the welfare state, dramatically increased police funding, and mandated the courts to follow extreme sentencing guidelines ensured that the prison pipeline would increase the number of people incarcerated in the United States from roughly 500,000 in 1980 to over 2.3 million by 2008.[70] As Elizabeth Hinton states, seemingly in answer to Michelle Alexander's *The New Jim Crow*, "the long mobilization of the War on Crime was not a return to an old racial caste system in a new guise—a 'New Jim Crow.' Rather, the effort to control and contain 'troublesome groups' through patrol, surveillance, and penal strategies produced a new and historically distinct phenomenon in the post-civil rights era: the criminalization of urban social programs."[71] An important part of this phenomenon is the criminalization of urban space, both real and imagined, with and through the perpetualization of blackness-as-risk. As the twenty-first century ushered in the war on terror, cities gained even more tools to surveil and criminalize residents, in the form of discursive practices centered on risk attached to blackness and increased funding for police and military-style equipment.

North County stands as a prime example of how blackness-as-risk has been deployed at a local level through cultural politics in order to differentiate and police bodies and space for profit through racist and "race-neutral" policies and practices. The processes that currently play out in this area illustrate a political economy of risk that employs highly developed logics of antiblackness and well-honed tropes of dehumanization to exploit and sort people and space. This results in areas that are able to hoard opportunity and poach resources while other areas bear the burden of environmental hazards, predatory lending, and limited access to basic services.[72] In response, and for the purpose of replacing lost funding and maintaining municipal autonomy, leaders in tiny majority-Black jurisdictions implement the same logics used against their cities to extract resources from Black residents through a continuous loop of catch-and-release policing. By the time Michael Brown (who was portrayed posthumously as a modern-day barbarian) was killed in Ferguson, Black residents of North St. Louis County had been living with the consequences of disinvestment and racialized municipal policing practices for more than thirty years. These practices are amplified by extreme geographic and political fragmentation and an unusually high degree of importance placed on local political autonomy in the St. Louis region. The specific ways that cultural politics and political fragmentation shape experiences of race and space in this region are taken up in chapter 2.

CONFLUENCE AND CONTESTATION

On the fifteenth of February AD seventeen hundred and Sixty four, they landed at a place which they thought convenient for the purposes of the Company, and immediately proceeded to Cut down Trees, draw the lines of a Town, and build the house where this Deponent [Auguste Chouteau] at present resides—Mr. Laclede on his arrival named the Town Saint Louis, in Honour of the King of France. . . . The Illinois [Inoca] Indians claimed the land where S'Louis now stands when this Deponent first came here.

—Auguste Chouteau, April 18, 1825, as recorded by Thomas Hunt

The cultural politics of race and space in the St. Louis metropolitan area today are embedded in legacies of fragmented governance and a fierce drive for local autonomy. The physical and political landscapes of this area are shaped by global contestations over territory, slavery, and trade, and the region has a long history of using the local courts and municipal law to police and reorganize racial, political, and economic hierarchies. The genealogies highlighted in this chapter follow the threads that run through these histories with a particular focus on early constructions of race and identity and later formations of spatial imaginaries and racialized policy. Also emphasized are narratives of development in North St. Louis County and the histories of demographic transition in this area. This chapter is not intended as a comprehensive history of the region or of North St. Louis County. Rather, it illuminates what I argue are important specificities and peculiarities that shape the physical, political, and cultural landscape of the region. These specificities and peculiarities are helpful for understanding contemporary practices and phenomena taken up in subsequent chapters, especially for readers who are unfamiliar with St. Louis.[1]

Colonization

French fur traders founded the original settlement of St. Louis in 1764 on the land of the Illinois (Inoca) tribes and adjacent to the ancient mounds of what has been described as the advanced pre-Columbian civilization of the Mississippian people.[2] Naming it in honor of King Louis IX, Pierre Laclede and Auguste Chouteau chose a location on the western bank of the Mississippi River just below the confluences of the Missouri and Illinois Rivers. Although they believed they had established the settlement for France, it was in fact added to the colonial possessions of Spain—as France had secretly ceded the Louisiana Territory to Spain at the end of the Seven Years' War in 1763.[3] It took four years for residents of St. Louis to learn they were subjects of Spain and six years before the Spanish showed up to govern the region. The Spanish, who governed the Louisiana Territory from New Orleans, initially planned to remove settlements on the upper Mississippi and install a series of forts; however, they reassessed their plans after observing the geography, size, and culture of St. Louis, choosing instead to build a fort near the settlement.[4]

By 1773, roughly four hundred French-speaking people and two hundred people noted as enslaved Africans and Indians lived in St. Louis.[5] Although the Spanish outlawed indigenous slavery in the Louisiana Territory in 1769, there was an apparent Spanish ambivalence regarding people already held in captivity, and French settlers and traders living in the territory were not prone to following Spanish law. Lieutenant Governor Pedro Piernas reported a backlash to the ban on slavery, and Spanish authorities allowed residents of St. Louis and surrounding towns to retain, as well as to take, both African and indigenous peoples into slavery, presumably to maintain relative peace in the Upper Louisiana Territory and obtain the cooperation of prominent French businessmen and slaveholders in the St. Louis community.[6]

According to written accounts, St. Louisans and residents in the Upper Louisiana Territory had a reputation for being especially cruel to Africans held as slaves. Amos Stoddard, who later became a commandant of the territory, observed that, from its inception, St. Louis developed a culture of particularly extreme brutality toward people of African heritage and stated that those enslaved in Upper Louisiana had it much worse than those in Lower Louisiana.[7] Stoddard noted that St. Louisans justified brutality by invoking culture and claiming that Africans were especially lazy and, unlike "Indians," required punishment to work. Stoddard attributed the particular brutality he witnessed in St. Louis to the settlers and traders who were drawn to the area and the necessary alliances traders made with indigenous tribes who routinely took slaves as a form of domination over rival tribes.[8] Representations of the "noble savage" versus the "subhuman African" are common colonial tropes. In colonial St. Louis, specific representations that utilized these tropes reflect the trading and logistical dependence of white fur traders on indigenous peoples and the relative degree of autonomy tribes maintained at that time. Enslaved African people, on the other hand, were viewed as disposable labor and treated as subhuman commodities with little agency and no rights. Writing about the state of enslaved African people in St. Louis, Stoddard states, "Good God! Why sleeps thy vengeance! Why permit those, who call themselves Christians, to trample on all the rights of humanity, to enslave and to degrade the sons and daughters of Africa!"[9] Stoddard goes on to argue that incompetence on the part of the Spanish and the constant turnover in leadership created a brutal environment that promoted the accumulation of personal wealth at all costs, rather than civic goals and governance. In his view, "the evils of the slave system in Upper Louisiana may, in a great measure, be attributed either to the want of energy or intelligence among the governors of that province. As their appointments were limited to short periods, seldom extending beyond five years, the accumulation of wealth was the predominant motive of their actions, and some of them did not hesitate at the means."[10] Stoddard, however, like many Americans who would be placed in leadership roles after 1805, viewed the Spanish government with contempt, and other records suggest that French-speaking founding families, rather than Spanish emissaries, dictated the political, social, and legal culture of Spanish colonial St. Louis.

The Spanish in fact found it difficult to govern the French-now-Spanish subjects who had no interest in living off the land and no desire to conform to the Spanish colonial model of planned self-sufficiency. Rather, pursuing the chase, trade, speculation, and the accumulation of property were at the center of civic life and shaped social and political relationships in the first several decades of the settlement's existence.[11] According to early French and Spanish documents, the small Spanish contingents sent from New Orleans to govern St. Louis were relegated to record keeping and resolving internal disputes—usually over the collection of debts or the ownership of land and people.[12] Legal scholars argue that while the legal system under Spanish rule performed the tasks of resolving disputes, allocating property, and providing structure for transactions, it did so with little formality, "with barely any reference to written law and with almost no resort to any authority beyond the unarticulated norms of the [French Creole] community."[13] Although lawyers working on behalf of the US government would later use Spanish code in attempts to sort out land claims and resolve disputes, Spanish code is rarely mentioned in existing legal documents of this period, and the granting of land generally did not follow processes identified by Spanish code.[14] This ambiguity of law led to much litigation contesting land and property claims in the century after the United States took control of St. Louis.[15] It also set the stage for a significant emphasis on local autonomy in the region and established a precedent by which the local courts were viewed as instruments of those in power, using local customs rather than the laws of the ruling nation-state as the basis for legal standing.

Between 1769 and 1800, St. Louis grew as a strategic trading post with direct access to the Mississippi, Missouri, and Illinois Rivers and as an important supply stop for people traveling from the eastern states and territories to points west of the Mississippi River. Fur trading remained at the center of commerce and, as J. Frederick Fausz's research shows, fur traders based in St. Louis built a trading conglomerate with Native American tribes, which reached across the middle of North America. Trade remained in the control of founding French families, including those of Auguste Chouteau and Pierre Laclede, who supplied furs to Europe and relied on Native American participation. The extended Chouteau and Laclede families developed elaborate financial systems through which trade licenses were issued and shares were calculated for each tribe.[16] Discipline was imposed on and by tribes through trade embargoes, enslaving captives of noncompliant tribes, and raping and marrying Native American women. Tribes that produced the most pelts and protected white fur traders by turning on other tribes were rewarded with substantial trading privileges. The Osage tribe, whose territory encompassed much of what would become the state of Missouri, developed a strong alliance with white traders in the Upper Louisiana Territory and, while they initially profited greatly in terms of favor and accumulation, the tribe ultimately suffered the greatest losses from disease, retaliation from other tribes, and division of their own tribe into two branches. Ultimately, the US government disregarded these alliances, and the Osage tribe lost what was left of their territory after losing much of their population.[17]

In 1800, France secretly took back control of the Louisiana Territory. Napoléon Bonaparte, having lost control and trade routes in what was considered the West Indies through slave revolts, believed that the vast territory would be more valuable as a tool of negotiation than as a part of the French Empire. As both the prize and the pawn of conflict in Europe for over a century, the Louisiana Territory was increasingly difficult to control from Europe in the face of US independence, westward expansion, and new forces impacting global trade policy—particularly the transatlantic slave trade that was building the southern cotton empire and greatly benefitting the US government.[18] As president, Thomas Jefferson believed American settlers pushing westward would gradually acquire the Louisiana Territory through nonmilitary means. When French troops arrived in New Orleans in 1801 to take possession and secure the city, however, panic set in among residents of the southern states and territories. Southerners in the United States feared reverberations of the Haitian Revolution and believed slave uprisings would follow across the southern US states if France abolished slavery in the Louisiana Territory. The Federalists, as the opposition to Jefferson, capitalized on the threat to slavery by demanding military intervention against France and calling for policies designed to secure slavery as an institution on the entire North

American continent. Jefferson responded by setting his sights on acquiring the complete territory through negotiation in order to nullify Federalist demands and maintain political power. In 1801, Jefferson sent Robert Livingston to Paris and John Baptiste Charles Lucas to New Orleans and St. Louis on fact-finding missions intended to facilitate covert negotiations with France over the Louisiana Territory.[19] In what was again a secretly negotiated deal, the United States purchased the Louisiana Territory from France in 1803. Shortly thereafter, St. Louis was designated as the seat of the Upper Louisiana Territory.

When J. B. C. Lucas visited St. Louis in 1801, he found a town of about 2,500 people and noted that it had a remarkably advantageous geographical location but lacked any civic or political organization.[20] As Eric Sandweiss observes in his highly researched account of early St. Louis, "by the time that formal Spanish rule [in St. Louis] came to an end in 1800, a widening gap had opened between the clearly delimited social and physical order that the government struggled to maintain, and the centrifugal force of diversified personal interests among the townspeople."[21] Composed of individual actors seeking opportunity, fortune, and property, the city embodied the values of westward expansion grounded in private enterprise, the accumulation of private property, and all forms of speculation. These values were overseen, however, by a few elite French Creole families that had direct ties to the original founders of St. Louis. Furthermore, forty years of distant and ambiguous Spanish colonial rule manifested as a localized legal system that privileged unwritten local norms over the rule of law. As a result, a culture that walks a paradoxical line between staunch economic individualism, entrenched hierarchies of bourgeois society based on familial ties, and a fierce desire for local autonomy became deeply rooted in the region and is still evident today.

By the time Amos Stoddard oversaw the transfer of the Upper Louisiana Territory in 1804 for the United States, there were 2,780 mostly French-speaking residents in the St. Louis region and approximately 500 people held in slavery.[22] The French flag symbolically replaced the Spanish flag for a few minutes at the transfer of power ceremony in St. Louis before the US flag was permanently installed, which must have been difficult for the French ruling elite. In his speech, Stoddard invoked a rhetoric of US civil liberties, exceptionalism, and civic duty while assuring St. Louisans that their customs would be respected, stating, "You are divested of the character of Subjects, and clothed with that of citizen—You now form an integral part of a great community," a distinction that, as Stoddard reminded them, came with many responsibilities.[23] Slavery was formally expanded at the time of the transfer by nullifying all Spanish restrictions that had been placed on the institution. As a result, the benefits of citizenship Stoddard spoke of were even more out of reach to the many mixed-race residents of the territory, who were clearly outside the strictly white male community Stoddard spoke of. The

Osage tribe, which had invested greatly in the promises of their white trading partners and alliances with the United States, also found that they were expendable and now "in the way." As Peter S. Onuf observes, "the history of Jeffersonian statecraft was one of ruthlessly exploiting regional power imbalances based on the convenient self-delusion that republicans operated on a higher moral plane than their corrupt European counterparts."[24]

Citizenship, Property, and Identity

Upon transfer to US authorities, property claims in St. Louis were in disarray, according to lawyers representing the United States, who had a positivist view of law and were charged with implementing the North/South, East/West grid of western expansion and distributing forty-acre parcels to white landowners. President Jefferson quickly appointed the French- and English-speaking J. B. C. Lucas as commissioner of land claims and territorial judge in 1805, with the hope of denying Spanish land claims and returning most of the land to US government control, from which new claims could be made according to the expansionist grid. Opposing these changes were the ruling junto of St. Louis—the elite French Creole landowners with power who had gradually acquired and developed the settlement footprint and held claims to large tracts of land inside and outside the city proper.

Officials from the Indiana Territory, where slavery had been abolished by the Northwest Ordinance of 1787, were placed in leadership roles in the newly acquired Upper Louisiana Territory, prompting rumors that slavery would soon be outlawed in St. Louis as well. As a result, wealthy junto landowners in St. Louis pressured Stoddard to formally follow federal slave codes, which, unlike most state and territorial laws, were vague and left much room for interpretation regarding which persons could be considered slaves. Soon after, US administrators officially adopted federal slave codes, resulting in much ambiguity regarding how circumstances of slavery, prior laws, and the timing of enslavement would be interpreted. Questions regarding racial mixing, unknown parentage, and physical appearance also had to be individually decided on a case-by-case basis.

The thirty-one-year fight of the Scypion women to gain their freedom from Joseph Tayon and the Chouteau family (the self-proclaimed and celebrated "first family" of St. Louis) is a cogent example of how these questions played out. When the judges J. B. C. Lucas and Rufus Easton, both of whom held African people in slavery, granted freedom in 1805 to two of the daughters of Marie Jean Scypion (a half-Natchez, half-African woman whose Natchez mother was held illegally in slavery during Spanish rule), they were acting on the precedent of Spanish slave code that people from native tribes could not be held as slaves and that slavery was passed through maternal routes. Testimony in that trial focused on the physical features of the deceased Marie Jean, who, by the accounts of several white women who had testified years earlier in Spanish court, "looked Indian."[25] When their sister sought a writ of habeas corpus to gain her freedom from a different Chouteau family member, her "owner" argued that the physical appearance of the sisters (who reportedly "looked Negro"), not the heritage of their mother, should be the determining factor regarding their African identity. He also cited limitations of gender, arguing that the testimony of the white women in Spanish court should be dismissed since US law did not permit women to testify in a case brought by a man. Lucas and Easton again ruled in favor of the enslaved women on the basis of new and old testimony that their mother had received consistent benefits throughout her life because of her known Indian heritage, as opposed to her appearance.[26]

Foreshadowing local politics in St. Louis today, members of the Chouteau family used their standing and the animosity between neighboring jurisdictions to secure warrants from county authorities for the arrest of the entire Scypion family after the St. Louis court granted freedom to the women and their children. Relying on the disregard nearby rural officials had for St. Louis governance, the Chouteau family convinced police in the county to arrest the Scypion family on the grounds that they were escaped African slaves once they left the jurisdiction of St. Louis. Pressured to revisit the case, Lucas and Easton acquiesced but required that a four-thousand-dollar bond (which Pierre Chouteau supplied) be pledged until the family's legal status could be sorted out again. The Tayon and Chouteau families were given a month to file suit establishing their legal rights, and they immediately filed petitions demanding a jury trial and custody of all three sisters and all their children.[27]

J. B. C. Lucas presided over the trial in 1806, and testimony relied solely on white male members of the community since, unlike in a Spanish court, non-white people and women could not testify against a white male citizen in US court. When Pierre Chouteau's brother-in-law was elected as jury foreman, there was little chance the jury of all white men would rule in favor of the enslaved women. On the basis of the jury's findings, Lucas denied all further motions for freedom and placed the women and all their children back into bondage. The debate that played out in court centered on whether or not the illegal enslavement of the original family matriarch, Marie Jean, superseded the plaintiff's property rights (the property being people). The court's finding—that the rights of property always supersede any rights of nonwhite persons—would become a central argument in local courts in the St. Louis region throughout its history. This argument continues today in the courts and in public discourse in response to the equally persistent question, Do the uncertain rights of Black residents in North St. Louis County outweigh the rights of cities to protect public and private property from the risk attached to abstracted Black bodies? Discursive responses to this question often center on concerns similar to those in the 1806 case, such as the authenticity and rights of local citizenship, and appeals to cultural norms. In the case of North St. Louis County, these norms are viewed through a white spatial imaginary of suburban citizenship.[28]

Twenty years after Lucas and Easton gave their final ruling, the Missouri General Assembly enacted a statute by which people held as slaves could sue for their freedom. The surviving members of the Scypion family again brought legal action. After ten years of appeals, the Missouri Supreme Court eventually upheld a lower court ruling to free them in 1836, on the basis of the original argument that Marie Jean Scypion's Native American mother was illegally enslaved under Spanish law.[29] Among many other things, this case illustrates how judges ruled inconsistently as they struggled to navigate confluences of law, cultural politics, and local practices within the local courts; how race was a fluid signifier across jurisdictional boundaries and cultural practices; and how constructed and imagined identities—such as "noble savage" and "subhuman African"—held the power to constitute legal rights. Today in St. Louis County, these legacies continue, as local judges oversee a racialized system that conflates law and cultural politics, race continues to be a fluid signifier, depending upon the work it performs, and constructed and imagined identities such as "urban" and "suburban" are conferred on people and space, resulting in disparate experiences of rights across the metropolitan geography.

The formation of the Missouri Territory in 1812 brought another shift in power in St. Louis when junto leaders were elected onto the new territorial council, which reversed the prohibitions and policies on prior land claims and put a large portion of the region back into the hands of the French Creole elite. Immediately following this change, a mad rush for land claims by both French Creole and St. Louis businessmen from the East Coast of the United States commenced in the wake of the New Madrid earthquake of 1812—the largest earthquake recorded in US history, which changed the course of the Mississippi River and damaged or flooded undeveloped land. Under the first disaster response act enacted by US Congress, the New Madrid Relief Act of 1815, all landowners who had suffered damage were granted the option to land in St. Louis County. Corruption regarding land deeds was already rampant in St. Louis culture, and three-quarters of the new claims utilizing this act were granted to people residing in St. Louis rather than to residents in areas affected by the earthquake. Investors in St. Louis bought up the damaged land immediately after the act was passed and before rural landowners learned of the opportunity afforded them. As a result, land claims stemming from the New

Madrid Relief Act would shape the boundaries of tiny municipalities in North St. Louis County more than a century later (figure 2.1).

Sixteen years after St. Louis was transferred to US control and eight years after Missouri became a territory, the Missouri Compromise was signed as a

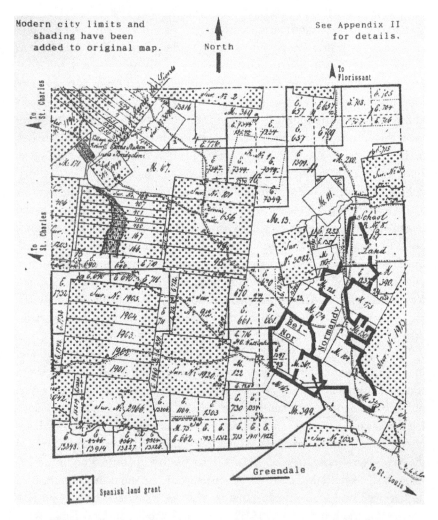

FIGURE 2.1 Land claims circa 1850 in an area of N. St. Louis County. The boundaries of Bel-Nor, Normandy, and Greendale are marked. Parcels marked with "Sur" (shaded area) are original Spanish land grants. Parcels marked with "M" were taken in exchange for property damaged in the New Madrid earthquake.

Harker August, *Greendale: History and Historical Atlas* (Greendale, MO: City of Greendale, 1996). Missouri Historical Society Library. Reproduced by permission from Alice August.

precursor for Missouri to enter the Union in 1820. The compromise made slavery illegal in the larger Louisiana Territory; however, in a congressional compromise to maintain the delicate balance in the federal government between free and slave states, it was agreed that Missouri would be admitted to the Union as a slave state while Maine would enter as a free state. The fight in Congress over the slave status of the territory versus the new state of Missouri prefigured the impending threat to the integrity of the Union and the eventual secession of the Southern states. Writing specifically in response to the debate that resulted in the Missouri Compromise, Jefferson lamented, "This momentous question, like a fire bell in the night, awakened and filled me with terror. I considered it at once as the knell of the Union. It is hushed indeed for the moment, but this is a reprieve only, not a final sentence. A geographical line, coinciding with a marked principle, moral and political, once conceived and held up to the angry passions of men, will never be obliterated; and every new irritation will mark it deeper and deeper."[30] Although Jefferson is speaking of a literal geographical line dividing the nation, these words haunt the physical geographical lines that divide white and Black spaces today.

Prior to Missouri statehood, landowners of French heritage (including the families of Auguste Chouteau and Jefferson's appointed land commissioner, J. B. C. Lucas) claimed large tracts of originally tribal land outside the settlement in what would become North St. Louis County. J. B. C. Lucas and his oldest son, Charles, allegedly gained many of these tracts by falsifying dates of claims under the New Madrid Relief Act. J. B. C. Lucas acquired 640 acres in North St. Louis County near the mouth of the Missouri River. The property comprised densely wooded rolling hills with many spring-fed streams running through prairielike valleys, which were said to have been traditional hunting grounds for several Native American tribes in the area. Lucas allegedly named the property Normandy because it reminded him of the province in France from which he came. There were several cities already established in the nearby area, including Florissant, which was founded in the late 1700s.[31]

North St. Louis County was shaped by another well-known figure in US history. When William Clark returned to St. Louis from his expedition with Meriwether Lewis, he was appointed superintendent of Indian affairs in 1807. Clark settled in St. Louis and would later be named governor of the Missouri Territory in 1812, but his primary duty prior to that was negotiating treaties with native tribes and "relocating" them from their land in the Louisiana Territory to reservations throughout the United States. To this end, Clark needed camping and hunting grounds for "Indian delegations" numbering in the hundreds in order to "make them comfortable and open to negotiation."[32] He purchased 1,231 acres from Auguste Chouteau just south of Lucas's Normandy in North St.

Louis County, which was said to include springs, groves, and ponds with excellent hunting.[33] When Clark acquired the land, the middle of which is present-day Pine Lawn, he is said to have called the area Minoma—the name given by local tribes because of its many sweet water streams and springs.[34] Clark built a colonial-style farmhouse on the site for his family, and it was on the hilltop called Counsel Grove, a name still used in the area, that many tribes ceded their land to the United States government. Upon his death in 1838, William Clark's land passed to his son Meriwether Lewis Clark, who later subdivided the property for private development, golf courses, and country clubs. William Clark, like many prominent St. Louisans, had at least one documented child with a Native American woman. His son, Tzi-kal-tza, was not recognized by Clark, nor was Tzi-kal-tza's mother, and neither benefited from Clark's estate.

Violence as Spectacle

As Jefferson had predicted, compromise would be brief, and Missouri would again figure largely in the debate over slavery and the events precipitating the American Civil War. When Dred Scott, an enslaved person residing in St. Louis, sued for his freedom in a case eventually heard by the US Supreme Court in 1847, the court ruled that slaves and their descendants were not protected by the US Constitution and could never be granted citizenship.[35] The decision essentially prohibited free states from granting privileges of citizenship to all Black people and added fuel to the fire in the US Congress, which was divided on the issue of slavery. The Dred Scott decision influenced the court's 1896 ruling in *Plessy v. Ferguson* that legalized racial segregation, the legacy of which is still starkly evident today.[36] Located at the geographical and cultural intersections between North/South and East/West, St. Louis walked the line on the issue of slavery for over a century, navigating between the self-interest of local slave-holding residents and an abolitionist rhetoric aimed at strengthening ties with leadership in Washington, DC, and maintaining business opportunities with entities in the North and the East Coast.

The years between Missouri's entrance into the Union and the Supreme Court decision on the Dred Scott case saw the expansion of the slavocracy in the South, which grew the economy of the entire Mississippi Valley. Sitting at another important crossroads of industrialization, transportation, and commerce up and down the Mississippi River, St. Louis played an important role in western development (particularly after the discovery of gold in California in 1848) and was an important market for all things, including enslaved Black bodies. More than two dozen slave dealers operated out of St. Louis, and people held as slaves brought a high price to work the fields in north-central and western Missouri. The *New York Tribune* remarked in 1855, "In no part of the Union is slavery more profitable than in Missouri and in no part of the Union do slaves bring more in the market, either to sell or hire."[37] Many prominent as well as average St. Louis families owned slaves and "hired" them out to companies and individuals who then paid wages back to the families. This included many of the men working in bondage on the riverboats up and down the Mississippi and Missouri Rivers. During the Civil War, St. Louis unsurprisingly continued to walk a line as a military post for the North and a home to many slaveholders and residents with Southern sympathies.

Prior to emancipation, countless people passed across the auction block on the steps of the St. Louis courthouse and were sent down the Mississippi River, and thousands more worked the fields of rural Missouri. The experience of urban slavery in St. Louis was varied, and the mixing of unfree and free persons occurred in public spaces as well as in church and other settings. A small but established Black aristocracy lived among white slaveholding society in St. Louis, albeit with significantly limited opportunities. A few were said to be among the wealthiest people in St. Louis because of business success and through inheritance, and many had known familial ties to elite white St. Louis families. In 1848, Cyprian Clamorgan, who was of mixed race, published a small book called *The Colored Aristocracy of St. Louis*, in which he used culture to argue that all people with African blood are not alike. As part of his argument, Clamorgan asserts that in St. Louis in particular, the long history of mixing along multiple transit routes amounts to the possibility that any St. Louisan might be traced back to Africa. He writes:

> The free colored people of St. Louis are surrounded by peculiar circumstances. Many of them are separated from the white race by a line of division so faint that it can be traced only by the keen eye of prejudice—a line so dim indeed that, in many instances that might be named, the stream of African blood has been so diluted by mixture with Caucasian, that the most critical observer cannot detect it. We, who know the history of all the old families of St. Louis, might readily point to the scions of some of our "first families," and trace their genealogy back to the swarthy tribes of Congo or Guinea. Such, however, is not our present purpose. Our business is with those who have the mark unmistakably fixed upon their brows.[38]

Clamorgan goes on to address the findings of the US Supreme Court in the Dred Scott case just one year prior to the time of his writing:

> According to the decision of Chief Justice Taney, a colored man is not a citizen of the United States, and consequently has no political rights

under the Constitution. . . . We shall not, in this place, call in question the judgment of the learned Chief Justice, who has in this State kindred of a darker hue than himself; but we may be permitted to show in what manner the political influence of the colored man is felt, and how in every important election, his interest is exerted on behalf of his favorite candidate.[39]

Clamorgan uses the rest of the text to describe in detail the success and influence that various members of the Black community had within the social, economic, and political structure of St. Louis because of their wealth and social standing. While clearly not a fan of slavery, Clamorgan, and the people he highlights, did not generally view the "Negro race" as equally deserving of rights or status. Physical appearance, social etiquette and cultural norms, and the ability to amass large amounts of money were the chief factors that determined who was worthy of equality. This theme of "Negro uplift" persisted and continues to play out today through a cultural politics that Black leaders in North St. Louis County use to determine which Black residents have access to the full rights of suburban citizenship.

Exemplifying a very different experience, William W. Brown was held in slavery in St. Louis during the same period of which Clamorgan writes. Brown was owned by a St. Louis businessman and hired out to a slave trader who amassed "gangs" of enslaved Blacks, transporting and selling them up and down the Mississippi River between New Orleans and St. Louis.[40] In *Narrative of William W. Brown*, Brown's accounts of slavery in St. Louis match Stoddard's earlier observations that life under slaveholders in St. Louis was just as brutal as the southern plantation experience. Brown places particular emphasis on, and describes in detail, the extreme brutality directed toward Black women and the denigration of their bodies, including that of his mother. Brown also foregrounds how enslaved and free Black people lived in close proximity to white residents in the city. He explains how white St. Louisans prided themselves on allowing their slaves to belong to the same church they themselves attended, offering them tea in the parlor one minute and viciously beating them in the kitchen the next. Regarding the "raising of slave stock" like livestock from Black women and the use of religion to ensure compliance, Brown writes:

> Who is it, I ask, that supplies them with the human beings that they are tearing asunder? I answer, as far as I have any knowledge of the State where I came from, that those who raise slaves for the market are to be found among all classes, from Thomas H. Benton [a US Senator who lived in St. Louis] down to the lowest political demagogue, who may be able to purchase a woman for the purpose of raising stock, and

from the Doctor of Divinity down to the most humble lay member in the church.

It was not uncommon in St. Louis to pass by an auction-stand, and behold a woman upon the auction-block, and hear the seller crying out, "How much is offered for this woman? She is a good cook, good washer, a good obedient servant. She has got religion!" Why should this man tell the purchasers that she has religion? I answer, because in Missouri, and as far as I have any knowledge of slavery in the other States, the religious teaching consists in teaching the slave that he must never strike a white man; that God made him for a slave; and that, when whipped, he must not find fault,—for the Bible says, "He that knoweth his master's will, and doeth it not, shall be beaten with many stripes!" And slaveholders find such religion very profitable to them.[41]

The campaign to publish slave narratives such as Brown's was part of efforts, mostly by northern white and free Black people, to abolish slavery in the United States by naming and revealing the degrees of inhumanity practiced and accepted by white Americans. Again similar to Amos Stoddard's observations regarding particularly brutal forms of violence practiced by settlers in the St. Louis region against enslaved peoples, Elijah Lovejoy, a white journalist originally from the East Coast, reported on the inhumanities regularly visited on free and enslaved Black people in St. Louis. He also published his opinions regarding the dangers of mob justice to civil society. Lovejoy's reporting in the *St. Louis Observer*, a Presbyterian paper, would ultimately lead to his death through the same violence. In April of 1836, Lovejoy and many others around the country were taken aback by the vicious lynching of Francis McIntosh, described as a free mulatto from Pittsburg. McIntosh was in St. Louis as a riverboat worker and had interfered while drunk in the arrest of other sailors who subsequently got away. When authorities attempted to take McIntosh into custody, he allegedly drew a knife, killing one man and wounding another. A mob quickly removed McIntosh from jail, tied him to a tree, and burned him alive. The diary of one purported witness stated that "the lower part of his legs were burnt partly off and when the flames had burnt him so as to let out his bowels, some asked him if he felt any pain, he said yes, great pain. It was 18 minutes after the fire was kindled before he died."[42] Similar to events following the death of Michael Brown, there were differing accounts regarding the details and justification (or lack thereof) of McIntosh's death, and a grand jury was called to investigate whether anyone should be brought to justice for the death. In the cases of McIntosh and Brown, nobody would be charged, and in both cases the victims were determined to be deserving of and responsible for what happened to them. Lovejoy was subsequently run out of town for his condemnation of the lynching and moved across the river to Alton, Illinois, where in 1837 his offices were burned down and he was killed by a similar mob. The particular brutality of mob activity in St. Louis was cited by the young Abraham Lincoln in 1838 in his address to the Young Men's Lyceum of Springfield, Illinois, stating that outrages committed by mobs

> in the State of Mississippi, and at St. Louis, are, perhaps, the most dangerous in example and revolting to humanity. . . . Turn then, to that horror-striking scene at St. Louis. A single victim was only sacrificed there. His story is very short; and is, perhaps, the most highly tragic, of anything of its length, that has ever been witnessed in real life. A mulatto man, by the name of McIntosh, was seized in the street, dragged to the suburbs of the city, chained to a tree, and actually burned to death; and all within a single hour from the time he had been a freeman, attending to his own business, and at peace with the world.[43]

White mobs would continue to terrorize the region well into the next century and, in 1917, East St. Louis, Illinois, was the site of one of the worst "race riots," otherwise described as the mass lynching of hundreds of Black residents by white mobs, in US history.[44]

Three years after Lovejoy was murdered for speaking out against lynching, the spectacle of killing "Negroes" in the St. Louis region continued as a spectator attraction, and those willing to pay could do so in style. As one advertisement from 1841 boasts, a steamboat was specially renovated and chartered for an exclusive all-day cruise to Duncan's Island in the Mississippi River, where, for the cost of one dollar and fifty cents, passengers could "see without difficulty" the execution of "Four Negroes" (three free and one enslaved) while enjoying the comfort of "every attention paid" (see figure 2.2). Some reports of the number attending the execution reached as high as twenty thousand in a city with thirty thousand people. After the hanging, the heads of the four men were cut off and displayed in the window of a drugstore in downtown St. Louis, presumably for the ten thousand who missed the gruesome event. The drugstore owner made plaster casts of the heads as part of the then-popular theory of phrenology, which attributes character and mental deficiencies to the shape of the skull.[45] The spectacle of the hanging, the description of the crowds and morbid details of death in the media afterward, and the display of the severed heads illustrate how "white self-reflection is produced from and instantiated through the staging of black bodily suffering," not unlike the spectacle of Michael Brown's body, left on hot asphalt for an entire afternoon.[46]

By 1870, St. Louis was the eighth-largest city in the United States.[47] Contentious politics continued around Black citizenship, immigration, transportation,

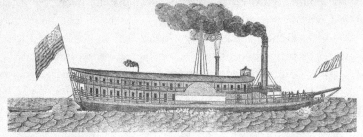

FOR SAINT LOUIS!

The Regular Steam Packet

EAGLE!

THE undersigned, having chartered the above Steam-boat, for the purpose of accommodating all the citizens of ALTON, and the vicinity, who may wish to see the

Four Negroes Executed,

At St. Louis, on *FRIDAY NEXT*, would inform the public that the Boat will leave this place at SEVEN o'clock, A. M., and St. Louis at a-bout FOUR, P. M., so as to reach home the same evening.

The Boat will be repaired and fitted up for the occasion; and every attention will be paid to the comfort of Passengers.

FARE FOR THE TRIP TO ST. LOUIS & BACK
ONLY $1 50 !!!

The Negroes are to be hung on the point of *Duncan's Island*, just below St. Louis. The Boat will drop alongside, so that ALL CAN SEE WITHOUT DIFFICULTY.

For Passage, apply to

W. A. Wentworth,
P. M. Pinckard.

ALTON, JULY 7, 1841

FIGURE 2.2 Broadside for a steamboat excursion to view the execution of four "Negroes," 1841.

and labor, and divisions between St. Louis city and the more rural county and
state were heightened throughout the short-lived Reconstruction period. Leaders of St. Louis city felt unduly governed by what they considered a backward
state legislature and rural county administrators, with particular resentment
toward "the authority of an antiquated and irresponsible power called a county
court."[48] The politically driven takeover of St. Louis city police by the state
prior to the Civil War was a significant point of contention that foreshadowed
contestations over municipal autonomy which relied on policing in the years
that followed. Furthermore, the largely antiurban and rural-leaning attitudes
within St. Louis County fueled animosity toward city residents, who were
viewed as sucking resources from state taxpayers. The relatively new and large
population of Irish and German immigrants that settled in St. Louis city in the
mid-nineteenth century initially opposed slavery and supported Union efforts
throughout the Civil War. Upon emancipation, however, immigrant labor
interests began to view large numbers of free Black workers moving northward
as a threat to wages and the terms of employment. Fueled by management,
which encouraged racial animosity, European immigrants changed course and
became a significant force in state politics against Reconstruction policies and
the rights of Black citizens in order to bolster their own claims to "white citizenship." These sentiments were invigorated by those opposed to labor rights
and efforts to organize, who consistently tried to pit white and Black workers
against one another.

The odd institution of the Veiled Prophet Ball and the secret society that
sponsors it, for example, were conceived in 1878 as a way to reestablish the hierarchy of elite St. Louis families and business owners in the face of Reconstruction and after significant labor strikes took place in the 1870s (see figure 2.3).[49]
By reinforcing class distinctions, white colonial heritage, and heteropatriarchy
in St. Louis, the ball was intended to further the rift between white and Black
workers and discourage efforts to organize the labor force. The Veiled Prophet
Ball might not be surprising in 1870s America; however, it continues in St. Louis
to this day and uses blatantly racist and misogynistic imagery, illustrating racialized practices that are deeply ingrained in the parochial culture of St. Louis
(see figure 2.4). As part of the ball, invited members of the St. Louis elite present their daughters to a secretly chosen "veiled prophet," loosely based on the
Veiled Prophet of Khorassan.[50] The prophet, whose identity remains unknown,
chooses the "queen of love and beauty," reportedly on the basis of her father's
influence in the community.[51] The list of queens from 1878 to today reads as a
who's who of elite families in St. Louis. In recent history, the ball has been the
focus of protests against racial and sexual oppression, most notably in the 1960s
and 1970s (see figure 2.5). In 1972, white members of the Action Council to

FIGURE 2.3 A poster for the Veiled Prophet Ball, October 6, 1878.

Courtesy of the Missouri Historical Society Library.

FIGURE 2.4   "Merrill Clark Hermann (center), the crowned Queen of Love and Beauty at the 130th annual Veiled Prophet Ball, rides in her float during the VP Parade as part of the Fair St. Louis festivities on Saturday, July 4, 2015 at Forest Park in St. Louis."

St. Louis Post-Dispatch, December 22, 2016. Photo by Huy Mach, 2015.

Improve Opportunities for Negroes posed as attendees and publicly unveiled the prophet.[52] As Clarence Lang writes:

> The unmasking sparked outrage among the city's civic leaders, and most media maintained their deference to the corporate elite by withholding the exposed official's name. Breaking ranks, the *St. Louis Journalism Review* disclosed his identity as Tom K. Smith, a Monsanto Corporation executive vice president and Civic Progress alumnus. Although entirely symbolic, the caper stripped a seemingly omnipotent icon of white capitalist hegemony of its mystique, and [temporarily] subverted the public rituals of power the gala had embodied since the nineteenth century.[53]

The ball was later the target of Ferguson protesters and Missourians Organizing for Reform and Empowerment, which launched an Unveil the Prophet campaign in 2015, aimed at exposing how powerful corporations and institutions in St. Louis support the oppression of African Americans, women, and queer individuals and directly profit from the prison industrial complex.[54]

FIGURE 2.5   "Percy Green of ACTION (Action Council to Improve Opportunities for Negroes) heralds the arrival on Oct. 3, 1969, of the 'black veiled prophet' and his queen at Kiel Auditorium, where the annual Veiled Prophet Ball was taking place inside. ACTION frequently picketed the Veiled Prophet organization as racially exclusive and elitist. In 1972 in the same building, it engineered an unmasking of the man playing the role of the veiled prophet."

St. Louis Post-Dispatch, December 23, 2018. Photo by Gene Pospeshil, 1969.

Divorce and Divergence

The rift between the city and the county and the legacy of political autonomy culminated when the Missouri electorate responded to requests from the City of St. Louis by ratifying a new state constitution in August 1875 that included provisions for the city to adopt a charter and establish the first example of constitutional municipal home rule in the United States.[55] The following year, a board of freeholders was elected to draft a city charter and develop a scheme for separation from St. Louis County. Although the 1875 constitution limited home rule charters to cities with over one hundred thousand residents, a precedent for formal municipal autonomy was set in Missouri when the charter and separation scheme narrowly passed. Later, the constitution of 1945 further liberalized provisions for gaining municipal autonomy, opening the door for even more tiny neighborhoods to incorporate.[56] In the years after 1875, St. Louis County would be carved up into as many as ninety-nine municipalities (as of the time of this writing, there are eighty-eight).

St. Louis County emerged from the "great divorce" from St. Louis city debt-free and with seemingly endless space to grow. The city, which had assumed the county's debt as part of the scheme of separation, was now contained by a permanent city limit with no possibility for future annexation, an agreement the city would soon come to regret.[57] Commuter development in the county began in earnest for wealthy St. Louisans when a rail line between St. Louis city and the outlying towns of Ferguson (established 1855) and Florissant was built two years after separation from the city. The Suburban and Electric streetcar line was also built into North St. Louis County soon after the rail line and development expanded to include elite planned neighborhoods in the Garden City tradition—with large lots, curvilinear streets, and restrictive covenants (see figure 2.6). Describing the developing North St. Louis County suburbs, Annie Orff's 1893 essay in the *Chaperone Magazine* (later the *American Women's Review*) describes the prevailing distinction between city and county and how the historical exclusivity of the area was translated into different suburban environments:

> The pleasure of leaving the chaos of the city on the Suburb and Electric car line comes to your mind as you are carried twelve miles through charming environments. . . . Having left the dirty, noisy city, this entrancing glimpse of arcadian splendor, is refreshing indeed. . . . The heart of the city dweller yearns for an abode of cleanliness, health, and repose such as is offered by these peerless suburbs. Its residents have the highest social standing, and include the most influential and wealthiest business men. Of course all objectionable features such as factories, dairies or any nuisance are excluded and objectionable people cannot be found here. Future immunity is secured by the requisite restrictions in all deeds to property, which ensure the most noble of neighbors. . . . This region is not one individual suburb, but a cluster of suburbs that appeal to different tastes and nobilities. This beautiful spot, which was chosen as a home by the illustrious William Clark, is now conspicuous because of a splendid residence of Governor E.R. Francis. That men of such unerring judgment, high standing, and moral fortitude should have chosen this, of all regions for a home, is significant.[58]

In keeping with representations of the city and suburbs at the time, the eight pages of Orff's article portrays the city as a chaotic place occupied by objectionable people with questionable cultural values and moral fortitude, whereas the untainted suburbs are home to only the most upstanding citizens. Nature and civilization are joint signifiers for suburban culture and space, with depictions of urban and uncivilized work as a racialized and moralized counterpoint. As described later in this book, the same cultural politics is used today in North St.

Louis County to "discipline" people moving from the city, on the basis of so-called moral arguments linking bodies to space.

The accumulation of unusually large tracts of land by single owners in North St. Louis County, much of which was held by the Lucas, Hunt, and Clark families, in close proximity to developed rail lines and roads drew investors looking for large open spaces with nearby transportation—for things such as cemeteries, golf courses, and country clubs. As a result, the development of the area worked in opposition to planning models that promote contiguous arrangements of rationally organized patterns or grids (see figure 2.6). It was, however, very conducive

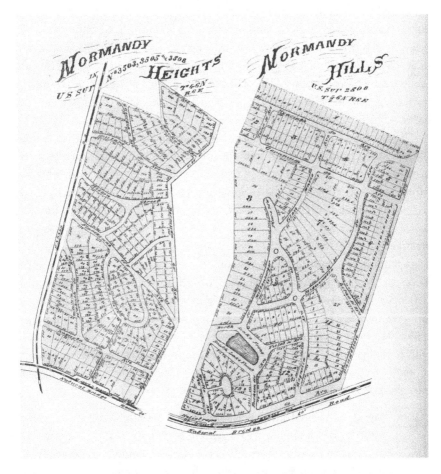

FIGURE 2.6   Plat map for Normandy Hills and Normandy Heights subdivisions (1893), examples of Garden City design in North St. Louis County.

Courtesy of the Missouri Historical Society Library.

to establishing small, insulated communities with minimal connections to surrounding neighborhoods.

Throughout the nineteenth century, a few towns and neighborhoods in North St. Louis County were formally and informally developed by and for African Americans who were excluded from other developments—except when they were held as slaves prior to the Civil War and as domestic and agricultural workers thereafter. Several of these communities existed in the early 1800s, when free Black people claimed small farming plots and others gradually settled around them, although this history has largely been lost. At least one Black community grew up around the slave quarters of a plantation in Ferguson following the Civil War. Most of the Black neighborhoods in North St. Louis County were eventually erased by newer development when the area became more desirable to white families and was shaped by corresponding government infrastructure projects. A few neighborhoods and blocks have maintained a continuous Black presence in St. Louis County, such as Whitney Street in Pagedale, areas of Rock Hill and Webster Groves, and the city of Meacham Park (annexed by Kirkwood). Kinloch, however, is the only historically Black city in North St. Louis County remaining today—albeit as a shell of its former self.[59]

The developer of the Kinloch Park subdivision in North St. Louis County in the late 1880s could not sell lots to Black families in proximity to whites because of white backlash against Reconstruction-era policies, although there were no formal laws restricting such sales. Capitalizing on the migration of Black people seeking jobs in St. Louis and the subsequent crowding in Black areas of the city, the company laid out a segregated subdivision exclusively for Black homeowners called South Kinloch Park in 1890. According to the *St. Louis Post-Dispatch*, Black families bought readily, but difficulty was encountered when banks refused to accept "Negro" notes as collateral for loans.[60] To get around the banks, the developer sold lots, or groups of lots, to whites who made small down payments and gave notes to cover deferred payments. The notes were accepted by the banks, discounted by the companies, and resold to Black buyers at double the price, with profits going to white investors.[61] Ads ran in Black and white newspapers promoting lots in Kinloch Park to Black buyers and white investors. One that ran after the turn of the century stated:

> The good colored people of South Kinloch are building themselves a little city of which they have a right to be proud. . . . We have been able to induce a number of white people of good standing to come in with us and cooperate with us to help with their money, influence, and good will to make South Kinloch Park a better place for the self-respecting Negro to live and make his home. We have given these good people a

big share of our profits in order to get their help and reward their good will toward the Negro.[62]

Although framed differently, the tropes of the self-respecting Negro and the celebrated goodwill of those willing to invest in Black communities continue to be perpetuated in contemporary narratives and practices in North St. Louis County today.

Fifty years later, fearing a rise in Black access to suburban areas, white Kinloch Park split from Black South Kinloch Park and became the city of Berkeley in 1938, when a second Black member was elected to the board of the segregated school district. In turn, South Kinloch incorporated as just Kinloch and was one of the first incorporated all-Black towns in the United States.[63] The new city of Berkeley surrounded Kinloch on three sides with physical barriers between the two cities. The existing city of Ferguson bordered Kinloch to the east. After losing its entire commercial tax base to Berkeley in the split, Kinloch suffered continued disinvestment after World War II and was eventually devastated by the expansion of St. Louis Lambert International Airport. Today, fewer than three hundred people live in Kinloch, down from 6,501 in 1960.[64]

Mapping Race and Risk

St. Louis entered the twentieth century as the fourth-largest city in the United States, hosting both the World's Fair and Summer Olympic Games in 1904. The city enjoyed international status and entertained hopes of winning a fierce competition with Chicago as the industrial and commodities hub of the Midwest. Although St. Louis ultimately lost its bid, largely because of transportation politics, a significant number of factories and other industrial facilities were built, including those involved in automotive and aviation development and manufacturing. Much of the industrial growth was located along the commercial rail line running through North St. Louis County to points north and west, which brought new residential developments selling small lots to middle- and working-class families finding jobs in the manufacturing industries.

As industrialization increased along with the in-migration of Black residents from the South, the protection of white neighborhoods became a primary concern in St. Louis city and county. In 1915 a petition for an ordinance to prevent "further invasion of white resident neighborhoods by Negroes and vice versa" was pushed by the United Welfare Association, which was organized around this issue and modeled the ordinance on a similar law in Baltimore upheld by the Maryland Court of Appeals. Letters and pamphlets passed out by proponents conflated race, class, and culture and likened the ordinance to fire insurance, asking, "DO YOU REALIZE that at any time you are liable to suffer an irreparable loss, due to the coming of NEGROES into the block in which you live or in which you own property? . . . While perhaps you have not yet been affected by this class of people coming into your neighborhood, you surely want protection against this growing danger which is more menacing than fire or the elements."[65] Spatial segregation was legalized when the ordinance passed in 1916 by voter referendum, making it illegal to move to a block whose population was more than 75 percent of a race other than one's own. The ordinance, however, was quickly struck down when the US Supreme Court ruled against a similar law in Louisville in 1917.[66] This spurred even more emphasis on local zoning and other means of excluding Black families, such as real estate practices and racially restrictive covenants, which remained legal until 1948.[67] Under the direction of Harland Bartholomew, who introduced and oversaw formal zoning and city planning in St. Louis from 1916 to 1953, an emphasis was placed on "protecting" white neighborhoods of single-family homes from people and activities of "vice." As Colin Gordon has meticulously detailed in his book, *Mapping Decline*, the St. Louis Real Estate Exchange maintained a particularly strong hold over the development and reach of restrictive covenants in the region and actively engaged in racial steering and blockbusting practices throughout the twentieth century.[68] When racially restrictive covenants were struck down in 1948, the Real Estate Exchange persisted in enforcing rules restricting members from selling homes to Black homebuyers in white neighborhoods. Real estate practices continued to reflect the claims that Black citizens were the ultimate threat to property values and framed antiblack actions as economically rational behavior. Although different language is often employed, I personally witnessed veiled steering practices when buying a home in St. Louis in 2003 and 2013, as real estate agents would refer to majority-Black neighborhoods as "transitioning," "bad," or "unsafe."

Facilitating the work of real estate agents, Bartholomew mapped St. Louis into tiered zones with "first tier residential" representing white neighborhoods with single-family homes that must be protected. The 1919 Zone Plan foreshadowed the early Chicago school maps (discussed in chapter 1), and subsequent zoning maps produced by Bartholomew's office reinforced the risk-assessment maps published by the Home Owners' Loan Corporation established in 1933. St. Louis is a particularly good example of how urban policies that produce and follow the mapping of risk historically attached to, and conflated with, blackness result in highly racialized geographies, even when race is not explicitly mentioned. In St. Louis County, many municipalities used zoning to effectively keep Black homebuyers out by requiring minimum lot and home sizes to keep the cost of land and building high. Advertisements for new gated developments continued to tout safety and were marketed to middle-class white families in St. Louis city (see figure 2.7).

FIGURE 2.7   Advertisement (circa 1930) for Bel-Nor subdivision, which was later incorporated as a village.

Courtesy of the Missouri Historical Society Library.

Following World War II, undeveloped areas of North St. Louis County were filled in by homebuilders and commercial developers capitalizing on the GI Bill and federally subsidized financing for white homebuyers, as well as federal infrastructure projects that facilitated transportation out of the city center. The housing in these post–World War II developments is smaller than the older Garden City developments and follows a grid, although each development adheres to a different grid based on major streets radiating from the City of St. Louis or surrounding landmarks. The physical landscape of North St. Louis County therefore consists of a patchwork of infill housing between large tracts of land with older developments, towns, religious and institutional grounds, industrial land and corporate headquarters, the University of Missouri–St. Louis, and St. Louis Lambert International Airport. As a result, the built environment of North St. Louis County is especially disjointed and noncontiguous, laying a physically fragmented groundwork for political fragmentation to follow.

Like the developments that preceded them, newly settled neighborhoods in North St. Louis County in the 1940s and 1950s tended to be ethnically and religiously homogeneous. White working-class neighbors and religious and cultural networks in ethnically divided areas of St. Louis city relocated to St. Louis County in similar proximities to one another, and developers often appealed to specific white European ethnic groups when advertising new homes.[69] Churches attended by ethnically homogeneous groups also followed congregants and relocated to the suburbs, prompting those left behind to follow suit. The suburbs were consciously and unconsciously viewed as means for ethnic minorities to claim or reinforce "whiteness" in contradistinction to "the dark races" left behind in urban space.[70] Consequently, the expansion of suburban developments occurred at a dramatic rate. In North St. Louis County, for example, the population of the municipality of Bellefontaine Neighbors grew from 766 residents to 5,200 in eighteen months. Between 1950 and 1952, 1,330 buildings were completed in this small city.[71] Expansion in North St. Louis County increased again after the University of Missouri established a campus on 128 acres within the boundaries of Bellerive, Bel-Nor, and Normandy, attracting thousands of students in addition to faculty and staff. Researchers at the university subsequently took particular interest in research issues in North St. Louis County. In keeping with a tradition of local independence and Missouri's spirit of home rule, municipal autonomy and local identity are highly valued in the St. Louis region. Residents often identify with their neighborhoods before, or in lieu of, St. Louis as a whole.[72] Prior to 1960, Missouri state law allowed existing local governments to easily annex adjacent land, but state laws also made it very easy for an area of any size to incorporate. As a result, a leapfrogging phenomenon of incorporation occurred in St. Louis County between 1940 and 1960, in which neighborhoods large and small incorporated as autonomous and semiautonomous first-, third-, and fourth-class cities and villages to avoid being joined with other communities that were viewed as a threat.[73] Incorporation was driven by a fear of cultural contamination linked to race, ethnicity, and religion and was rooted in what was understood as a fundamental right of local autonomy and the concept of home rule within the political culture of the region. The 1948 Supreme Court ruling on *Shelley v. Kramer*, which emanated from St. Louis and made racially restrictive covenants unenforceable, added fuel to the fire of municipal incorporation sweeping St. Louis County. Many unincorporated developments in St. Louis County had restrictive covenants, and residents viewed municipal governance, particularly zoning championed by Bartholomew, as a means to maintain housing restrictions that discouraged demographic changes after 1948.

Neighborhoods in North St. Louis County tended to be smaller because of physical fragmentation, and so the area ended up with an exorbitant number of tiny cities that were essentially incorporated neighborhoods, some with fewer than one hundred homes. Formal and informal histories describe this patchwork of cities as tiny fiefdoms where fierce politics play out over very little power. Community pride and the desire to control one's immediate environment with people perceived as like-minded meant that collaboration across municipal boundaries was not easily achieved (see figure 2.8). This resulted in a vast duplication of services, including police departments and municipal courts, across a relatively small geography.

FIGURE 2.8   Cartoon by George E. Coates, mayor of the city of Beverly Hills in North St. Louis County, 1981.

Courtesy of the Missouri Historical Society Library.

"Negro Invasion"

Soon after the rash of incorporation and even before the Fair Housing Act of 1968 opened up previously walled-off areas to African Americans, Black residents were moving to neighborhoods in the county in proximity to Black areas in north St. Louis city. Many Black families faced intimidation tactics. For example, in 1963, David L. Thompson was the first Black man to move with his family to the city of Jennings. According to newspaper reports, several windows of their home were smashed with rocks within the first week, they received multiple death threats, and the Jennings police had to step in to protect the family.[74] An emergency meeting was organized to encourage Jennings residents not to panic and sell their property to more Black buyers. Robert Dieckhaus, who lived on the same block as the Thompsons, told a *St. Louis Post-Dispatch* reporter, "The only way to beat this is to forget that they're there. Put up a fence and get a dog, but don't throw rocks. If you try to run, the real estate people will make a profit at the expense of a lot of us who cannot afford to take a loss."[75] The editorial writer of the local newspaper, who used her column to encourage Jennings parents to instruct their teenage children not to engage in violence against the family, also received death threats and required protection from the Jennings police. The president of the NAACP, who spoke out on behalf of Thompson and lived in nearby Pagedale, received multiple bomb threats and was given protection by the Pagedale police department during the same period.[76]

A handwritten document in the archives of the Missouri Historical Society, titled "Normandy's Black History," describes another side of Black homeownership in North St. Louis County at this time, stating:

> By 1964, Garfield and Lincoln schools had a significant number of Black children. The James Price family is typical of many Black families who moved into the Normandy area in the 1960's. When James and Maggie and their two sons moved onto Dardenne Street in Pine Lawn, only two Black families lived on their block. Ten years later, in 1974, only one white family remained. Dr. Wright, the principal of Garfield school, recalls that nearly every house and yard improved in appearance after streets became Black. Mrs. Price said they felt like pioneers in those early days but that Pine Lawn and the Normandy area have made a good home.[77]

Civil rights legislation—specifically the Fair Housing Act of 1968—opened up more suburban areas to Black homebuyers by 1970. Because of continued racial steering by realtors and discriminating lending practices, many of the programs initiated through the Fair Housing Act perpetuated segregation.[78] White suburbanites and institutions across the United States also resorted to new tactics to limit the potential for Black citizens to buy homes in historically white neighborhoods. As documented by multiple published studies between 1973 and 1976, St. Louis County policy makers, suburban municipal leaders, and grassroots organizations attempted to subdue public panic and slow the "inevitable social and physical decline" resulting from the influx of African American families from St. Louis city into the perceived all-white county.[79] Task forces were assembled and meetings took place between residents, civic leaders, and academic researchers. The momentum of white residents out of North St. Louis County in the early 1970s was accelerated by media attention directed toward "racial tensions" at Normandy High School in 1970, when more than sixty Black students were suspended following an in-school protest after a Black female student was hit with an object in the lunch room.[80] Well-documented blockbusting tactics by local real estate agents who routinely called residents and sent mailings intended to scare white homeowners into selling their homes added to the white exodus.

In 1973 six North County subdivisions complained to county authorities that white residents were continuously harassed by real estate agents pressuring them to sell, leading to unsuccessful efforts by county council members to pass legislation prohibiting blockbusting practices. Real estate interests defeated the legislation.[81] This occurred at the same time demolition had begun to dismantle thirty-three eleven-story buildings at the Pruitt-Igoe public housing site, which put more pressure on areas open to Black residents and prompted middle-class Black families to leave the city. According to researchers, administrators, and leaders, many areas "fell quickly" to "negro invasion," with some areas reaching 70 percent "Black occupation" by 1975.[82] This was the same vocabulary of war used by realtors in St. Louis city just after the turn of the century and by the Home Owners' Loan Corporation to establish risk ratings for home loans beginning in the late 1930s.

As other areas in St. Louis County opened to middle-class Black families, demand slowed in North County and many homes were sold without needed repairs by alarmed sellers to speculators and investors looking to turn homes around quickly for a profit. These homes were cosmetically improved literally overnight or on a weekend and sold or rented to unsuspecting Black buyers or tenants at the market rate.[83] Because of hidden problems with many of these homes, new homeowners faced unexpected repairs and system replacements that some were not able to afford. In other instances, the interim owner would divide rooms without a building permit and sell the house as a five-bedroom house, for example, instead of a three-bedroom. New owners were subsequently charged with occupancy violations based on the number of rooms on record with the city.[84] Many homes were purchased as rental properties, and absentee landlords tended not to maintain them, instead renting to lower-income Black residents when problems arose. The US Department of Housing and Urban Development, which had increased Federal Housing Administration lending to white homebuyers in this area between 1950 and 1970 (allowing lower requirements for white borrowers), also participated in this trend since repossession rates had also increased.[85] Upon repossessing homes, the department sold off unimproved properties to investors at reduced prices, increasing the number of flipped properties and prevalence of slumlords. Nevertheless, the depreciation of the housing stock in this area was often attributed to the increase of Black residents, rather than discriminatory policies and predatory investment practices. The overnight sales occurring in many areas of North St. Louis County made it difficult for municipalities to oversee housing quality. This in turn led to more ordinances directed at property and Black homeowners—including occupancy permit ordinances aimed at excluding larger (Black) families.[86] If people not listed on the occupancy permit of a residence were found to be spending nights, the owner was subject to fines. In order to receive an occupancy permit, the new occupant must remedy all "problems" found in the city's property inspection. Without an occupancy permit, families could not move in and children were also not eligible to be enrolled in the public schools. Occupancy permit requirements continue across North St. Louis County today.

Documents show designations of high-risk lending areas in North County zip codes (redlining) by the Federal Home Loan Bank Board, which further decreased conventional lending to qualified Black residents. This provided openings for mortgage investment companies to make high-interest loans to investors and Black buyers. These companies could provide Federal Housing Administration–certified loans, although the requirements they placed on borrowers and properties tended to be less strict than those imposed on conventional lenders. When foreclosures occurred, the companies collected their money and handed the property over to the Department of Housing and Urban Development, which in turn started the process over again by selling the property quickly. Although saving and loan associations were generally not making conventional loans to residents in "transitioning neighborhoods," they were making short-term interim loans to investors at high rates and buying Federal Housing Administration–insured loans on the secondary mortgage market—turning them back to the administration when foreclosures occurred.[87] Most people, however, would not learn of very similar lending practices that bundled government-secured high-risk loans and sold them as safe investments until thirty years later, when a national foreclosure crisis immobilized the US economy. Predatory lending that led to foreclosures and disproportionately impacted North St. Louis County was occurring long before 2008, and once again, North St. Louis County foreshadowed trends that would eventually reach a critical mass in the larger region. Not surprisingly, this area was further devastated by the inordinate number of foreclosures during the crisis that hit in 2008.

As with the most recent foreclosure crisis, Black residents, rather than the institutions driving disinvestment and predatory lending, were blamed for the deterioration of physical property, loss of home values, and a declining tax base. Throughout the 1970s and 1980s, Black homeowners were targeted with ordinance violations for property and occupancy infractions that were initially aimed at curbing blight associated with new Black occupants. Eventually ordinances would be crafted to target not just property but also what could be designated "living while Black," or practices associated with Black culture, in order to generate as much income as possible and make up budget deficits brought about by disinvestment and white panic fanned by the real estate market. These tactics are detailed in chapter 3. Adding to municipal shortfalls and policing-for-revenue practices, the county-wide sales tax shifted from a point-of-sale model to a distribution model in the late 1970s. This change penalized communities losing population and benefited the growing cities to which white residents were moving. Federal urban austerity policies throughout the 1970s, discussed in chapter 1, also meant fewer resources for areas facing disinvestment, and the federal government ended many municipal tax-sharing mandates throughout the Reagan era, leaving struggling cities in North St. Louis County further stranded. In spite of pushes for consolidation by academic researchers and regional policy makers, stressed cities generally feared consolidation and increasingly turned to policing and the courts in order to balance annual budgets and maintain municipal autonomy.[88]

Throughout the 1970s school districts in North St. Louis County lost students at a higher rate than neighborhoods were losing white residents because white families pulled their children from the public schools. By the early 1980s it was clear the Normandy School District, which serves much of North St. Louis County and was 85 percent Black in 1981, was on its way to becoming an all-Black district. The district had not received a tax increase since 1969, and two attempts to raise the school tax were voted down in the late 1970s. The defeat at the polls was attributed to the fact that the majority of white residents either did not have school-age children or did not send their children to Normandy schools.[89] Private and parochial schools in the area saw vast increases in white students. The Reverend Robert A. Ottoline, pastor at St. Ann Catholic Church, whose school received many of the new white students, told a St. Louis Post-Dispatch reporter in 1981, "Let's face it, there's not going to be any white people moving here and sending their children to Normandy schools."[90] Ottoline saw his parish as a stabilizing force for surrounding neighborhoods, providing a public service for white families who would otherwise face the decision to either move or send their children to schools with high numbers of Black children. In response to a question regarding why St. Ann School was thriving when other Catholic schools were in decline, he said, "We have the numbers, we have the whites, and we have money. That's the only way we make it." Ottoline acknowledged, however, that the tendency for municipalities to resist cooperation and keep to themselves was not a Black/white issue. Regarding the tendency for municipalities to not work together, he said, "Forty or fifty years ago, when everybody out here was white, they had that same problem."[91] This statement suggests that, although Black leaders were later blamed for stubbornly holding on to political autonomy, to the detriment of their residents, the inward-looking trend of coveting municipal independence is rooted in the history of this region.

Poaching and Policing

One of the most influential pieces of Missouri legislation with regard to the experience of residents in North County today was passed in 1969. This legislation allowed cities in Missouri to levy a municipal sales tax (if passed through a city-wide vote) on top of the relatively low state sales tax. Although subsequent legislation replaced the 1969 version, the designations of cities under the new legislation depend on whether or not cities sought and won local sales tax initiatives under the initial law. Upon passage of the 1969 legislation, most cities in the St. Louis region almost immediately passed a local sales tax, and many approved lower property tax rates at the same time. The vast fragmentation of the region and tiny size of many cities promoted a cannibalistic approach to sales tax revenue, as cities poached businesses and shoppers from surrounding municipalities in order to tax point-of-sale dollars and pay for services in their own jurisdiction. Cities unable to attract commerce became part of a tax-sharing pool that is distributed to municipalities on the basis of population—which was also in decline in North County. Cities that can attract commerce have been able to drastically reduce property taxes, thus passing the cost of local government to shoppers who often live outside municipal boundaries. This has created vast disparities between the winners and losers of a continuous sales tax war in St. Louis County.[92] In 2016, sixty-nine of the (then) ninety-two local governments in the county listed sales taxes as their primary source of revenue.[93] Not surprisingly, the majority of the cities that do not rely on sales tax because of a hollowing out of their tiny commercial districts are located in North St. Louis County. Residents of these cities must travel to other communities—sometimes several miles away—to buy groceries and other necessities and pay a sales tax of between 7.5 and 10 percent for which they will receive no benefit. Meanwhile, their own property taxes remain the highest in the county and they experience the highest rate of policing for revenue, as discussed in chapter 3.[94]

The dependence on municipal sales tax and measures established under Missouri state law that preclude the equitable collection and distribution of resources means that developing and maintaining thriving commercial districts is not just generally advantageous to cities, it is essential for the funding of municipal budgets. For this reason, competition for economic development is fierce, and vast incentives are offered to developers and retail businesses by municipal governments that are in a position to lure commerce away from weaker communities, thus increasing spatial disparities. Developers and businesses often call the shots and hold tiny cities hostage with the threat of leaving or not investing, in a manner similar to the way sports teams operate in larger cities. Tax increment financing (TIF) is frequently used throughout the United States to attract development, but because Missouri state law allows sales taxes in addition to property taxes to be captured by TIF, this mechanism is particularly attractive to both cities and developers in the St. Louis region.[95] Furthermore, under Missouri law, the creation of a TIF area requires only municipal approval, whereas other states have a more rigorous regional approval process to ensure TIF is used in the manner it is intended—for public rather than private good. Consequently, it is common to find TIF areas in relatively affluent neighborhoods throughout the region. In a particularly notorious example in St. Louis County, an upscale area of the county seat, Clayton, was deemed blighted in order to secure a TIF district. According to the group Better Together, over two billion public tax dollars have been diverted to developers in the past twenty years using TIF to subsidize private developments in the St. Louis region.[96] Although North St. Louis County covers more than one-third of the physical geography of the city and county area and many of its neighborhoods fit the conventional definition of *blighted*, of the 168 TIF projects carried out in St. Louis city and county, only 13 are located in North St. Louis County.[97]

There is a direct relationship between a loss of sales tax revenue through poaching and dis/investment practices and an increase in the amount of revenue generated through predatory policing and the courts.[98] Not surprisingly, the same cities that have lost the sales tax war are at the top of the list when it comes to per capita predatory policing practices. As predatory policing practices were made public as a result of Ferguson protests, Black leaders were blamed for abusing the municipal courts. The questionable role and power of municipal courts in Missouri as laid out in the state constitution, however, including gray areas concerning whether municipal courts should act more as criminal or civil courts, impacted North St. Louis County long before Black leaders were elected to offices. T. E. Lauer described the problem of municipal court ambiguity in 1966 in his argument for municipal court reform in Missouri, which did not transpire at that time.[99] Lauer identified inherent conflicts of interest, a clear lack of procedure and standards, little uniformity across municipalities, consistent duplication of laws, strangely particular ordinances across municipalities, and an alarming disinterest in the spirit of justice. In addition to observing "matters of peculiar local importance," Lauer also revealed that abuses by the municipal courts have a long history. He states:

> While our criminal law makes an increasing claim to adhere to the theory that rehabilitation of the offender is the proper end of criminal justice, municipal ordinance violators are dealt with almost as though the twentieth century had never happened: the offender is punished by the imposition of a fine or jail sentence. And failure to pay a fine will cause the offender to be remanded to jail, there to "lay it out." But ordinance

violations are trivial matters, we will say; they are only civil matters and surely the fine or imprisonment cannot amount to much. An examination of the statutes, however, discloses that in third and fourth class cities an offender may be punished by a fine of one hundred dollars and imprisonment in the "city prison or workhouse" for three months.[100]

Lauer also makes clear that predatory policing and abuses by local lawmakers in conjunction with municipal courts have existed in Missouri for more than fifty years. He notes that "the number and variety of municipal ordinances in force in Missouri municipalities is astonishing," and "in many cases ordinances have been enacted which parallel or duplicate the state law."[101] Lauer further theorized that any reform would be met with significant resistance from cities because "not only would this reform diminish the importance of the municipal court, but more importantly it would cause a loss of revenue to municipalities."[102] More recent manifestations of predatory policing and court practices, however, have taken a racial turn both statistically and rhetorically.[103] Since Lauer's article was published in 1966, the most egregious municipal court practices, such as jail time for failure to pay and the funding of municipal budgets through the courts, were greatly reduced across the state, including in many majority-white areas of West and South St. Louis County through reform measures.[104] These practices have increased, however, in North County at roughly the same rate as the increase in the Black population.[105] From specific types of ordinances (e.g., against sagging pants and barbecuing in the front yard) to justifications for policies (e.g., statements such as "these people don't know how to act in the suburbs") to employing dehumanizing practices and tropes (e.g., leaving a body in the street for four and a half hours and labeling it demonic and animalistic), the criminalization and dehumanization of Black people and the spaces they inhabit conveniently justifies significant increases in court-generated revenues.[106] These revenues make up for the substantial disinvestment and loss of sales tax revenues that result from the historical risk attached to blackness. This is the basis of the double bind Black residents find themselves in today.

In outlying and larger municipalities of North St. Louis County, such as Ferguson and Florissant, transition in the demographics of residents and leadership (from white to Black) lagged behind smaller communities that were closer to Black neighborhoods in St. Louis city. By the time the teenager Michael Brown Jr. was shot by a white Ferguson police officer in 2014 in Ferguson, the city was 67 percent African American as compared to over 90 percent in many of the surrounding cities, and it had maintained its majority white leadership. The demographic misalignment of the population and the leadership was often cited as contributing to the unrest witnessed after the shooting and subsequent data produced by the Department of Justice regarding extreme racialized policing practices in Ferguson.[107] Although this misalignment did not help racialized tensions in Ferguson, the presumption that the policing of Black residents based on suburban norms was specifically carried out by white leadership is proven incorrect by the fact that even more extreme forms of racialized policing practices are carried out in multiple cities in North St. Louis County with all-Black leadership.[108] Chapters 3 and 4 describe and document these practices as well as looking at many of the nuanced factors that impact the experiences and responses of residents and leaders in this area.

The Region Today

Today the St. Louis metropolitan area consists of fifteen counties in two states with approximately 2.8 million people.[109] Encompassing over nine thousand square miles (map 2.1), the region includes over 300 local governments and 165

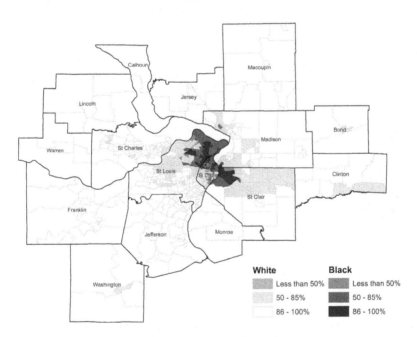

MAP 2.1   St. Louis city and the fifteen counties that make up the St. Louis metropolitan area. Areas that are less than 50 percent white or Black are color-coded according to the majority of a single race reported in that census tract. US Census data, 2013–17 American Community Survey. (Note: the author recognizes that the use of color, rather than black and white, is preferable when representing demographic information but was limited by the requirements of publication.)

TIGER/Line shape files prepared by the US Census Bureau, 2018. Map by Alexis Sheehy.

school districts with the highest number of taxing authorities in the nation, at 26.8 taxing units per 100,000 people.[110] St. Louis County, at just under one million people, is by far the most populated county in the region although geographically one of the smallest, covering just 524 square miles. Established as a district in 1804, when the Upper Louisiana Territory was transferred to US control, and as a county in 1812 when the Missouri Territory was formed, St. Louis County is the oldest county in Missouri. The City of St. Louis, which separated from the county in 1876 because of differing political priorities discussed earlier in this chapter, spans 66.2 square miles and has a population today of roughly 315,000 residents, down from a high of 856,796 in 1950.[111]

There are eighty-eight municipalities in St. Louis County today (map 2.2), of which eighty-one maintain independent courts, sixty-one have independent police forces, and all provide some level of basic services. More than half (forty-six) of the eighty-eight municipalities are located in the northern fifth of the county footprint,

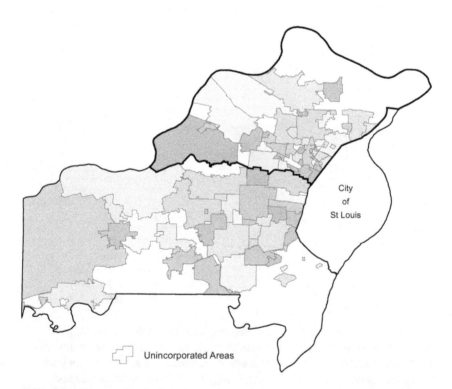

Unincorporated Areas

MAP 2.2   Municipalities of St. Louis County, Missouri as of 2018. The area known as North St. Louis County is outlined in bold. Source: US Census, 2013–17 American Community Survey.

TIGER/Line shape files prepared by the US Census Bureau, 2018. Map by Alexis Sheehy.

to the north of Olive Boulevard in the area known as North County (map 2.3). This area covers roughly 50 of the 524 square miles in St. Louis County. Of the forty-six municipalities located in the area of North St. Louis County, twenty-five can be found within a twelve-square-mile area known as the Normandy suburbs, roughly defined by Page Avenue, Interstates 70 and 170, and St. Louis city limits. People driving on interstates or thoroughfares in this area may cross seven or eight city limits in a one-to-two-mile stretch.[112]

Black residents make up 24 percent of the population in St. Louis County—up from 2.7 percent in 1960. More than 80 percent of the Black population lives in North St. Louis County, which is majority Black, and many municipalities in North St. Louis County are over 90 percent Black.[113] As discussed above, demographic shifts were rapid in this area following civil rights legislation, and several municipalities inverted within a twenty-year period—from over 90 percent white in 1960 to more than 90 percent Black by 1980—with the most dramatic shifts occurring in the mid-1970s.[114] Today, demographic mapping of race, income, and poverty levels (maps 2.4, 2.5) as well as education, workforce, health, and amenities reveals a consistent line dividing North St. Louis County from the rest of the region.

The genealogies outlined in this chapter reflect the interconnected global histories of chattel slavery, colonial and imperial expansion, and capitalist

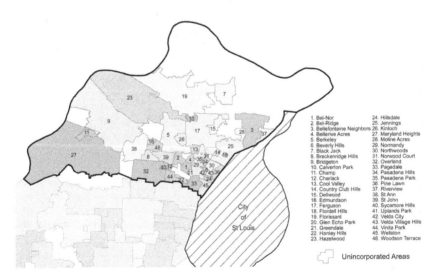

MAP 2.3   The area known as North St. Louis County as of 2018. Forty-six of the eighty-eight cities in St. Louis County sit within this footprint. Source: US Census, 2013–17 American Community Survey.

TIGER/Line shape files prepared by the US Census Bureau, 2018. Map by Alexis Sheehy.

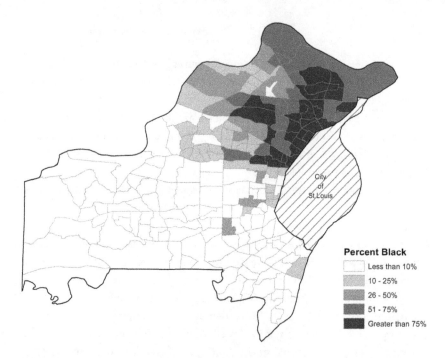

MAP 2.4   St. Louis County, percent Black. Source: US Census, 2013–17 American Community Survey. (See note, map 2.1)

TIGER/Line shape files prepared by the US Census Bureau, 2018. Map by Alexis Sheehy.

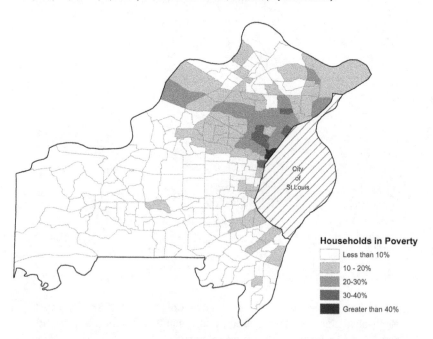

MAP 2.5   St. Louis County, poverty rate. Source: US Census, 2013–17 American Community Survey. (See note, map 2.1)

TIGER/Line shape files prepared by the US Census Bureau, 2018. Map by Alexis Sheehy.

development. In keeping with these histories, Black residents in the suburbs of North St. Louis County are disciplined as less-than-human, profit-generating bodies by tiny cities that have been stripped of resources and struggle to provide basic services except for an ever-expanding police force. A fierce desire for self-governance and municipal autonomy, a persistent tradition of parochial hierarchies, a peculiar reliance on the local courts, and the perpetual conflation of blackness and risk are legacies that result in specific forms of cultural politics and racialized practices across a highly fragmented geography. The chapters that follow in this section describe and examine the double bind of blackness—as a signifier of risk and as a means of exploitation and profit—that has led to conditions such that "if you were to design a place whose sole purpose was to create and maintain a system of racialized poverty, it would look like this."[115]

RACIAL STATES AND LOCAL GOVERNANCE

> My son was in the hospital and I got a ticket for a "water closet." No one at the court knew what that was and I'm still paying on it. I was locked up for a day and a half for a water closet and my eight-year-old son was in the hospital. Also, the police maced my dog when they came on my property. They said they had the right to do that.
>
> —Black woman, resident of Normandy, Missouri

> They are crazy about writing tickets out here—just giving tickets to people for nothing. My eighty-five-year-old grandmother got one like that. It's to fill up the courthouse and fill out the books.
>
> —Black woman, resident of Velda City, Missouri

The production of racialized disparities in and through space is not unique to St. Louis. In fact, to some extent and as detailed in chapter 1, the sorting of people and space is something all metropolitan areas have in common. North St. Louis County is, however, especially revealing with regard to how municipal governments are critical instruments in the remaking of the modern racial state and processes of subject-making in twenty-first-century US cities. As discussed in chapter 1, cities have assumed the role of administrating urban austerity policies and increasingly act as the gatekeepers of citizens' rights. Using formal and informal policies and real and perceived forms of discipline and surveillance to construct hierarchies of power that appear rational and routine, tiny municipalities in North St. Louis County use similar narratives of propriety, risk, and property to police residents, extract revenue, and create new forms of statecraft under the banners of maintaining order and preserving municipal autonomy.

Although shockingly racialized policing and governing practices in North St. Louis County were exposed by protesters in the city of Ferguson, cities across this area have been carrying out and perfecting similar practices for decades. Ferguson, in fact, does not represent many of the nuanced issues at work in most of the tiny majority-Black cities across this geography. In addition to having one of the few majority-white leaderships, Ferguson, unlike its neighbors, enjoys relatively stable commercial areas, including a revitalized shopping district that brings in a steady stream of the much-coveted sales tax upon which Missouri cities rely.[1] After a contested annexation between 1956 and 1964, it became home to the Fortune 500 company Emerson Electric, which employs over 1,300 workers and provides the municipality with another stable, albeit limited, source of tax revenue.[2] Furthermore, as a chartered city founded in 1855, Ferguson has a greater degree of political autonomy and taxing authority relative to the tiny third- and fourth-class cities and villages in North County, most of which incorporated after World War II and have limited power but seemingly unlimited economic liability.

This chapter argues that municipalities with majority-Black populations are often both victims and administrators of highly racialized practices that differentiate, oppress, and exploit nonwhite communities. This argument is based on data showing that municipalities with higher percentages of Black residents are more likely to have their resources poached by adjacent cities with majority-white populations. The data also show that the residents of these cities experience more extreme forms of political, economic, and physical violence at the hands of local administrators and police, and that the forms of predatory policing in these areas are often obscured or deemed economically rational. As this chapter illustrates, formal and informal manifestations of the law in North St. Louis County use imaginations of suburban space, or a white spatial imaginary, as a basis for the policing of behavior and property in order to generate essential funds that keep tiny cities solvent.[3] This policing for revenue also relies on age-old tropes of Black deviance and the illegibility of Black suffering. In this way, the function of policing is not "applying the law, but . . . obtaining a normal behavior; conformity," which local leaders exploit in the hope of maintaining hard-won yet politically and economically tenuous Black municipal autonomy.[4] What follows are detailed accounts of the racialized means and extreme measures cities in North St. Louis County use to extract money and resources from Black citizens. These practices have been developed over many years in response to wholesale disinvestment and the poaching of resources out of Black communities. Also considered are the ethical arguments and discourses concerning municipal dissolution of majority-Black cities, with particular emphasis on the relationship between municipal poaching, predatory policing, and suburban race-making.

Evelyn and Patrice

Evelyn is a sixty-eight-year-old Black woman who has lived in North County for twenty-six years. She inherited the house she was living in from her long-time boyfriend, who died fifteen years earlier, struck by a car while walking near his home on a street with no sidewalks. I got to know Evelyn over a period of three years when she participated in the "services for seniors" project that my students organized as a way to engage with residents and learn about the community. In addition to the time I spent chatting with her while sitting between her two toy poodles on a worn red couch, my students would often come to class and relay how Evelyn had stuffed them with donuts and shared stories that put their own lives in stark perspective. Two of my male graduate students from China became particularly attached to Evelyn, and one continued to ride the bus to visit her long after the semester ended. Every time I saw her, she effusively thanked me for sending "those nice Chinese boys" to help her around the house.

By the time I got to know her, Evelyn had received multiple municipal citations for property-related infractions. My students were helping her address a long list of violations she could not afford to take care of on her own. Evelyn believed she was being harassed with citations because her son, who lived in another house in the same municipality, had vocally supported the candidate who had attempted to unseat the current municipal alderperson in the previous election. She believed this because she had never received a citation until her son had become politically active. After that she had received eight notices of violations of local codes and several letters from the municipality threatening more fines and the possibility of losing her house if she did not comply. Most of the citations were cosmetic, not safety related. They included demands that she paint her front and back door, paint the foundation of her house, and rewire the exterior lighting on her house. Evelyn also relayed a story about a time when she was in her yard trimming a rosebush and the alderperson drove by her house. According to Evelyn, the alderperson stopped upon seeing her in the yard and told her she should worry about her weeds and not her rose bush and she had better paint her front door right away or receive another citation. Evelyn found the exchange very unsettling and moved between visible anger and tearful anxiety as she recounted the experience. When I asked the alderperson who had stopped in front of Evelyn's house about the incident, they stated that all residents of the city were treated equally and the city had the right to protect safety and property values by issuing citations to "people that don't know how or don't want to take care of their property."

Property violations were not the only experience Evelyn's family had with predatory policing. Evelyn's youngest child, Patrice, had accumulated eight traffic violation citations in the course of two years, four of which were for the same violation—a faulty muffler—received in four different municipalities over a few weeks. After moving in with her mother, Patrice was working two part-time jobs as well as getting her children to three different schools outside the district because she wanted them to finish the school year where they had started. She shared, "I couldn't take off work or not get those kids to school to go get my muf-fler fixed. But that's how it is. It's like flies on shit. You got one problem with your car and they will be on your ass in an instant because they want to get at every-thing you got, which is really nothing." Because she worked evenings, Patrice could not attend three of the court dates, which were all held one evening each month. On the one evening she could attend, she had to make a decision regard-ing which ticket to take care of, since two court dates were on that same night. She also could not make arrangements to take care of tickets other than physically showing up at court since the cities did not provide online payment methods, nor did they provide another means to pay. Consequently, Patrice had three warrants issued for her arrest even after she emptied her bank account of eight hundred dollars to pay fines and fees. "If all that hadn't happened," she said, "I could have fixed my car. Maybe even moved out of my mother's house."

Patrice unfortunately had firsthand experience with warrants and understood why she did not want to find herself again in a cycle of municipal jailing. Three years before I met Patrice, she had gone through a similar experience. As she explained,

> When my tail light was busted out, the same thing happened which is also why I don't want to show up at courts because, who knows, they may ship me over to Jennings and throw me in jail when I try to pay a fifty-dollar ticket in Velda City. Or they'll take my driver's license away until I can pay and if I lose my car, I lose both my jobs and then I lose my kids. That's how it works. The last time, I got pulled over for no reason at all. The cop was just driving behind me running my plates. He saw there was a warrant in St. Ann and I ended up in jail there. They told me I had to pay a thousand-dollar bond in cash. I was living on my own then and actually doing okay. My mom took my kids but they couldn't get to school. I wasn't allowed to shower for the whole ten days. There was like fifteen of us in there, coming and going, and not enough beds for everyone. People were peeing and heaving and bleeding right in where we were supposed to sleep. I haven't never seen nothing like that. It was literally like animals in a cage. It took ten days for my mom and brother to get the money together. By that time, I'd lost my job. As soon as St. Ann got their money, they drove me over to Pine Lawn and booked me into jail there. The bail there was set at five hundred dollars and there was no way my mom and brother could get more. I had to call my ex-boyfriend, the father of my youngest two to get me out. I'd been trying to get away from him for years but I don't have any-body else after my mom and my brother so I ended up going back with

him. After that, everything just all fell apart. Maybe I was lucky though because I know people who go through four or five jails and they still owe thousands of dollars. I don't know what's going to happen though if I get pulled over again. I have to think real carefully about when and where I drive. Damn, I wish I could leave St. Louis.

Draconian Practices and Debtors' Prisons

Stories like those of Evelyn and Patrice that detail Black citizens' experiences with the police, housing inspectors, municipal courts, and jails—and the impact of those institutions on their lives—were told to me time and again through interviews and during informal conversations.[5] However, prior to the sustained protest movement following the death of Michael Brown Jr. in Ferguson, few policy makers, journalists, or anyone else was interested in hearing these accounts. Nevertheless, residents consistently described a geography of local legal systems designed to criminalize and entrap people in a web of seemingly endless fines and fees for routine traffic and nontraffic ordinance violations that disproportionately impact poor Black residents. The intergenerational effects on Evelyn's family went even further, as she recently told me stories of her son's latest encounters with traffic stops and warrants, as well as her granddaughter's encounters with the Ferguson police department as a peaceful protester.

Ironically, one of the few acts of collaboration between a patchwork of municipalities that typically refuse to cooperate with one another is a database of municipal warrants, which leads to a leapfrogging jail population across jurisdictions. People described similar inhumane conditions and practices in numerous jails. Common complaints included the lack of personal hygiene implements such as a toothbrushes, towels, or soap; the refusal to accommodate requests to use the bathroom or to shower; the refusal to provide feminine hygiene products to women; vast overcrowding and unsanitary conditions; and taunts, including racial, gendered, and homophobic slurs. Many stories ended with the loss of jobs, housing, and even children. Several stories told by the media ended tragically when individuals hung themselves in municipal jails out of despair.[6]

It is not uncommon for an individual to rack up hundreds of dollars in fines, as did Patrice, for failure to pay or failure to appear in court for a single infraction that many of us have committed at no cost. For example, a woman from Pasadena Hills waits in line each month at the municipal court to make a twenty-five-dollar payment on a thousand-dollar debt to the city because she let her pit bull urinate in her own front yard without a leash and was unable to pay the initial fine, leading to a warrant for her arrest. Twenty-five dollars represents 12 percent of her monthly grocery budget, and she will need to appear in court on the one designated night every month for more than three years to pay off the fine. If she misses a night, she faces arrest and more fines. Another woman interviewed outside the Pagedale court stood in a long line to pay $30 toward what she said was a $350 cumulative fine for moving into her house after dark without a permit and failing to list her boyfriend, who occasionally spent the night, on her occupancy permit. She has spent an evening every month standing in line for the past eight months. If she does not show up to pay her installment, she will face jail and more fines. "This month I was short," she said. "I had to borrow from my neighbor who knows what this city does to people. But now I owe her and the city. If I could move, I would."[7] More examples of how Black residents, including many older people, describe their experiences with policing across this geography follow.

Black man from Hazelwood (aged 46–55)

I've had horrible experiences with driving in North County. I don't even get tickets when I get pulled over because they can't find anything to ticket me for. They just pulled me over and harassed me. People don't even go to the county solely for that reason.

Black man from Florissant (aged 26–35)

You've got be 100 percent cautious around here. It's not a good feeling driving around like that. You feel that anxiety. In Country Club Hills I missed a court date, so when I came in they held me and locked me up. It was embarrassing. So much pressure here, it'll make a grown man cry. It'll break you down like cancer.

Black man from Ferguson (aged 66–75)

I've lived here for nine years and I own my home. I've had very bad experiences with the police. I'm actually suing the Ferguson police department right now. They came to my house because they wanted to speak with my son. They knocked on the door and said they had a warrant but they didn't. They threw me down on the floor and handcuffed me. They found my son and tased him. It turns out the Berkeley police wanted to talk to my son, so the Ferguson police just came in like that. I got a lawyer and went to court and they dropped the charges because they never had a warrant.

Black woman from University City (aged 56–65), regarding North County

I was walking with my grandson to his day care at our church in North County one morning. He was wearing his rain boots and after I dropped him off

I thought, "What if he wants to play outside and he needs his shoes?" So I turned around (in the church parking lot) to go home and get his shoes. The police stopped me and the officer said I had made a "sudden move." In the county they are looking for Black people. In the city Black people blend in.

Black man from Normandy (aged 56–65)

My wife drives a 2015 Taurus, I was driving it and I got stopped for driving while Black. The officer said my sticker wasn't high enough on my license plate. I told him that the sticker was put on by the dealer when we bought the car. I actually called the dealer and he confirmed it but I still got a ticket. So I walked to the police station and spoke to the chief. I explained how I got the ticket and he tore it up. It's a good thing I know how to talk to the cops or that could have turned out differently.

Black woman from Ferguson (aged 56–65)

I had a bad experience with Calverton Park. My son was stopped there on his way to work, and I was called. He was cited for "improper lane usage" after the cop put his lights on to pull him over! He hadn't actually done anything wrong until he was pulling over. It was just a "random" stop.

Black woman from Vinita Terrace (aged 56–65)

My boyfriend used to come over and he would get tickets constantly for parking too often in the community. We went to court and they told us that he would continue to get tickets and he should stay in a hotel. We're still paying for those tickets. I wanted to do community service but I couldn't because I was working a job. . . . There's only certain hours you can do it.

Black man from Hanley Hills (aged 56–65)

They definitely target you on small issues out here: trash, grass, stickers. It keeps you on pins and needles in order to keep things straight all the time. I got a ticket for paying my trash bill [to an independent company] thirty days late. I actually paid it before getting the ticket so I went to the court and showed them all the paperwork that I had paid it and they dismissed it. Other people were there were paying seventy-five- and one-hundred-dollar fines for not paying their trash bills.

[His female partner added,] They've got someone working at the city who calls the trash company to find out who hasn't paid on time and they send them a ticket. That's just lazy, unfair, and unjust. People could use that money to pay their trash bill but instead they have to give it to the city for a fine.

Children and the parents of minors are not allowed in most courts, and police are assigned to keep order, which many residents say amounts to constant harassment while waiting.[8] Cases of those who can afford an attorney are heard first. When those who cannot afford an attorney finally appear, the most common directive to those unable to pay, according to those interviewed, is to immediately step out to call every friend and family member they can think of to bring money so they won't have to "be detained."[9] Not coincidentally, payday loan establishments have cropped up next to many municipal courts, in addition to bail bondsmen, to take advantage of family members who do not have the resources to pay the fines and fees of those jailed. One municipal judge in this area points to this practice as particularly effective because the city receives more of what is owed, stating that "if people didn't break the law they would not have these problems."[10] This is ironic coming from someone who works for a municipality that has not filed the required data for multiple years or adhered to the cap on municipal financing set forth by the Macks Creek Law, with no consequences.[11] Another judge handed brochures to residents for his brother's traffic school as a means to settle tickets.[12]

The threat of jail time and the inability to move because of economic constraints ensure that municipal court payments are a priority for residents, regardless of the limitations of their monthly budgets and the sacrifices required to make these payments, including food for themselves or their families.[13] In many cases, the absence of opportunities for formal employment leads residents to turn to informal economies in order to pay fines. This fact exposes another reading of theorizations regarding the uses of the wageless class.[14] Because of the "taxation-by-citation" structure of municipal financing in these small cities, informal economies are a primary source of funding for municipal budgets. Selling food subsidies and blood, bartering, receiving compensation for listing nonfamily dependents on tax returns, hustling products of questionable origin, doing hair and nails, taking out payday or car title loans, and borrowing money from equally struggling family members as well as friends and neighbors are all examples of how residents coble together resources to pay fines, fees, and bail for minor infractions.[15] As a result, cities remain financially solvent by extracting resources gained through informal economies. While extreme, this phenomenon is not unique to St. Louis County. When Eric Garner resisted arrest for selling individual cigarettes on a Staten Island street corner to stay afloat, saying, "This stops today," he was referring to the perpetual criminalization of his attempts to make ends meet. Like Michael Brown, who, according to his companion Dorian

Johnson was fed up with being harassed by police for "walking while Black" in North St. Louis County, resistance led to death.

Reports and news coverage have also revealed that some city leaders and police chiefs set monthly citation quotas for police officers based on budgetary shortfalls, and many cities routinely plan future budgetary increases based on projected increases in arrest and fine quotas by police chiefs (figure 3.1).[16] I personally witnessed one city leader calling the police chief and demanding that police officers come to a certain area and write more tickets. I witnessed the same official calling the mayor to report specific addresses for visits from the housing inspector because the residents "didn't have the right attitude" during interactions.

MEMO

Date: April 18, 2014

To: Edmundson P. D. – Sergeants and Patrolmen

Subject: Traffic tickets

In the past several weeks, the Board and I have noticed a marked downturn in traffic and other tickets being written by your department. It is correct that we have no quotas and want only "good tickets" written. However, we do have a record of your past performance to compare to your current performance and the picture that I see is a very disappointing one.

I wish to take this opportunity to remind you that the tickets that you write do add to the revenue on which the P. D. budget is established and will directly affect pay adjustments at budget time.

It is and has always been the desire of myself and the Board to provide a safe and pleasant work place with good compensation and benefits for everyone. However, our ability to continue doing this is being compromised by your work slow down. I realize that your work production records are directly affected by many extenuating circumstances and those factors are always accounted for as your work records are reviewed by myself and human resources.

As budget time approaches, please make a self evaluation of your work habits and motivations, then make the changes that you see that will be fair to yourself and the city.

Thank you

Calm E. Gwaltney

Mayor John Gwaltney

FIGURE 3.1 Letter from the mayor of Edmundson, April, 18, 2014.

St. Louis Post-Dispatch.

Over the past ten years, most cities in this geography have averaged more than one citation per every one resident per year. Many average four to five citations for every one resident, with some issuing as many as ten citations per resident on average every year.[17] Leaders have adamantly insisted that all policing is carried out and citations issued in the interests of safety and the protection of individuals and property. While the number of citations written in North St. Louis County cities trended upward between 2004 and 2014, a dramatic decrease occurred in all but two cities between 2014 and 2015 (see table 3.1). According to city leaders interviewed for this research, these data suggest that residents in North St. Louis County became more compliant between 2014 and 2015, which coincidentally corresponded with over fifty media articles, as well as state legislation, aimed at exposing and remediating predatory policing practices—brought about by Ferguson protesters following the death of Michael Brown Jr. In 2015, new guidelines were passed by the Missouri legislature stipulating that all revenue generated from court fines and fees over 12.5 percent of the general operating budget of a city was to be given to the local school district. If, as leaders have consistently argued, Black residents "don't know how to behave in the suburbs" and need to be policed for purposes of public safety and the protection of property, then the same leadership should, in theory, continue to police citizens and turn the excess revenue over to struggling schools. Interestingly, when cities cease to directly profit from policing, policing decreases substantially.

The data from St. Louis County show a distinct trend: the higher the percentage of Black residents in a city, the higher the percentage of the municipal budget is derived from court fines and fees. In the two majority-white cities that are exceptions to this trend, the cities of Bella Villa and Calverton Park, Black motorists make up a significant number of traffic stops relative to the municipal demographics, meaning that Black residents are still policed for revenue in majority-white cities (see table 3.1). Poor white residents of St. Louis County are also concentrated in unincorporated areas, making it more difficult to assess whether or not these residents are impacted by policing for revenue through the county court.

Although table 3.1 reveals that the city of Ferguson is by no means the worst offender in terms of budgetary funding from policing or citations per resident, the Ferguson protests led the US Department of Justice to review municipal practices in the city. It found that "Ferguson's law enforcement practices are shaped by the city's focus on revenue rather than by public safety needs. This emphasis on revenue has compromised the institutional character of Ferguson's police department, contributing to a pattern of unconstitutional policing and has also shaped its municipal court, leading to procedures that raise due process concerns and inflict unnecessary harm on members of the Ferguson community."[18]

TABLE 3.1 Demographic and policing data for twenty-four cities in North St. Louis County, eight selected cities in larger St. Louis County, and the City of St. Louis

MUNICIPALITY · POPULATION · AREA	% BLACK	% BELOW POVERTY LINE	% OF TRAFFIC STOPS INVOLVING NONWHITE INDIVIDUALS, 2005–15	% OF NONTRAFFIC VIOLATIONS ISSUED TO NONWHITE INDIVIDUALS, 2009–14	% OF BUDGET FROM FINES & FEES, 2013	AVERAGE TOTAL VIOLATIONS PER PERSON PER YEAR, 2005–14	% CHANGE IN # OF TRAFFIC VIOLATIONS, 2014–15	% CHANGE IN # OF NONTRAFFIC VIOLATIONS, 2014–15
Bel-Nor 1,499 people 0.63 sq. miles	46	8	78	79	11	2.65	–43	–37
Bel-Ridge 2,715 people 0.80 sq. miles	85	27	74	City set prohibitive cost for obtaining data	25	2.57	–47	–13
Bella Villa 729 people 0.13 sq. miles	1	6	12	Data not requested	57	9.6	–66	–58
Bellerive 188 people 0.33 sq. miles	43	1	Not reported	93	29	3.01	–77	–67
Berkeley 8,971 people 4.97 sq. miles	82	22	63	Data not requested	11	1.34	–62	–8
Beverly Hills 574 people 0.09 sq. miles	93	29	93	95	26	10.29	–49	–32

Black Jack 6,929 people 2.6 sq. miles	81	11	Not reported	Data not requested	4	0.22	−49	−24
Calverton Park 1,293 people 0.40 sq. miles	42	10	72	Data not requested	66	4.17	−74	−75
Charlack 1,363 people 0.26 sq. miles	35	9	58	City set prohibitive cost for obtaining data	29	3.44	−21	−65
Clayton 15,939 people 15.9 sq. miles	8	8	35	Data not requested	3	0.48	−44	−27
Cool Valley 1,196 people 0.47 sq. miles	85	11	92	92	29	3.04	−53	−15
Ferguson 21,201 people 6.22 sq. miles	67	23	82	City set prohibitive cost for obtaining data	14	0.91	−75	−69
Des Peres 8,373 people 4.32 sq. miles	1	3	15	Data not requested	4	0.44	−16	−16

(Continued)

TABLE 3.1 (Continued)

MUNICIPALITY • POPULATION • AREA	% BLACK	% BELOW POVERTY LINE	% OF *TRAFFIC STOPS* INVOLVING NONWHITE INDIVIDUALS, 2005–15	% OF *NONTRAFFIC VIOLATIONS* ISSUED TO NONWHITE INDIVIDUALS, 2009–14	% OF BUDGET FROM FINES & FEES, 2013	AVERAGE TOTAL VIOLATIONS PER PERSON PER YEAR, 2005–14	% CHANGE IN # OF *TRAFFIC VIOLATIONS,* 2014–15	% CHANGE IN # OF *NONTRAFFIC* VIOLATIONS, 2014–15
Greendale 651 people 0.21 sq. miles	69	19	12	91	11	1.72	–34	–20
Hanley Hills 2,101 people 0.36 sq. miles	85	26	85	92	11	0.69	–50	–46
Ladue 8,521 people 8.55 sq. miles	1	1	16	Data not requested	4	0.53	+10	+65
Maplewood 8,046 people 1.56 sq. miles	17	15	15	Data not requested	9	1.51	–37	–11
Normandy 5,008 people 1.85 sq. miles	70	23	75	90	41	4.01	–17	–28
Northwoods 4,227 people 0.71 sq. miles	94	23.2	76	City set prohibitive cost for obtaining data	26	1.53	–28	+5
Olivette 7,737 people 2.78 sq. miles	24	4	45	Data not requested	4	0.41	No change	–9

Pagedale 3,304 people 1.19 sq. miles	93	30.2	85	City refused to provide data*	18	2.14	-30	-23
Pine Lawn 3,275 people 0.61 sq. miles	96	33.6	79	City refused to provide data*	48	5.88	-1550	-14
St. Ann 13,020 people 3.20 sq. miles	22	13.3	40	Data not requested	37	1.25	-52	-19
St. John 6,517 people 1.42 sq. miles	24	12.1	24	64	24	1.96	-15	-10
Sunset Hills 8,496 9.14 sq. miles	2	4.8	11	Data not requested	6	0.42	+17	+14
Uplands Park 445 people .007 sq. miles	96	16.9	Not reported	Data not requested	24	4.27	-99	-93
Velda City 1,420 people 0.16 sq. miles	95	24.8	92	City set prohibitive cost for obtaining data	22	3.58	-40	-36
Velda Village Hills 1,005 people 0.12 sq. miles	99	29.5	99	99	10	0.93	-13	-46

(Continued)

TABLE 3.1 (Continued)

MUNICIPALITY · POPULATION · AREA	% BLACK	% BELOW POVERTY LINE	% OF TRAFFIC STOPS INVOLVING NONWHITE INDIVIDUALS, 2005–15	% OF NONTRAFFIC VIOLATIONS ISSUED TO NONWHITE INDIVIDUALS, 2009–14	% OF BUDGET FROM FINES & FEES, 2013	AVERAGE TOTAL VIOLATIONS PER PERSON PER YEAR, 2005–14	% CHANGE IN # OF TRAFFIC VIOLATIONS, 2014–15	% CHANGE IN # OF NONTRAFFIC VIOLATIONS, 2014–15
Vinita Park 1,880 people 0.72 sq. miles	65	22.5	76	City set prohibitive cost for obtaining data	12	1.37	+85	−7
Vinita Terrace (merged in 2016) 277 people 0.06 sq. miles	73	15.2	Not reported	89	52	6.61	−23	−46
Wellston 2,313 people 0.93 sq. miles	95	43.5	Not reported	City refused to provide data*	12	2.65	−35	−16
Warson Woods 1,962 people 0.58 sq. miles	1	5	7	Data not requested	3	0.38	−44	+41
City of St. Louis 319,294 people 66.0 sq. miles	49	25	67	Data not requested	2	0.57	+11	−18

Sources: 2010 US Census Data, https://www.census.gov; US Census Data, American FactFinder, 2013–17 American Community Survey, https://factfinder.census.gov/faces/nav/jsf/pages/index.xhtml; Missouri Courts Annual Statistical Reports (Supplement-Municipal Division), https://www.courts.mo.gov/page.jsp?id=296; Better Together Municipal Courts Report, https://static1.squarespace.com/static/59790f03a5790abd8c698c9c/t/5c4b0260ebbe8fdff77c74b/155242403815/BT-Municipal-Courts-Report-Full-Report1-%281%29.pdf; Missouri Attorney General's Office, Vehicle Stops Reports, https://www.ago.mo.gov/home/vehicle-stops-report; independent request for court data to selected municipal courts in accordance with the Missouri Sunshine Law (by author).

Note: Shaded rows indicate cities in St. Louis County that are outside the area considered North County.

* In violation of Missouri Sunshine Law.

The report then describes in great detail the extent to which the police harassed the city's Black population. The police, for example, regularly accosted residents for what might be termed "sitting in a car while Black" and then charged them with bogus crimes such as failing to wear a seat belt in a parked car or "making a false declaration" that, for instance, one's name was "Mike," not "Michael."[19] Officers seeking promotion were told to keep in mind that their numbers of "self-initiated activities" (random stops) would have a significant effect on their future success on the force. The report cites several internal documents encouraging lieutenants and sergeants to tell officers wanting promotions that decisions would be based on the number of these stops.[20] Meanwhile, residents issued citations often lost their jobs and livelihoods because of court appearances, fines, and jail time. Justice Department investigators also discovered that Ferguson municipal court did not "act as a neutral arbiter of the law or a check on unlawful police conduct." Instead, it used its judicial authority "as the means to compel the payment of fines and fees that advance the city's financial interests."[21] If these are the conclusions drawn in one of the least predatory cities in North County, the question arises: How much worse are conditions in cities issuing ten times the number of citations per person each year?

As discussed above, recent reports and media attention focused on Ferguson often suggest that the death of Michael Brown and the unrest that followed were largely due to a racial mismatch between leadership and the residents of Ferguson. Scholars and journalists have used this imbalance to explain the hyperpolicing and unjust treatment of residents that led to mistrust between residents, leadership, and the police. This dynamic, however, does not explain similar and (as table 3.1 reveals) even larger degrees of predatory practices in predominantly Black cities in North St. Louis County that have all-Black leadership. To highlight a comparison from table 3.1, police officers, building inspectors, and judges in Pine Lawn, a community of 3,275 people which is 96 percent Black and has an all-Black leadership and significantly "more Black" law enforcement, issued more than nineteen thousand traffic tickets and over nine thousand nontraffic ordinance violations (eight violations for every one resident) in 2014.[22] In the same year, fines and fees in Pine Lawn composed 48 percent of the city's budget, well above the 30 percent cap mandated by the Macks Creek Law. In comparison, the city of Ferguson, with a population of 21,200, wrote 11,800 traffic violations and 11,900 nontraffic ordinance violations in 2014 (roughly one violation for every one resident), with fines and fees making up 22 percent of the municipal budget.[23]

In spite of the fact that it is unconstitutional to jail someone solely because they are unable to pay fines and fees, many courts jail individuals without holding the required hearings on their ability to pay, a clear violation of those individuals' constitutional rights.[24] More often courts threaten to jail individuals, without intending to follow through but hoping fear will entice them to take out payday or car title loans (loan establishments are conveniently located near municipal courts), dip into rent or grocery money, sell government-issued subsidies in the informal market, or borrow from friends and family members whose financial status is also precarious.[25] Interviews with North County residents and a review of court procedures reveal some of the varied ways cities pressure desperate residents to find ways to pay fines and fees for nonviolent offenses, even when they lack the financial means. For example, citizens found guilty of a traffic violation in Beverly Hills must pay the fine in full or be jailed until someone shows up to pay the fine.[26] Similarly, it is well documented that Pine Lawn and Jennings have routinely jailed people for weeks and even months without a change of clothes or toiletries for failure to pay a speeding ticket.[27] Northwoods will demand and hold the driver's licenses of residents parking within city limits but unable to pay for the required city parking sticker. Residents in Velda City or St. Ann who are pulled over with a warrant for failure to appear in court must pay the fine on the spot or face arrest and being held until the assigned court date weeks later.[28]

While most residents I interacted with had frequent encounters with the police, the majority have given up on calling authorities when they are victims of, or witnesses to, a crime, stating they do not trust the police to act in their best interest. One woman interviewed for this research recounted a time when she called the police because her neighbors were arguing and she feared for the woman's safety. By the time the police arrived, the neighbors were quiet, but she ended up in handcuffs because she refused to let police search her house. While she was handcuffed, the police searched her house unlawfully and then cited her for multiple housing infractions. When she complained to city officials, the housing inspector showed up at her house three days later and issued additional property violations, which she interpreted as retaliation and a warning.[29] In another more publicized case, a mother called the police because her mentally disturbed son had a knife and was threatening to hurt himself. The police arrived and coaxed him out of the house; he was carrying the knife and a bible. When he refused to drop the knife, he was shot dead.[30] Many people I spoke with stated that they would not call the police voluntarily, "no matter what," because they feared they or someone else would be wrongfully arrested or killed.[31] "There is no way in hell I would call the police even if I was dying," one woman told me.[32] Judging from statements by almost every respondent that voluntarily calling the police was entirely out of the question, officers appear to have plenty of time for police-initiated stops.

The fragmented geography and postage-stamp size of many cities in North County often mean that residents experience what Patrice has described—amassing several violations from multiple cities, often on the same day for the same infraction, such as having a broken taillight or faulty muffler. Residents comment on "the fact you can get pulled over in one jurisdiction then just cross over into another and in five seconds get the EXACT same ticket as you just did."[33] Another stated, "In the county you can get ticketed almost every other day. I have tickets from municipalities I didn't even know existed. Turns out, I was driving through five different towns when I thought it was all one—because they are literally the size of a football field." Yet another said, "I've been stopped three times in one week in three different municipalities on my way home from work because my windows were tinted. It is ridiculous. The only way you know you're entering a different city is a different police officer stops you."[34] Again, while extreme, these experiences are not unique to North St. Louis County. For example, the 2016 shooting of Philando Castile, who reportedly was stopped for a broken taillight and subsequently shot to death in front of his girlfriend and her daughter in his car in Falcon Heights, Minnesota, revealed how Black residents in suburban Minneapolis also experience hyperpolicing. Castile had been stopped fifty-two times and issued eighty-six violations in fourteen years for minor traffic infractions and had paid thousands of dollars in municipal fines and fees.[35] As was the case in several instances involving North St. Louis County residents, witnesses claim that Castile's taillight was not broken. And as in the case of Michael Brown, whose physical appearance was seemingly blamed for his death, after the Philando Castile shooting the officer claimed that Castile's "flared nostrils" resembled those of a suspect in a robbery.

Residents throughout North County point to tickets that do not list court dates, or list the wrong court date, as intentional attempts at creating confusion about how to settle tickets or ploys to prevent citizens from appearing for court dates and thus to accumulate more fines or warrants for their arrest.[36] Many also explain the difficulties they have encountered when trying to obtain information from part-time courts, which lack full-time staff, hold court only one or two nights each month, and often do not maintain websites. Others describe confusion created by the existence of multiple courts in a small geography, each with a different set of policies and practices. The biggest factor residents name for not appearing in court is fear of jail time for inability to pay, which many, like Patrice, have either experienced themselves or know about from others who have been jailed. Other reasons for not appearing include lack of childcare, since most cities do not allow children in court, and the inability to get to the court for fear of receiving another ticket while driving there.[37] As a result, the number of people who live with anxiety over warrants for their arrest or mounting fines for small infractions in multiple cities is staggering. This dramatically affects decisions residents make, such as when and where to drive and whether or not to use public space and amenities, such as parks.[38] Public transportation is lacking in this area, which was developed as a series of commuter suburbs for people with cars. Food deserts are common since many grocery stores relocated to more affluent communities, and many people described sending their children to the nearby gas station to buy snacks for meals because they did not want to use their cars to drive several miles for groceries out of fear of being pulled over.[39]

For those residents who do attempt to take care of violations immediately, stories of frustration, barriers, and jail time are surprisingly normal.[40] Many cities in North County issue so many violations that they often have several hundred cases on a docket for one court evening, with some courts averaging five hundred cases per docket.[41] On court nights people can be found lined up and down the street of the court building for hours, waiting to take care of a ticket. Many who were interviewed on those evenings worried while they waited that they might end up in jail that night because they did not come with enough money. Others explained that they constantly lived on the edge because of payment plans that took years to pay off. Many residents shared the sentiment of a woman who said, "Money-wise I've practically gone broke multiple times. Court fees and paying fines constantly over minor things has really taken a toll on me and him [referring to her son]."[42]

While the recent focus on North St. Louis and St. Louis County has been directed at traffic violations and warrants, many people are not aware of the many other methods by which municipalities in this area collect fines and fees and even take possession of property. These types of nontraffic and property violations have increased greatly over the past ten years and, like traffic violations, disproportionately affect nonwhite residents.[43] When Senate Bill 5 was passed in March of 2015, capping the amount cities can collect from *traffic-related* fines and fees at 12.5 percent of the total municipal budget, many feared that cities would seek to replace lost revenue by increasing the number and costs of nontraffic violations issued. In light of preliminary data, this is a valid concern, since the number of traffic violations plummeted while nontraffic citations increased significantly over the six-month period after the law went into effect.[44] In 2016, the Missouri legislature passed modifications to the bill, which added nontraffic violations to the limits set on revenue generated through the courts.[45] These types of nonviolent violations target property and behavior and include infractions in the following areas: manner of walking, wearing sagging pants, playing loud music, leaving toys or wading pools in front yards, playing in the street, having basketball hoops or barbecuing in front yards, drinking alcohol within fifty feet of a grill, installing mismatched curtains, loitering in a park, failure to secure a trash can lid, failure to keep grass at a certain length, allowing individuals not listed on occupancy permits to spend the night, owning a nuisance dog, telling someone's future, and failure to contract with the private trash collection company. The idea that someone could potentially land in jail for failure to appear in court or for the inability to pay for a citation for mismatched curtains seems implausible, yet residents questioned about this possibility emphatically stated, "Yes, that could happen for sure."[46]

Cities also use bizarre interpretations of the International Property Maintenance Code to cite hundreds of homes for specific infractions. According to the data, cities tend to choose a pet infraction each year.[47] For instance, in 2010 the city of Normandy cited 110 homes for "failure to paint sign pole," citing ordinance 505.020, which adopted the international standards for property maintenance requirements. This was in addition to the 303 homes that received citations for "violating minimum housing standards," with reference to the same ordinance (505.020). But the only wording in the international standards that comes close to the language about failing to paint a sign pole in the Normandy ordinance is a clause stating that all exterior metal must be painted with rust-resistant paint. The following year, no houses received a "failure to paint sign pole" citation in Normandy; however, eighty-one homes were cited for "failure to paint the front of a rear door," again using ordinance 505.020.[48]

One could argue that the practices outlined above are not race-based since, as one leader put it, "we're all poor and we're all Black."[49] This argument, however, would be shortsighted, since the reasons that these cities give for resorting to policing for revenue and the predatory policing tactics employed by administrators are dependent upon perceptions of race and realities of race-making. While tiny cities in North St. Louis County with more diverse populations claim that the inordinate number of traffic citations written to Black drivers is due to the number of Black nonresidents driving through their boundaries, the same cities disproportionately cite Black residents for housing and nontraffic violations. Of the eight municipalities that complied with a request for data regarding nontraffic ordinance violations, all of them issued a larger percentage of citations to Black residents than the overall percentage of Black residents in their jurisdiction.

For example, Greendale has a population of 651 residents and is 69 percent Black. Between 2012 and 2014, 91 percent of all nontraffic violations were written to Black Greendale residents. The city of Bellerive has a population of 254 people and is 43 percent Black. Between 2012 and 2014, 93 percent of nontraffic violations were written to Black residents of Bellerive. The city of Bel-Nor has a population of 1,500 people, of whom 43 percent are Black. Between 2012 and 2015, 79 percent of nontraffic violations were issued to Black residents of Bel-Nor. In Cool Valley, 85 percent of the 1,196 residents are Black, but Black residents receive 92 percent of nontraffic violations. Normandy, with a population of 5,008 residents, of whom 70 percent are Black, issues 90 percent of nontraffic citations to Black residents. Finally, the city of Pasadena Park has a population of 470 people, of whom 60 percent are Black, and issues 78 percent of nontraffic violations to Black residents.[50] The issuing of nontraffic ordinance violations to a disproportionate number of Black residents feeds the cycle of traffic violations, since whenever a police officer stops a Black driver, for any or no reason, the likelihood is high that the driver will have an outstanding warrant for failure to pay a nontraffic violation. It is interesting to note that seventeen municipalities either did not comply with my request for specific data concerning nontraffic citations (in violation of the Missouri Sunshine Law) or demanded more than five hundred dollars to provide data. This response led me to wonder whether or not disparities in noncompliant cities are higher than the disparities among cities complying with my request.

Policing the Suburban Crisis

In 1978, Stuart Hall, along with four coauthors, published *Policing the Crisis: Mugging, the State, and Law and Order*, which asserts that real and perceived crime rates cannot be viewed independently from the institutions that aim to control and report on crime.[51] The book examines the politics of policing—using mugging to look at the relationships between a rhetorical "moral panic" and policing campaigns in the context of colonial and imperial legacies of human differentiation through race-making. The authors argue that agencies such as the police, the courts, and the media do not passively react to a given crime situation but "are actively and continuously part of the whole process."[52] Forty years later, this conceptualization is useful for looking at the case of North St. Louis County, where municipal leaders, police, and the courts not only participate in the process of criminalization but, to a large extent, have created specific ways to criminalize Black behavior for economic purposes. Utilizing tropes of deviance, residents are moved from rights-bearing citizens to rightless criminals through the active policing of a rhetorical "suburban crisis," which works in tandem with equally powerful imaginations of suburban space and norms.

The crisis in the suburbs rhetorically promoted by municipal leaders stems from the very real economic crisis brought about by plummeting property values, hollowed-out commercial districts, and the evaporation of state and federal funding outlined in chapter 2. Leaders, municipal judges, and city attorneys, however, frame the crisis as a public safety issue and, in response, assert their "fundamental right to protect private property" and "maintain their sovereignty."[53] According to these narratives, the astronomical number of citations handed out—which is ten to twenty times higher than in white suburbs—is strictly due to the inability of Black residents to follow simple rules and the tendency of these residents to engage in behaviors said to threaten safety, devalue property, and discourage private investment. Taking the conflation of property values and public safety even further, one mayor argued that failing to maintain an aesthetically pleasing property was absolutely a public safety issue because it lowered overall property values and put other people in economic danger.[54] Consistently invoking the rights of the city itself, leaders, judges, and city attorneys claim that residents would have nothing to complain about if they would just "act right and take care of their property."[55] Blaming residents for the predicament of lost investment and framing aesthetic concerns as public safety issues shifts the focus of responsibility away from public and private actors that have abandoned this area and ignores the blatant poaching of resources practiced by more financially stable cities in the region. It also follows a long history of linking blackness to risk and blaming Black residents in North County neighborhoods when self-fulfilling prophecies of decline occur after investment moves elsewhere.

While much has been written about the criminalization of poverty and the many economies of the prison industrial complex, residents of North St. Louis County are perpetually punished for the loss of economic viability brought about by their sheer presence in space and subsequently suffer exploitation that preys on their own financial hardships.[56] In this way, cities must necessarily "catch and release" poor residents in order to maintain a steady stream of revenue through what amounts to legalized extortion. Comparing municipal practices to criminal racketeering, a class action complaint against thirteen cities in North St. Louis County makes the following point:

> [Cities] have abused the legal system to bestow a patina of legitimacy on what is, in reality, extortion. If private parties had created and implemented this scheme, enforced it by threatening and imposing indefinite incarceration, and milked poor families of millions of dollars, the law would punish them as extortionists and racketeers, and the community would take steps to prevent them from exploiting the most vulnerable of its members. These predatory practices are no more legitimate— indeed are more outrageous—when state and local government actors perpetuate them under cover of law.[57]

In contradistinction to the concept of whiteness-as-property—the legally protected rights associated with a white privileged identity—blackness-as-risk erodes, and in some cases suspends, the rights of Black citizens so that perceived risks may be contained, controlled, and limited in the interests of economic and physical security.[58] As Cheryl Harris showed more than two decades ago, whiteness holds tangible and enforceable rights.[59] In her now-classic essay "Whiteness as Property," Harris examines the many ways white privilege is constructed and enforced in, and through, legal interpretations that do not explicitly rely on racist doctrine. The ways in which eminent domain is exercised and upheld in spite of legal challenges by communities of color, using legal claims of "public good" and "highest and best use," exemplify how whiteness-as-property determines what is considered good or best for people and space.

Blackness-as-risk can be understood as the inverse of Harris's argument. The association of blackness with risk permeates all levels of decision-making, from individual to institutional, in a society where historical constructions of race determined whether one was free or unfree and where one drop of Black blood stripped individuals of the privileges afforded white subjects.[60] In a more blatant example of the legal ramifications of blackness-as-risk, less than 1 percent of police officers who shoot and kill unarmed people of color are charged with a crime, and even fewer are convicted of wrongdoing. This statistic alone shows how the risk associated with blackness is understood as sufficient reason for the use of deadly force.[61] The risk associated with blackness can be clearly seen in North County, from structural disinvestment and the hollowing out of middle-class suburbs to the legalized killing of unarmed Black residents.

Beyond the essential framework of antiblackness, another useful theorization for understanding the phenomena found in North St. Louis County is Michel Foucault's concept of a punitive society and the use of fines (defined as the taking of property—real and monetary). The four tactics of state violence identified by Foucault in *The Punitive Society: Lectures at the Collège de France, 1972–73*,[62] which create an everyday penal system within normative society, are on bold display throughout this geography:

1. *Exclusion from the right to live somewhere.* Residents of North St. Louis County find their right to a place to live compromised through multiple property violations, harassment, loss of income, and in some cases, the confiscation of their homes. Many residents find that the so-called right to the suburbs afforded by the Fair Housing Act of 1968 does not apply to them, and they end up returning to St. Louis city, where they report there is significantly less harassment. As one mayor in North St. Louis County put it, "Having a place to live is a privilege" and not a right.[63]

2. *Compensation from subjects for what is lost by "the state."* As described in this chapter, residents are made to compensate cities for lost revenues brought about by disinvestment linked to the risk associated with their very bodies.

3. *Public acknowledgment of a sovereign power and authority and the marking of the subject.* Residents are made to understand the power of what many

mayors expressed as "sovereign cities" and marked as deviant—publicly harassed and humiliated—through constant police stops and draconian court policies.

4. *The literal denial of physical and individual freedoms—confinement.* Jail time and the denial of individual freedom are frequent threats and part of the reality experienced by countless people across this geography. Many residents are further confined by the inability to move due to economic constraints.

Foucault goes on to argue, "What has to be brought out first of all in the analysis of a penal system is the nature of the struggles that take place around power in a society."[64] He asks, "What forms of power are actually at work for power to respond to infractions that call its laws, rules, and exercise into question with tactics such as exclusion, marking, redemption, or confinement?"[65] The criminalization of normal behavior and extreme policing of minor infractions, as well as everyday practices that oppress the opportunity to live freely, are some of the forms of power at work in this area, which reveal how governance and governmentality operate at the most local and mundane levels of society. In this way, the racial state is a local state of affairs. Moments of extreme violence, such as the death of Michael Brown, are eruptions of quotidian practices that create the conditions of possibility for racialized police brutality.

A Hollow Prize of Black Political Autonomy

The people of North St. Louis County understand the history, policies, and politics described in this chapter, and their experience defies the notion that race is becoming increasingly less important in the United States. Many people I spoke with also believe that the implications of race today are less about skin color and personal prejudices and more about the power to control in ways that keep one group over another, which has always been a fundamental purpose of race-making. This perspective explains why structures of antiblackness are implemented by Black leaders using white spatial logics. In addition to the scathing review by the Department of Justice regarding racist and race-based practices and culture in both the municipal administration and police department of Ferguson, other reports prompted by Ferguson resistance also cite racialized practices. For example, the findings presented in the report from the Ferguson Commission, released in September 2015, squarely focus on race.[66] After a year of research and listening to communities, the report began by stating, "We know that talking about race makes a lot of people uncomfortable. But make no mistake: This is about race."[67] Remarkably, the commission was made up of a bipartisan cross-section of community leaders, residents, and law enforcement representatives appointed by the governor of Missouri to report on the underlying causes of, and possible proactive responses to, unrest in Ferguson. Although there are 189 calls to action listed in the report, which was supposed to focus on Ferguson, the authors make clear that the report is intended to read as a narrative about racial inequities found in the history, policies, and practices of the St. Louis region.[68]

The report is somewhat unusual because it is intended to directly address the causes, as opposed to merely the consequences, of tensions. Governor Jay Nixon's executive order establishing the Ferguson Commission stated, "The unrest and public discourse set in motion by the events of August 9 in Ferguson, Missouri underscore the need for a thorough, wide-ranging and unflinching study of the social and economic conditions that impede progress, equality and safety in the St. Louis region."[69] The Ferguson Commission, in its own words, specifically embraced the call to be "unflinching." This meant "listening, often uncomfortably, to the personal stories shared by citizens who came to our open meetings, and by people we interviewed throughout the process of developing this report.... Many of the stories were frustrating, depressing, infuriating, deflating, and heart-wrenching. We are committed to honoring those stories, and facing those truths, throughout our work and in this report."[70]

The 203 pages of the report present the same depressing data regarding the interconnecting disparities of race and class in the St. Louis region that my research reveals and similarly attaches the experiences of marginalized residents to specific data and analysis. As a "living document," commissioned at the highest level of state government, the report is an important resource for understanding the degrees of racialized experience in the St. Louis region, with an emphasis on North St. Louis County. How the report will impact change and whether or not recommendations will be implemented remain to be seen. The fact remains that dehumanized Black bodies continue to be used as revenue-generating reservoirs, just as they have been used historically. The 2018 victory of Wesley Bell in the Democratic primary for St. Louis County prosecutor has provided hope to some that change is occurring. Almost four years to the day after Michael Brown was killed in Ferguson, Bell, a Black candidate who ran on a reform platform, unseated the seven-term white incumbent, Bob McCulloch, who was highly criticized for his handling of the police shooting that killed Brown. Although many people calling for reform in St. Louis County cite this outcome as a major milestone, the fact that Bell worked for many years as a municipal judge and prosecutor in multiple small cities across North St. Louis County and oversaw many of the practices described above is rarely mentioned.

Although cities are fighting to maintain the status quo, it is clear to municipal leaders that their world is changing. Less clear is whether change will come in the form of actually remediating inequitable and unconstitutional practices, finding alternative ways to exploit residents, or dissolving cities. In the three years following Ferguson unrest, municipal leaders attempted to preemptively "reform themselves" in closed-door meetings with judges and attorneys, in the hope of convincing state legislators and the Missouri Supreme Court that court reform can be internally addressed. In spite of the findings of an extensive audit and public meetings held by a working group of the Missouri Supreme Court that found vast problems with municipal courts in St. Louis County, few reforms are slated for implementation other than telling cities to do a better job.[71] Several leaders of small villages and third- and fourth-class cities complain their sovereignty has been infringed on by the state.[72] This consistent invocation of sovereignty suggests that the culture of fiefdoms in this fragmented area and the Missouri tradition of defying Dillon's Rule continue to frame leaders' perceptions (and confusion) regarding sovereignty, hierarchy of power, and structure of law.[73] However, the fact that cities have more or less been able to pass laws and conduct business as they wished for so many years certainly supports the conception that local governments can act as fiefdoms. In this way, municipalities continue to operate as racial states of "sovereign subjects" caught in perpetual cycles by which residents fund their own oppression in order for cities to survive.

Black leaders claim that policing is not about race or class in majority-Black cities where the leadership is all Black. However, the same leaders do cite race when challenging recent reform measures. A dozen municipalities, most of which are very small and majority Black, brought a lawsuit against the state, claiming Senate Bill 5 violates their constitutional rights.[74] The cities won the lawsuit by arguing the state is taking away an important revenue source without funding the law it has passed.[75] The lawsuit reveals how some municipalities will be vastly more affected by the law than others, and, in the end, many will cease to exist. Indeed, small Black cities will be the first to be erased and merged with other cities or dissolved into unincorporated St. Louis County, which shows how race directly impacts issues of autonomy and democracy at the smallest scale.[76] It also harkens back to a long history of erased and disempowered indigenous populations and Black communities throughout history and particularly in the St. Louis region.[77] This situation, however, is both a classic double bind and a zero-sum game if the question at hand remains: Should small Black cities be allowed to oppress and harass residents because otherwise their questionable right to exist will be violated? Arguing that Black leaders have a right to oppress Black constituents because they themselves are Black is an ironic twist in the logics of racial equality and illustrates the limitations of pursuing a "racial democracy." Clearly, municipal leaders, Black or white, should not be allowed to construct systems by which cities are funded through violence. However, setting majority-Black cities up for certain failure is equally troubling and reveals the degree to which blackness-as-risk operates within the economic structuring and norms of the United States.

Proponents of municipal consolidation are calling for what they see as the natural end to cities that do not serve the interests of residents. Majority-Black cities, as the worst offenders of predatory policing practices and the least capable of competing in the game of municipal solvency, will be the first to be dissolved under proposed reforms. The arguments used to promote consolidation focus almost entirely on the symptoms of municipal insolvency—specifically, predatory policing—and not on the cause, and certainly not on the question of historical responsibility. Those who have long supported consolidation plans view the unrest that reverberates from Ferguson as a political opportunity to highlight the very real consequences of political fragmentation, such as municipal dysfunction, inefficiency, greedy administrators, and racist practices, as they push for regional consolidation.[78] In 2019, proponents of merging cities in St. Louis County, and merging the county with St. Louis City, capitalized on the momentum created by Ferguson unrest and attempted reunification under a single metropolitan governance, something administrators across St. Louis County are vehemently fighting against. It is assumed by many in these discussions (in the media and public forums) that residents will be better off as citizens of unincorporated areas of St. Louis County or larger municipalities, and perhaps that is true. However, consideration is not generally given to how municipal space functions as a racializing force or what new race-making situations may emerge under alternative forms of oversight. The latest effort toward city-county reunification failed after revelations of corruption, backroom deals, and other forms of misconduct emerged.[79]

It appears that any discussions will remain centered on the consequences rather than the causes of predatory practices, and Black leaders will continue to be used as scapegoats for the vast inequities and suffering residents endure. While it is difficult to find much sympathy for Black leaders who intentionally prey upon their own citizens, what they claim is true. Majority-white cities in St. Louis County will remain unaffected, whether or not the state is eventually able to enforce Senate Bill 5 or similar legislation. Cities in North St. Louis County that have hung on to white populations or bolstered commercial districts and capitalized on corporate investments, such as Emerson Electric and Express Scripts (headquartered in Ferguson and Berkeley), will likely weather current reform measures. The culture of fragmentation will continue to be promoted and defended by those who can afford to claim autonomy in the St. Louis region, and small Black municipalities will dissolve or be annexed into neighboring cities.

Lawsuits arguing that the state has not funded the law created by Senate Bill 5 potentially shift the focus to a different question: What is the obligation of the state or the county to ensure certain levels of funding for cities with no alternative sources of revenue—especially cities with historically oppressed populations?[80] This could also shift the focus to how the roots of inequality lie in the myriad ways Black residents have been isolated through legal forms of segregation and the legal gutting of resources from minority-occupied areas. Another shift in this line of questioning made by some reformers is, Should any of these tiny municipalities—Black or white—exist, in light of the costs and benefits to the region and the disparate experiences they create across a relatively small geography? The debates over localism versus regionalism are of course not new; however, the extreme practices, disparities, and violations of individual rights revealed in the case of North St. Louis County support arguments for regionalism by vividly illustrating the devastating consequences of "the favored quarter" or, in this instance, the favored fragments.[81] These, however, were not the arguments of the lawsuit brought by municipalities and not the reasons that leaders discursively use. Rather, according to the arguments made in the case and consistently made by municipal leaders, the purpose of the lawsuit was solely to declare Senate Bill 5 unconstitutional and return to business as usual. Simply focusing on municipal autonomy versus regional governance in terms of remediating disparity does not acknowledge the historical and prevailing weight that blackness carries with it.

The work that blackness-as-risk performs is experienced by people like Evelyn and Patrice in their everyday lives and justifies multiple technologies of the modern racial state.[82] The case of North St. Louis County challenges academic tendencies to draw distinct boundaries around violence and the state, and illustrates how technologies of policing and control operate within civic society at multiple scales of governance, particularly at the scale of the local.[83] These technologies of policing blackness *in and through space* are reinforced by the fact that individuals and institutions are economically rewarded when they separate themselves from perceived risks associated with nonwhite people and groups. Black city administrators tasked with the responsibility of reducing risk and maximizing economic stability in their jurisdictions are thus incentivized to engage in racialized practices that lead to complex contradictions and dilemmas when cities become majority Black. In North County, the economic risk associated with Black residents creates an additional double bind for leaders of majority-Black cities, because they must either work against the individual interests of their residents or risk losing Black political autonomy by operating outside the prevailing economic models. As a result, actions or inactions that disadvantage already disadvantaged groups are justified through appeals to risk management and fiscal responsibility by civic and corporate administrators, who are subsequently represented as rational actors.

As for Evelyn and Patrice, Evelyn has since moved out of Missouri and lives with her brother in Birmingham, where she grew up. Patrice still lives in her mother's house, which Evelyn is trying to sell, but "after what's owed on it in fines," the city may as well have it, she said when I contacted her by phone. "I swore I'd never go back to the South," she went on. "But nobody should have to live like that."

DISCURSIVE REGIMES
AND EVERYDAY PRACTICES

In every society the production of discourse is at once controlled, selected, organized and redistributed by a certain number of procedures whose role is to ward off its powers and dangers, to gain mastery over its chance events, to evade its ponderous, formidable materiality.

—Michel Foucault, *The Order of Discourse*

There is no racial divide in the city of Ferguson—that is the perspective of all residents in our city—absolutely. This community is absolutely supportive of what we've been doing and what we're doing moving forward. . . . Black or white, we're all middle-class citizens who believe in the same thing.

—Ferguson mayor James Knowles, August 19, 2014

Stories like those of Evelyn and Patrice, described in the last chapter, illustrate the degree to which race, space, and identity are mutually constituted and policed in metropolitan space and the disparate outcomes that are produced. The debates over how to define and study urban and suburban space, as well as whether North St. Louis County is urban, suburban, or something in between, go beyond simply qualifying physical geographies or mapping demographics, and beyond the relentless need scholars have to codify space. These distinctions reveal how space—as imagined, represented, and lived—is highly political and carries out specific types of work.[1] The fact that suffering is tolerated, or even expected, within certain spaces yet deemed intolerable in others illustrates the interdependencies between racial and spatial meanings, as well as the ways in which the intelligibility of race and differentiations of the value of life—those who must live and those who could die—are produced in and through space. As this chapter shows, space can be recodified over time or overnight, depending on the intended work spatial distinctions perform and the discursive processes used to link social and cultural practices to race and space.

The practices of policing residents for revenue in North St. Louis County rely on specific deployments of the suburban imaginary—producing respectable middle-class citizens, protecting private property, and upholding the aesthetic and cultural norms of suburban space. The discursive regimes at work in North St. Louis County determine what is known and what remains unknown about it, as well as what can and cannot happen within these boundaries. When the mayor of Ferguson stated that "we are all middle-class citizens who believe in the same thing" five days after Michael Brown died, he erased approximately half his constituency by coding "we" as middle-class and gesturing toward a whiteness that accompanies middle-class "beliefs." Michel Foucault points out, "each society has its regime of truth, its 'general politics' of truth: that is, the types of discourse which it accepts and makes function as true."[2] In the months following August 9, 2014, Mayor Knowles practiced a general politics of truth that appealed to a white spatial imaginary of Ferguson—as white and middle-class—in spite of the changes that had occurred. It was the same politics of truth used to extract thousands of dollars from residents and it was the politics that led to Brown's death. Although the discursive regime overseen by Knowles in Ferguson reflects practices everywhere, it illustrates the multiple scales of society in which regimes of truth operate. It also illustrates that "truths" occupy space and what is true can become false by simply relocating what we are talking about. In this way, North St. Louis County demonstrates Stuart Hall's observation that "each regime of truth *makes difference function discursively*," and, "by making difference intelligible in this way, each regime marks out human differences within culture in a way that corresponds exactly to how difference is understood to function in nature, that is 'naturally.'"[3]

Discursive power extends well beyond language. Discourses are the historically and contextually specific ways people interact with the world, view the world, and conduct themselves with other people.[4] Discourses of space are always discourses of race. Foucault underscores this point when he states that discourse is "a battle that has to be waged not between races, but by a race that is portrayed as the one true race, the race that holds power and [feels] entitled to define the norm, and against those who deviate from that norm, against those who pose a threat to the biological heritage."[5] The processes that lead to racial formations (as conceptualized by Michael Omi and Howard Winant) constitute discursively determined regimes of truth.[6] This is an important point made by Hall when he argues that "what is at stake is not whether there is some ultimate or final truth about the meaning of race to be found in the knowledge produced by science, but that our object of investigation shifts to examine the historical forms of knowledge that produce the intelligibility of race."[7] P. Khalil Saucier and Tryon P. Woods remind us, however, that "the originating and grounding name of racism is 'black' and yet the critical scholarship on racism persistently asserts otherwise."[8] In this way, generalized racial formation theory that misidentifies antiblackness is yet another regime that inflicts racialized trauma. In North St. Louis County, the historical association of *blackness* with risk rooted in the afterlife of slavery establishes the discursive grounds (and physical ground) that determine degrees and rights of citizenship.

An emphasis on "good suburban citizens" is clearly part of the politics of truth used by leaders in North St. Louis County to justify state violence. Antiblackness, which is historically dependent on a dialectical construct of civilization and its other, as discussed in chapter 1, is thus embedded in a localized understanding of citizenship and the terms for belonging. Modern interpretations of good citizenship based on capital accumulation further set the terms for good suburban subjects as functions of self-reliance and consumption that reinforce a self-perpetuating cycle of capitalism (which, following Cedric Robinson, is always racialized).[9] As Aihwa Ong observes, being a good citizen of a capitalist society means reducing one's burden and, therefore, it is one's *civic duty* to be economically productive and a good consumer.[10] The discursive qualifications of space are similarly dependent on the logics of development and capital such that the space of North St. Louis County, which is associated with subsidization, disinvestment, and loss of population, is inherently coded as inferior.

The Normandy Schools Crisis

In the fall of 2013, the residents of suburban North St. Louis County found themselves in the crosshairs of the urban schools debate in Missouri when the Normandy School District (NSD) lost its accreditation after eighteen years of provisional status. Both state and school officials explained the district's demise as stemming from its inability to deal with unfortunate "urban problems"—or, in less polite terms, "the ghetto mentality that plagues the area"—to quote the language used to refer to things such as a high proportion of female-headed households, violence, and supposedly rampant drug problems (although statistics show that rates of violence and drug activity in the area are comparable with those in South St. Louis County).[11] Due to housing insecurity caused by multiple intersecting factors, discussed in chapters 2 and 3, mobility rates of residents and functional homelessness, which are often represented as problems of urban space, are two of the biggest challenges faced by the district. The superintendent at the time embraced the urban identity and repeatedly called for the use of alternative metrics in evaluating teacher and school performance in "an urban district that has many external challenges."[12] Referring to the NSD controversy, the executive director of the group hired by the Department of Education to analyze statewide transfer laws stated, "We don't have any urban school districts in America that serve all of its kids well."[13] This statement identified the NSD as an urban district and reinforced that "urban" is how education officials describe failing schools regardless of their location.

When officials on the Missouri State Board of Education met to decide the accreditation status of the district, deliberations failed to bring up the fact that only three years earlier the same board had merged a failed district into the then-failing NSD. When the board dissolved the Wellston School District in 2010, it was 100 percent African American, and more than 95 percent of its students came from impoverished families. The question at that time was which district(s) would receive the "urban" student population made up entirely of poor Black children from North St. Louis County. Rather than face political pushback by sending students to thriving majority-white districts throughout the county, the board opted to send all of Wellston's children to the Normandy School District, which both Stanton Lawrence (the NSD superintendent at the time) and the board said was just beginning to see significant improvements in student achievement. Given the overwhelming data regarding the performance of impoverished Black children in highly segregated and underfunded schools, it is difficult to imagine that the board actually believed that combining two failing districts composed of poor Black children was going to improve the educational opportunities for the children involved or help the NSD reach accreditation. Many would later argue that the board was fully aware that the NSD would not survive the merger.

In spite of the unprecedented decision by the state board of education, which passed up any opportunity to partially desegregate St. Louis County schoolchildren, the merger of two failing and virtually all-Black districts did not result in any lawsuits filed by civil rights advocates or federal intervention, which is likely what the board was banking on. The NSD attempted to welcome the Wellston students into its schools, but the decision to merge the Wellston district with Normandy sealed the fate of children in both areas and cleared the way for the board's action two years later, when it declared the NSD nonaccredited and set in motion a state take-over. This, according to Lawrence, who resigned upon the board's decision, is the "school reform of punitive disparity."[14]

Shortly after the NSD and the Riverview Gardens School District—also in North St. Louis County—lost accreditation in 2013, the Missouri Supreme Court upheld the state's Student Transfer Program, requiring unaccredited districts to pay transportation and tuition costs set by the receiving districts (ranging from $9,500 to $21,000 annually per student) for any student requesting to transfer to an accredited district. In this way, the Student Transfer Program encourages students to desegregate themselves yet forces already failing districts, rather than the state, to pay for it, taking much-needed resources away from the students left behind. More than one thousand Normandy students (approximately 25 percent of the district population) transferred to schools in what were rhetorically represented as the "authentic suburbs"—according to media reports of the transfer process and public hearings.[15] Consequently, the NSD ran out of money in the spring of 2014. A hotly contested emergency funding bill was passed by the Missouri legislature in March 2014 in order to keep the district open through the academic year. The battle over funding was largely framed as a debate about whether Missouri taxpayers should be responsible for bailing out "failing urban schools," which happened to be located in historically white suburban space. As a bankrupt district, it was subsequently restructured by the state board of education, which suspended all contracts, temporarily placed it outside accreditation standards, and renamed it the Normandy Schools Collaborative. This prompted a new set of court actions and student transfer debates because it was technically (and strategically) no longer a district and therefore did not have to pay for student transfers or follow other requirements set for Missouri school districts. Prior to taking over the district, the state argued that students should be allowed to transfer and that the Normandy and Riverview Gardens districts had to pay any range of tuitions demanded by receiving districts. After the state takeover, however, the Department of Elementary and Secondary Education successfully argued that only students that had transferred in the prior school year would be allowed to remain as transfer students. Tuition for those students was negotiated at a lower rate by the state.

Race, or more accurately, racism—whether couched in euphemisms or actively invoked—was unequivocally at the center of both formal deliberation and ad hoc discussions regarding the NSD, including who would be blamed, who should determine the district's fate, who should pay for actions taken, and whose responsibility it is to educate "poor, urban kids" inconveniently located in St. Louis County.[16] The reactions of parents and other residents in North County, which were divided between those choosing to leave the district and those choosing to stay, as well as the reactions of residents in the receiving districts, were highly racialized. After attending a public hearing in the majority-white Francis Howell School District, which was slated to receive most of Normandy's transfer students via busing, one Normandy resident commented, "When I saw them screaming and hollering like they were crazy, I thought to myself, 'Oh my God, this is back in Martin Luther King days,' they're going to get the hoses out. They're going to be beating our kids and making sure they don't get off the school bus."[17] The statements by white parents that this resident was responding to included, "I now have to worry about my children getting stabbed? Or taking a drug? Or getting robbed? Because that's the issue"; "We don't want [these kids] at Francis Howell."[18] Ironically, prior to the transfer program the Francis Howell School District reported seventeen incidents in which a student had a weapon in 2013, as compared to six reported by NSD, and Francis Howell had ninety-six drug incidents compared to eleven at NSD.[19]

In discussions that took place in the NSD area, the topic of racism was highly vocalized by residents and played down by state administrators. At the public hearing held by the Department of Elementary and Secondary Education to introduce and defend the choices "under consideration" for the district, a long line of parents and students waited their turn to voice frustration and anger for "being set up to fail."[20] The history described in chapters 1 and 2 was here invoked by residents who opposed the educational policies of the districts. Speakers accused the department of "putting chains around our ankles," perpetuating separate and unequal education, and intentionally splintering the Black community, since those choosing to transfer were pitted against those choosing to stay in the district. Several speakers compared putting the fate of the all-Black district in the hands of mostly white state officials to slavery, with one stating, "All that's missing is the whip," and several residents compared their grandchildren's experience in North St. Louis County to their own experience growing up in the Jim Crow South, based on similarities of forced segregation and being put in situations that guaranteed failure.[21] In the audience impromptu arguments broke out between Normandy residents regarding whether the district should be taken over by the state or absorbed into other districts through busing. Parents and administrators from Francis Howell School District also felt compelled to show up and voice opposition to "urban kids" being bused to suburban schools, citing support for community schools and forming unlikely alliances with Black residents advocating for keeping their kids in their own communities. Local and national media picked up the controversy, including a *New York Times* article and slide show focused on the racial conflict and a PBS web series that featured the debate in a segment asking what had changed since *Brown v. Board of Education* and the March on Washington fifty years ago.[22]

Controversies in the Missouri state legislature and in public debate over how to define and deal with underperforming schools are ongoing, but North St. Louis County has lost its suburban status, except when representations are intended to either lament that which was lost or highlight bodies-out-of-place. The physical space of this area has remained unchanged, so it is clear that the processes by which suburban space becomes urban and the work these spatial distinctions perform exist more within the realms of discursive and representational space than in physical space itself. Discursive and representational space would come to play an even bigger role a few months after the state take-over of the Normandy School District.

"Riots" in the Suburbs

Michael Brown was a student at Normandy High School during all of the events described in the preceding section. He graduated on August 3, 2014, after the highly politicized 2013–14 school year ended and immediately after the Normandy Schools Collaborative took over as a state-run entity. According to media accounts of the Normandy schools crisis and Normandy High School, Brown graduated from an urban school with urban problems. Five days after he graduated, however, Brown lay dead on what was reportedly a suburban street in the same geography, shot by a white police officer in front of Canfield Green Apartments in Ferguson. Many of the same media outlets that had cast the Normandy and Riverview Gardens school districts as urban suddenly referred to the area as "a quiet suburban community in greater Saint Louis" or described "riots in a St. Louis suburb" when covering protests and militarized police responses that followed Brown's death. The rhetorical transformation illustrates the work of space and how certain things are expected to happen in some places but not in others. The fact that people had taken to the street and were met by a fully militarized police force had to be explained by something's being out of place. As with the coverage of the schools crisis, representations of events in Ferguson relied on well-understood spatial signifiers—such as *riotous* (Black), *quiet* (white)—to evoke a contrast of differentiated racialized stereotypes, often without mentioning race. Articles published in national media outlets mused about how something so good (Ferguson in its so-called heyday) had gone so bad. Some cited "urban decay" and "ghettoization" as the reason "rioting" had moved to the suburbs, insinuating that Black people, and not the disinvestment and disparity that follows Black people, ruin nice suburban places and enact violence, even though most violence in North St. Louis County is enacted by public institutions.[23] An article in *Time* magazine titled "How Ferguson Went from Middle Class to Poor in a Generation" appeared on the same day Governor Nixon ordered the National Guard to Ferguson and just a few days after Mayor Knowles had claimed middle-class status for all residents. Lamenting "the demise of suburban Ferguson," and warning that something similar could be coming to a community near all Americans, the journalist stated, "In 1990, Ferguson, Mo. was a quiet middle class suburban enclave north of St. Louis with a population about three-quarters white. In 2000, the town's population was roughly split between black and white with an unemployment rate of 5%. By 2010, however, the population was two-thirds black with unemployment exceeding 13%. . . . Demographic transformation came fast and stark to Ferguson, Missouri. So what happened?"[24] The journalist identifies "fast and stark" demographic transformation as the answer to his question, "What happened?" to the "quiet middle class suburb." He does not reference fast and stark disinvestment in the community. Nor does he correlate its "demise" with relentless and often violent hyperpolicing of Black residents for lost revenue. Instead, he equates decay and unemployment with the mere presence of Black people and presumably their culture.

The discursive regimes at work in the Normandy schools crisis and the media coverage of Michael Brown's death establish the norms and hierarchies that "orchestrate, delimit, and sustain that which qualifies as 'the human.'"[25] As Judith Butler argues, the construction of the human is not a simple dialectic. Rather, it is produced "through a set of foreclosures, radical erasures, that are, strictly speaking, refused the possibility of cultural articulation. Hence, it is not enough to claim that human subjects are constructed, for the construction of the human is a differential operation that produces the more and the less 'human,' the inhuman, the humanly unthinkable. These excluded sites come to bound the 'human' as its constitutive outside, and to haunt those boundaries as the persistent possibility of their disruption and rearticulation."[26] The sets of foreclosures, radical erasures, and policing of cultural articulation, which create urban subjects in suburban space, operate in relationship to relative proximities to blackness and thus determine degrees of the human, the inhuman, and the humanly unthinkable in and through space. The constitutive outside, however, does indeed haunt the boundaries of space in North St. Louis County and it did disrupt foreclosures and rearticulate possibilities in this area and beyond.

Imagining Suburbia

Dianne Harris, in her book on postwar suburbia, shows how the perceived and actual development of post–World War II US suburbs for a specifically white middle class was not only highly orchestrated by institutional policy and real estate markets but also seared into the psyche, imagination, and normative assumptions of the US public through calculated promotion and representation that both produced and maintained normative middle-class ideals as synonymous with white culture.[27] In this way, the suburbs became defined as white space in opposition to "dark urban space," in spite of the fact that US suburbs have always maintained surprising diversity. Extending this argument, Margaret Garb, in her book on housing reform in Chicago between 1871 and 1919, uses historical data to convincingly argue that the link between race and cultural perceptions of home ownership began much earlier than the post–World War II era: "Even at the turn of the [twentieth] century, a single-family house set on a tidy yard was fast becoming a mark of household health, respectability, and morality," where perceptions of respectability worked in relationship to whiteness.[28] The obsession with the single-family house and the importance of property was institutionalized by New Deal–era housing policy and instilled over time in US culture, which viewed home ownership as a fundamental right of white citizenship and a distinguishing factor of white culture. The systematic denial of home ownership to nonwhite citizens through both exclusion and lack of facilitation resulted in vast disparities in individual and family wealth since property ownership and appreciation are fundamental tools for passing assets between generations.

In fields that study metropolitan space, scholars' recent coinage and frequent use of the term *suburban ghetto*, which was subsequently picked up by popular media, is intended to describe what happens when the suburban imaginary (as opposed to the actual suburbs) loses its middle-class white status and becomes a container of poor nonwhite people or specific ethnicities—as the ghetto has been theorized.[29] This illustrates the need scholars feel to qualify low-income nonwhite suburbs as something other than authentic suburbs.[30] In fact, anytime suburban space does not fit the imagination of white middle-class space, qualifications follow within scholarship and the popular media: for example, working-class suburbs (white but not middle class), affluent suburbs (white and upper-middle class), Black suburbs (middle class but not white), immigrant or ethnic suburbs (meaning non-European ethnic immigrants, since European immigrants overwhelmingly settled the first US suburbs), suburban ghettos (Black and poor), and barrio suburbs (Latinx and poor).[31] In the same way that whiteness is the invisible "unraced" racial norm, the nonqualified suburbs are assumed to be white and middle class. A quick review of the table of contents of the first and second editions of *The Suburban Reader*, which is organized chronologically, correlates to what a literature review of suburban space reveals. That is, the economic qualifications of the suburbs entered the discursive space in the late 1800s, whereas ethnic, racial, cultural, and often racist qualifications appeared around the 1940s, when challenges to housing discrimination and opposition to racial covenants were gaining political traction.

In addition to defining the suburbs as white, the suburban imaginary is also a gender-conforming situation. Feminist scholars have shown how the suburbs produce and reproduce heteronormative assumptions about families and patriarchal hierarchies concerning the place and role of women.[32] Therefore, areas with majority-female heads of households cannot be "the suburbs." As Mary Jo

Wiggins has shown, antiblack assumptions concerning non-white inferiority are also reinforced in Black suburbs because Black suburban residents lose real benefits and perceived status when investment and amenities go elsewhere.[33] In this way, Black people, as opposed to other factors, are held responsible for the risk associated with Black space and the "rational" disinvestment that rhetorically recodes Black suburbs as something other than suburban. Journalists, politicians, and those speaking out within the public sphere, such as attendees at the forums held to address the ongoing Normandy schools crisis, join urban scholars in attaching the connotation of "subpar space" to Black people by requalifying suburban space as suburban ghettos or as urban space. By linking the loss of suburban status to the departure of white people, to new cultures of poverty, and to supposedly natural processes of "benign neglect,"[34] spatial imaginaries are constructed and maintained that assume (1) authentic suburbs cannot exist without the presence of white people; (2) authentic suburbs cannot coexist with Black culture; (3) authentic suburbs cannot exist without heteronormative families; and (4) policy *naturally* redirects resources to other areas by way of color-blind capitalist logics (although capitalist logics are inherently raced). The race-making situation of the suburbs, as evidenced in North St. Louis County, supplies an exemption to antiblack spatial practice and policies through a discursively produced cultural politics that trades in the criminalization of Black residents, tropes of respectability, and policies that intentionally diminish the basic rights of Black citizens. In turn, leaders who find themselves charged with local governance in the unfavored "urban" quarter of suburban St. Louis County avoid dissolution by exploiting powerful racialized imaginaries concerning suburban and urban space.[35]

Imagining North St. Louis County

The recodification of North St. Louis County—from suburban to urban, and sometimes back again—relies on geographical imaginations directly tied to discursive representations. An imaginative geography, as Edward Said explains, "legitimates a vocabulary, a universe of representative discourse peculiar to the discussion and understanding" of a place.[36] Imaginative geographies establish and maintain difference—familiarity and otherness—of bodies in space and are integral to forming and understanding identity as well as power. Through the stories told about places, dramatic boundaries are constantly drawn and redrawn on physical space at multiple scales through imaginative processes.[37] The history of development in St. Louis is an excellent example of how individuals are

expected to be in some places but not in others, and disciplinary means are necessary to keep individuals and groups "in place."

As civil rights legislation opened up neighborhoods and schools to Black
families, new discourses of certainty needed to be produced in conjunction
with official antiracisms and emergent global political economies appearing in
the wake of global postcolonial restructuring. Jodi Melamed observes that "in
contrast to antiracist struggles led by social movements, official US antiracisms
since World War II" (such as the desegregation of neighborhoods and schools)
"have disconnected racism from material conditions" through control over constructions of rationality and discourses of certainty.[38] The prevailing viewpoint
became that if something appears to be economically rational, it is not racist.
A case in point is a statement such as "I don't dislike Black people, I just don't
want my property values to go down."[39] This is the reframed, race-neutral racial
order that establishes the discursive terrain by which Black residents moving to
St. Louis County were and are denied the full benefits of suburban citizenship
through the reordering of material resources in St. Louis County in ways that are
considered rational and routine.

Although the initial rhetoric and subsequent reports published in the early
1970s regarding what was happening in North St. Louis County demographically
referenced race by referring to "Negro" populations, these arguments and representations assumed, without specific explanations, that "Negro" space, regardless
of class, was risky space.[40] Clearly it had to do with numbers. If only a few of the
most highly qualified and "best-behaved" model "Negro" families moved into
the suburbs, the inevitable desegregation of space could be said to have occurred
successfully with limited consequences to the white spatial logic. In fact, this
is how the idea was promoted by white liberals who helped pass the Fair Housing Act of 1968.[41] However, the statistical threshold of this logic was extremely
low. When many blocks in North St. Louis County quickly became majority
Black, a new logic swiftly took its place. The historical link of blackness with
risk was critical to maintaining racial hierarchies because it depersonalized and
obscured antiblack practice—again, the refrain "I'm not racist. I'm just practical."
The idea that Black space is something to be feared and avoided did not require
explanation, and representations of the dark ghetto conveniently provided an
imaginative geography that linked Black culture to what was occurring in North
St. Louis County. As Derek Gregory points out, the ways in which anxiety, fear,
and fantasy produce, reproduce, and transform imaginative geographies through
discursive practices go beyond simple classifications or reclassifications of space.[42]
In North St. Louis County, economic "considerations" and demographic "transition" provided a common narrative regarding the struggle over space; however,

the discursive use of anxiety and fear created the fantasy that fundamentally transformed the everyday lives of all residents across this geography.

Anxiety, fear, and fantasy were certainly documented by a frenzy of academic research and reports published between 1973 and 1976, outlined in chapter 2. As municipal leaders attempted to control narratives, curb white panic, and slow what they believed would be an inevitable social and physical decline of the area, academic studies in the 1970s employed the same vocabulary of war used to promote racial zoning laws in St. Louis city in 1915 and describe the area as "falling" quickly to "Negro invasion."[43] The Federal Housing Administration and the Home Owners' Loan Corporation guidelines that established risk ratings for lenders perpetuated the war analogy. With racial homogeneity at the top of the risk assessment list, documents stated that neighborhoods "invaded" or "infiltrated" by African Americans had lost, or would lose, all value and succumb to the presence of a "Negro colony."[44] Subsequent writing on this area continued the narrative regarding the "fall" of communities brought about by "racial tipping"—the ratio of Black residents that guarantees an area will eventually become all Black.[45] Using terms that appeared again in the 2014 article in *Time* magazine (quoted above) on the "fall" of Ferguson, a local observer remarked that by the end of the 1970s, "Ghetto spillover (stretched) almost all the way across the county in a northwesterly direction."[46]

By the 1970s, the urban core was no longer the perceived sole container of Black space in St. Louis, although, as shown in chapter 2, Black people had lived and formed communities in St. Louis County since before St. Louis city was founded.[47] The rapidly changing "demographic makeup" distinctly challenged the local suburban imaginary and spatial identity of many people who had grown up in North County. Where did you go to high school? is a question famously understood in St. Louis as a way to locate a person's social and economic status, and St. Louisans place particular emphasis on spatial identity, a concern that harkens back to the area's history of physical, political, and economic fragmentation. Three people interviewed for this research who graduated from Normandy High School in the 1950s, at a time when the school was virtually all-white and academically outperformed every other high school in the region, described the ways by which they had recalibrated their attachments and decoupled their identity from the space in which they had grown up. "I don't tell younger people that I went to Normandy High School because I just don't want to have to explain that it was a totally different school. It was a different universe," a white woman stated. "Older people get it—get the history," she went on, "so I might tell older people." The two men (both white) I interviewed also described the area as "unrecognizable" because "you know, it's just not a place you'd want to go now," one of them explained. "When we have class reunions there's always the question, Do we even go back to the old neighborhood?" All three people described an initial fight for, and subsequent relinquishment of, space in terms of imagined geographies of "our space" and "their space." All three also expressed the ways in which anxiety, fear, and fantasies of what might happen discursively unified many people as "us" as opposed to "them." As one man stated, "A choice had to be made by every one of us. Either we maintained what we had created for ourselves in spite of them, or we left. In the end we had no choice. It was now their place."[48]

The white spatial imaginary is not just policed by white individuals, as chapter 3 has shown. Many of the Black mayors interviewed for this research made distinctions between suburban space and urban people, consistently citing suburban norms as the reason people and space must be policed.[49] With statements such as "People from the projects must be taught how to act in the suburbs," and "People who don't know how to mow their grass have no business living in the suburbs," Black leaders employ a form of suburban respectability politics that is specifically spatial. In addition to municipal autonomy, the incompatibility of people and space came up repeatedly as the reason for excessive numbers of citations issued in this area and the reason that nothing needed to change. Variations on the argument that "people who can't act right in the suburbs need to go back to the ghetto" are common refrains that reinforce the racialized dialectic of urban and suburban space.[50] Discursively deploying spatial signifiers, mayors and alderpersons, when asked to describe their cities, most often said something like "We are a small suburb with big urban problems." Expectations of home ownership and property rights were also commonly cited. Patrick Green, who identifies as African American and is the mayor of Normandy, used cultural politics from both a white and Black perspective when he explained,

> People can use their house as a weapon by not doing what they're supposed to. Having a place to live is a privilege. A home is a privilege. It comes with responsibility. Our laws and ordinances are intended to protect the city when people don't uphold their responsibilities. . . . The question should not be, Why are police giving out so many tickets? The question should be, Why are so many people breaking the law? . . . The state says we can keep giving out all these tickets but now we're supposed to turn the money over [to the schools]. That's slavery, making you work for the land. . . . When they came to talk to us they accused us of being the number one city in the ticket scheme. That's like calling us niggers.[51]

This statement reveals the conflation of multiple spatial and racial tropes and identifications used by municipal leaders to justify racialized practices for the purpose of meeting fiscal responsibilities. The concept that having a place to live is a privilege is derivative of the idea that homeownership is quintessential to the American Dream and the common trope that minority citizens expect to receive everything from the welfare state. The idea that the rights of property trump all other rights stems directly from the neoliberal concept that property rights and the right to protect "the city" are always elevated above personal rights; the responsibilities that come with having a place to live, in this case in the city of Normandy, fall under the unstated expectations of suburban citizenship. Equating the requirement (of Senate Bill 5) to turn money from fines and fees that exceed the legal limit over to the public schools with slavery is an interesting take on "working for the land" and also conflates the work of race and space in this area. Mayor Green and several other mayors in North St. Louis County consistently contend that being singled out or cited as a number one abuser of "taxation by citation" is due to the racial makeup of these cities and is motivated solely by racism. As chapter 3 illustrates, these claims have merit; however, they are significantly undermined by the suffering residents experience as a result of these practices, which rely on a generalized tolerance of suffering in Black space.

Spatializing Identity

Contradictory categorizations—suburban versus urban—are both claimed and deployed, sometimes interchangeably, by residents of North St. Louis County, depending on the work they perform, the identities they mobilize, and the distinctions they are intended to make. This is clearly evident in the attitudes, opinions, and spatial practices of residents in North St. Louis County. Residents interviewed for this research (N=105), who were randomly intercepted in various locations across the geography, were asked a number of questions regarding whether they perceive North St. Louis County as suburban or urban; how they define urban versus suburban; whether, and how, they see differences between Black experience in St. Louis County versus St. Louis city; what their experience has been with policing practices; and whether or not they support municipal consolidation measures.[52] Among other things, these interviews show distinct differences with regard to perceptions of space—as urban or suburban—between Black residents (N=85) and white residents (N=20). Differences were also evident in the ways Black and white residents quantified and codified space and their perceptions of whether, and how, Black experience differed between St. Louis County and St. Louis city. While gender did not stand out as a significant factor, the age of respondents did appear to correlate with specific responses.

The distinctions respondents made about urban and suburban space were significant. When asked whether they believed North St. Louis County was urban or suburban, 65 percent of Black respondents stated that North St. Louis County is urban, while 100 percent of white respondents defined it as suburban. Interestingly, when white residents living outside North St. Louis County (but in the region) were interviewed in a separate study (N=16), most (78 percent) defined specific areas in North St. Louis County as urban.[53] Regarding why North County is urban, one older Black man (aged 66–75) from Normandy stated what many Black respondents shared in various ways: "The neighborhood was suburban when I moved in, now it's urban. It's because the people have changed, and the diversity. There are more Blacks in urban places than whites." Another respondent, a Black woman (aged 56–65) from Pagedale, like many respondents, equated urban and suburban with changing class status. She said, "This area is urban, it's not suburban at all. In our neighborhood, people don't have enough money to be suburban. . . . People in the suburbs do things because they want to while in an urban area they do things because they HAVE to." A middle-aged Black woman from Ferguson associated suburban space with the quality of services and equated changes in services with racial changes: "I was the second African American on my block in Ferguson twenty-seven years ago. When I arrived it was suburban and the services were really high quality. As the racial makeup changed, the services got much worse." A young Black man (aged 20–25) simply said, "This area is urban because no white people live here at all."

These descriptions suggest that, in the perception of these respondents, space can easily change, or be recodified, from urban to suburban and back again, depending on who lives there and what they are doing. This supports the argument that space is codified depending on the messages being sent regarding class and race and that it can change quickly, depending on who controls the narrative. The data also showed that space is actively racialized and that Black residents view themselves as contributing to the reclassification of space (i.e., "Black people live here [so it is urban]," or "white people live there [so it is suburban]"). Furthermore, according to respondents, once an area is qualified as "the ghetto" or "the hood," as many described North St. Louis County, it must be urban.[54] This is an important finding because it corresponds with Black residents' lowered expectations for the space in which they live.

Regarding definitions of suburban space, Black respondents across age and gender groups most often said things like "It's quiet," "It's not as busy," "White people live there," "It's wealthier," "It's cleaner," and "It's more close knit." Similarly, regarding urban space, Black respondents observed things like "It's busier/ noisier," "Black people live there," "It's poorer," "It's the hood," and "It's more crowded." When asked to define and describe the differences between urban and suburban space, Black residents overwhelmingly cited experiential, demographic, and behavioral characteristics—things that can change quickly—rather than physical qualities of space, such as density, building typology, or green space.

White residents of North St. Louis County were more likely to base definitions of urban and suburban on physical definitions—things that do not change quickly—such as density, residential or commercial uses, and amount of open space. When asked to define suburban space, white residents most often said things like "There are single-family homes," "It's residential," or "It has more open space." Unlike Black respondents, none of the white respondents directly cited race in their responses. Regarding urban space, white respondents said things like "There are apartment buildings," "Things are closer together," and "You don't need a car." White residents interviewed for this research largely lived in communities that have recently shifted to majority Black, such as Ferguson, but live in predominantly white neighborhoods. These residents were also more likely to cite changes in the community and unrest as things they dislike about living there. They did not, however, describe the area as urban, presumably because they themselves still live in the community and identify as suburban citizens, citing more permanent features as evidence of suburban conditions. This hypothesis is based on the fact that whites living outside North St. Louis County were more likely to describe the area as urban, citing different types of physical evidence such as abandoned buildings, defunct commercial districts, and trash. While the sampling of white residents both inside and outside North St. Louis County was relatively small, responses suggest that once white residents had moved out of the area, they perceived it as urban rather than suburban. Age is also a determining factor, as older Black residents living in the area for more than ten years (N=15) were more likely to describe their community as suburban and to cite "outsiders moving in" as one of their dislikes. Black residents under the age of fifty-five overwhelmingly stated "the police" as the thing they disliked the most about living in North St. Louis County.[55]

Another significant distinction between Black and white respondents is the perception of Black experience in the county versus the city. Ninety-four percent of Black respondents across age and gender said different experiences did exist, and of those, virtually all stated that it is easier for Black people to live in the city than in the county. Black respondents cited better experiences with the police, not being stopped on a regular basis, not being harassed for everyday activities, and "blending in" as the most common reasons why this is the case. The specific question, Do you think African Americans have a different experience in the city versus the county? led to comments such as "Oh yeah, it's definitely easier in the city," "Yes, you don't get stopped and harassed in the city," "They leave you alone in the city," and "Out here [in the county] you gotta watch what you do more. Just basic things like walkin' down the street. It's not that way in the city." Many people went into detail:

Black man from Bellefontaine Neighbors (aged 18–25)

Young people in the city can walk around freely without being worried about being stopped because they look like they are up to no good. In the county, if you walk in a group with your friends you have to hope that there isn't any cops around. They will stop you and ask you what you are doing and where you are going.

Black woman from Cool Valley (aged 46–55)

Black people in the city don't have to deal with nearly as much as you would if you lived in the county. They are way more petty in the county. They have too many petty laws out here, whatever law they can make to get money out of you they will. In the city they just don't care. Both experiences are tragic.

Black man from Northwoods (aged 18–25)

Definitely. I've been trailed by police in the county so many times I can't even count. Not here in Northwoods because the officers know me, but in other parts. The county uses people for revenue. The city police watch for actual crime.

Black man from Ferguson (aged 18–25)

On a certain level, things are nicer in the county. Everybody wants to come to the county until they deal with the police here.

Black woman from Hanley Hills (aged 18–25)

The city is trying to maintain order. The county is trying to make money. In the city you are not treated as badly by the government.

The majority of white respondents (75 percent) stated that there was no difference for Black people living in the city versus the county. Of the 25 percent of white respondents who believed there was a difference, virtually all said it was easier for black people to live in the county, saying things like "It's nicer out here," and "There's less crime."[56] One white man from Ferguson between the ages of forty-six and fifty-five, stating something similar to several other white respondents, said, "Yes, blacks definitely feel safer here. It's safer for their sons and daughters. I've never met anyone who is unhappy. St. Louis city can be a terrifying place. You don't have to worry about that here even over on Canfield. I hang out over there a lot." Similarly, a white woman from St. John between the ages of fifty-six and sixty-five said, "I'm sure they feel safer here in the county than in the city. They can get a better education and they have all these nice parks they can use. St. John has its own police department but I'm also within walking distance to five other municipalities that all have their own police departments too." I found it interesting that white residents felt they could speak so definitively regarding Black experience, despite the fact that their perceptions were more or less the opposite of those of Black residents on this topic.

In and Out of Place

In light of the answers of both Black and white respondents to questions regarding the relative difficulty or ease of living in the city and the county, as well as differing opinions regarding what they liked and disliked about living in North St. Louis County, the primary factor for differing opinions appears to be experiences with the police and expectations of behavior and norms between city and county (see table 4.1). Virtually all Black respondents described multiple forms of harassment by the police in St. Louis County that either they or people they knew had recently experienced. These experiences shaped their attitudes toward where they lived and the stories they told others and themselves about this place. Their experiences also shaped how they viewed what they had sacrificed versus what they had gained by living in the county and the expectations they had in both places. Many stated that they wished to move back to the city but could not, because of lost investment in their homes or their reliance on a friend or family member with whom they lived.[57] Experiences with the police elicited the longest and most impassioned responses from Black residents. Some people were angry and some were shaking when they shared their stories. While there are many experiences included in this chapter, there were many more shared in the interviews that were not included.

While almost every Black respondent had a personal story regarding policing and their expectation of being stopped, white respondents in general had a positive view of the police. White residents stated that they believed leaders and the police had their best interest in mind and they said that public safety should be at the top of leaders' priorities. White residents most often cited racial tensions and change as what they liked least about living in North St. Louis County. One white respondent who had lived in an unincorporated area of North County for forty-seven years said the thing she least liked about living there was "the perception that I live in the ghetto."

Regarding leadership, Black respondents overwhelmingly disagreed that municipal leaders acted in the best interest of their community, while virtually all white residents said the leaders of their municipality were doing a good job. Black residents identified money and greed as the only reasons for the amount of citations and court fees handed out in North St. Louis County, while white residents largely agreed with the narratives of municipal leaders that public safety was the sole reason for the types of policing that took place.

Black woman from Woodson Terrace (aged 46–55)

I don't buy into it when they talk about public safety. Hell yeah it's about money. At any given time you can see someone pulled over, almost all the time. I've seen it for over ten years—they bank on it.

Black woman from Dellwood (aged 46–55)

Where is the danger to public safety all those leaders are talking about? All I see right now are bogus tickets being given to people in the area for crazy reasons. I believe they give these tickets to fund themselves, yes I do. How else are they going to get all that military equipment they use on us? WE pay for it.

White respondents generally agreed with the public safety argument that leaders repeatedly made. Echoing statements made by several other white respondents, a white woman from Pasadena Hills between the ages of fifty-six and sixty-five said, "I think the leaders are just interested in keeping the city safe. There are high standards for homeowners and they keep things real nice. They have all of our best interests at heart. You have to hit people in their pocketbook if you want to make an impact and get their attention. They use money to get people's attention, but it's all about safety and keeping this a nice place to live." Similarly, another white woman between the ages of fifty-six and sixty-five stated, "I've worked with companies that have contracts with the police, so I have good experiences. I believe the policing is done for public safety or because someone is a suspicious person. I believe that it's for public safety. Police seem to serve the public good. None of them are very well-paid, and the job comes with danger. I have to believe they want to make a difference. But you can have bad apples in every profession." Unlike the many firsthand experiences shared by Black respondents above, this respondent's opinions were based on what she "had to believe," since that was what she most often heard. Another white respondent, a man in his sixties from Calverton Park, expressed his assessment, which, like many others', used a cultural explanation. He said,

> I've never been targeted because I'm not Black. I have a hard time believing it's about hatred. It's because they get more calls from those communities. I know police and they're trained to take control, and sometimes force needs to be used. I was stopped with my son in his car and the officer gave me the opportunity to say why I was speeding. That impressed me. I ride a Harley, and when cops approach me in my leather it's my role to put them at ease. Black culture does the opposite. They get belligerent immediately. If one guy has a knife and the other has a gun, you know who'll win.

There were of course exceptions to how Black and white respondents answered, and some viewpoints of both Black and white residents did occasionally fall outside the polarized pattern that can be seen in the data. For example, when I asked a white woman from Bel-Nor between the ages of forty-six and fifty-five whether city leaders had motives beyond safety when policing residents, she stated, "I doubt their motives are all that conscious or stated. They don't really think about it. I think the people setting policy don't understand the context of people's lives that are being affected. There's a disconnect. The people affected are basically invisible to them." Not surprisingly, Black respondents were overwhelmingly in favor of municipal consolidation while white residents were almost entirely opposed.[58]

TABLE 4.1 Selected questions and answers to survey conducted in North St. Louis County (N=104*)

Q: Do you consider North St. Louis County to be urban or suburban?

	BLACK	WHITE
Urban	64%	0%
Suburban	26%	75%
Mixed (both)	10%	25%

Q: Do you think African Americans have a different experience in North St. Louis County than in St. Louis City? If so, why?

	BLACK	WHITE
Yes: It is easier in the city than in the county.	91%	5%
No: No difference	9%	70%
Yes: It is easier in the county than in the city.	0%	28%

Q: What do you like best about living in North St. Louis County?[†]

	BLACK	WHITE
It's quiet.	51%	0%
Nothing	25%	0%
My house	11%	10%
My neighbors	6%	0%
It's safe.	3%	10%
Community events	2%	15%
Everything	0%	20%
The parks	0%	3%
My neighborhood is gated.	0%	12%
The police	0%	30%

Q: What do you like least about living in North St. Louis County?[†]

	BLACK	WHITE
The police	45%	0%
My neighbors	13%	10%
It's racist.	13%	0%
There's no shopping (no stores).	9%	0%
There's no transportation (need a car).	7%	0%
There are no sidewalks.	6%	0%
It's disconnected (no community).	3%	5%
It's dark.	2%	0%
Crime	2%	5%
Unrest	0%	45%
Nothing	0%	20%
Things are changing.	0%	15%

Q: How do you define suburban space?[†]

	BLACK	WHITE
Quiet (peaceful)	45%	5%
Wealthier (people are better off)	25%	0
White people live there.	25%	0
Clean	17%	0
Not dense (single-family homes)	14%	4%
Classier people live there (more upscale).	12%	0
Safe	12%	3%
Close knit	11%	5%
Not diverse (people are all the same)	9%	4%
Better schools	8%	4%
Need a car	6%	0
More families	3%	3%

(Continued)

TABLE 4.1   (Continued)

Q: How do you define suburban space?†

	BLACK	WHITE
People own their houses.	3%	12%
Residential	3%	46%
More older people	3%	0
Bigger yards (bigger lots)	2%	15%
Bigger/nicer houses (more bedrooms/bathrooms)	3%	12%

Q: How do you define urban space?†

	BLACK	WHITE
Busy/lots of activity	28%	12%
Black people live there.	25%	0%
Poorer	23%	0%
Dirty	17%	0%
More crime	15%	4%
Police don't harass people.	15%	0%
Congested/crowded	14%	2%
Diverse (lots of different people)	11%	1%
Good transportation	8%	1%
More young people	6%	0%
The ghetto (people don't dress well, not upscale)	5%	0%
Cheaper	4%	0%
Apartment buildings	4%	28%
Commercial	4%	8%
Vacant	4%	12%
Less space (more dense)	2%	36%

Note: Respondents were randomly approached in public settings (light rail stations, markets, community events, etc.) and asked whether they would participate in the anonymous survey. The answers listed (or something similar) were offered by the respondents and were *not* multiple choice.

* Respondents self-identifying as Black N=79; respondents self-identifying as white N=25.

† Respondents' first answers are listed.

† All respondents' answers are listed.

The link between white people and imaginations of suburban space, and the requalification of space when Black people arrive, is clear from the responses of both Black and white respondents. Black residents clearly state this distinction in explicitly racial terms. While Black residents who do not experience the benefits of so-called suburban living view North St. Louis County as urban, as do whites who have moved out of the area, white residents who claim suburban identity view this area as suburban. Although white respondents never mentioned race, they tended to code this area as suburban until they moved, at which point the area became urban in their absence. In contrast to Black respondents, white respondents used many different ways to signify race without ever naming it. This careful use of language illustrates how color-blind racism and "postracial" discourse are practiced. It also testifies to the power of liberal humanism to narrate and obscure racialized conditions.[59]

While most Black respondents said North St. Louis County is urban, they also stated that it is easier for Black people to live in St. Louis city, which they also identified as urban. This reveals that recodifying North St. Louis County as urban has not made it easier for Black residents to live there. It also suggests that the recodification of historically white suburban space produces disruptions that lead to specific phenomena and experiences for Black residents that do not occur in spaces that are historically associated with Black people, since Black respondents clearly state that it is "easier to live" in St. Louis city. While Black urban space carries with it an expectation of suffering (as discussed above), so-called urban space in general has also been shown to have a higher threshold of tolerance for diversity and difference,[60] and, as many respondents described it, Black people are expected to live there. But the intersection of urban people and suburban space creates a contradictory set of expectations, as well as varying degrees and experiences of suburban citizenship. The transformation of North St. Louis County, or at least parts of it, from suburban to urban space—in the discursive spaces of public debate and in the minds of the residents themselves—has meant a lowering of expectations for Black residents living under draconian practices, such as debtor's prisons, which come to be viewed as normal. As a middle-aged Black man from Pine Lawn shared, "It was worse until the Mike Brown incident and then it became known what was happening to people. It shouldn't have been happening in the first place—so much that people got used to it. But they did get used to it."

This is an important observation, given that several reports, such as the one published by the Manhattan Institute in 2012, have declared spatial segregation to be essentially over.[61] On one level, the fact that North St. Louis County is majority Black can be interpreted as proof that anyone can live in suburban communities. This interpretation of data assumes that space and spatial mobility are experienced and inhabited in the same way by all people and groups. Given the reality of experiences described above, North St. Louis County is an example of bait-and-switch policy in which urban residents claim benefits in the suburbs only to find that they are not only urban once again, but also held financially responsible for the losses municipalities incur when space is recoded.

Urban space, when it is deployed as the container of "dark" bodies, is understood as the disposable space of the city, the pornotopology, the native colony, inhabited by dark bodies and enjoyed by others—where anything goes but where residents are restricted and controlled. Under these circumstances, as discussed in the introduction to this book, discursively produced spatial imaginaries of white and Black space reinforce a biopolitical construct that works to divide the city into those who *should* live and those who *could* die.[62]

The recodification of space from suburban to urban means not only that Black residents expect that they will be treated badly, but also that administrators and policy makers can erase entire communities, and that people outside this area can ignore practices that would not be tolerated in other locations. In this way, physical and discursive spaces intersect to produce a cultural politics that rationalizes both "fast" and "slow" state violence.[63] In North St. Louis County, discursive spatial regimes control, select, organize, and redistribute power relations, material outcomes, and identity based on the risk historically attached to blackness. These discursive regimes not only objectify residents but also critically influence how individual subjectivities of both leaders and residents are formed and re-formed.

POLITICS AND POLICING
IN PAGEDALE

It's *who* you're bringing in and what they're accustomed to. They
come with what they're used to. Where they come from, they were
doing what they want and nobody is teaching them another way to do
it. We have a better chance in the county with our little municipality
of enforcing the laws that teach people how to live. It's the teaching
that we have.

—Alderperson, City of Pagedale

The City of Pagedale represents an extreme example of how discourses of
race and space are deployed in North St. Louis County, yet its history also represents a complicated intersection of race, generation, and gender in suburban
space. City officials in Pagedale pass and enforce ordinances that promote
"suburban aesthetics" and white cultural norms, as well as targeting circumstances of poverty and Black culture. They do so using a consistent rhetoric of
public safety and property rights, which began soon after the first developments
began to appear in this area. Whereas traffic violations make up the vast majority
of policing-for-revenue practices in North St. Louis County, Pagedale has historically policed space and property, in addition to writing traffic tickets. Pagedale also sits at the far end of the spectrum in terms of the rate of demographic
change that occurred between 1960 and 1990 and the demographics of people
elected to office after 1970. For example, in 1970, Pagedale was 23 percent Black,
and by 1972, Black women had begun running, albeit unsuccessfully, for elected
office. Ten years later, Pagedale received national attention when it became the
first city in the United States to elect an all-Black, all-female leadership in 1982.
By 1990, Pagedale was 93 percent Black, and the city has continued to elect all-
Black and majority-female leaders. At the other end of the spectrum in North
St. Louis County, Ferguson, as a much larger and older city with a long history
of segregating itself from the neighboring historically Black city of Kinloch, was
1 percent Black in 1970. In 2014, Ferguson was 67 percent Black and maintained
an all-white, majority-male leadership.

In 2010, the City of Pagedale had a population of 3,304 and was 94 percent African American, with a per capita income of $11,005. Although the city covers just 1.19 square miles, it is one of the larger municipalities in North St. Louis County (see maps in chapter 2). Most of the small bungalow homes were built in the 1940s, and during that time, many working-class families of German and Polish descent moved to Pagedale from St. Louis City. A large Lutheran church was built next to the public park in the center of the city and directly across from the city hall. Page Avenue, for which the city was named, ran through this area prior to development, as did the old fur trading route of St. Charles Rock Road. Several houses also dotted the agricultural landscape prior to 1940, including the home of Nicholas Craig, a formerly enslaved African American who moved to Whitney Avenue around 1900.[1] Probably because of the Craig family's residence, Whitney Avenue was developed in the 1940s as one of the few African American streets in St. Louis County, and adjacent streets that connected to Whitney Avenue were gated off to prevent access from the block of Black families.[2]

Pagedale was incorporated as a fourth-class city in 1950, after the neighboring city of Wellston threatened to annex most of the developed unincorporated area. Across the small geography, there are roughly 1,400 small homes, two commercial districts, an industrial zone along a railroad that bisects the city, several churches, and a large Lutheran cemetery. Several large factories, distribution centers, and headquarters were located in midcentury Pagedale, including the Lever soap factory, the Production Engineering Company (a gun manufacturer), the Stix, Baer, Fuller department store service warehouse, and Hill-Behan Lumber national headquarters, which together provided several hundred jobs in the area. In keeping with the suburban imaginary, advertisements for new homes in one development in Pagedale, which targeted white working-class families, touted "clean neighborhoods, quiet streets and a fruit tree planted in every yard."[3] Almost immediately after incorporation, the City of Pagedale began to experience demographic change.

In 1962, the first of several factories in the city moved to an outlying area that offered attractive tax and infrastructure benefits.[4] Concurrent with the relocation of major employers throughout the 1960s was the momentum of the civil rights legislation and overcrowding in Black communities in the city of St. Louis, which exerted new forces on suburban municipalities to open their boundaries to Black homebuyers, as discussed in chapter 2. As was the case in cities across the United States, the push of Black families beyond the central city and into the suburban context was met by much resistance from white residents, politicians, and real estate agents in Pagedale. Violence and threats toward individuals and families, veiled exclusionary policies, and blatantly racialized real estate and lending practices were common and aimed at keeping Black people "at bay." Many incidences of vandalism and threats (including death threats) aimed at Black families moving in and whites "selling out" were documented in Pagedale and relayed by former and current residents.[5] Realtors were mandated to sell the *right property* to the *right people* or risk losing their licenses.[6] Neighborhood and municipal meetings were routinely called by white homeowners to discuss what could be done to thwart the "Negro invasion" discussed in chapter 2.[7] While some of the resistance was unapologetically racist, most arguments in Pagedale steered the debate toward economic factors and the right to protect the value of property that was perceived as threatened by "undesirable" people and lifestyles.[8] In 1970, the Legal Aid Society became involved in complaints against the City of Pagedale regarding occupancy permits. Several Black families, specifically Black women, alleged they had been harassed by the city for having more than four children, allowing visiting relatives to temporarily stay at their homes, and having babysitters occasionally spend the night when a parent was working nights.[9] At the time, the leadership in Pagedale was all white men, and the Legal Aid Society threatened racial charges against the city. One of the women involved in the complaint, who was the first Black homeowner on her block, said her white neighbors constantly called the city to harass her, stating, "It has been the most miserable year of my life . . . because of my white neighbors."[10] Although reports of animosity toward Black families were not uncommon, records indicate that Black mothers were most often the ones making claims regarding harassment by neighbors and by municipalities over ordinance violations.[11]

The demographic transition from majority white to majority Black throughout North St. Louis County was swift, but demographic transitions in municipal leadership occurred much more slowly. In areas like Pagedale, which had become majority Black by 1975, elections in which Black candidates sought to unseat white leadership were still highly contested. Politics among white leaders in Pagedale was notoriously contentious, and backroom deals, outbursts at city council meetings, violence outside city halls, arrests, and restraining orders were routinely reported on.[12] Black candidates began running unsuccessfully for office in 1970. In 1972, the city was reported as 70 percent Black and an all-Black slate for mayor and three aldermanic positions was on the April 4 ballot, which included Mary Louise Carter, the current mayor of Pagedale.[13] The Black mayoral candidate, Roosevelt Clossum, stated he was running to halt white flight from Pagedale by restoring confidence in the city government. He stated that there were seventy to eighty vacant homes in Pagedale because of white flight and that four white families on his own block had moved in the span of a week.[14] All the Black candidates were defeated and Black candidates would continue to run and be defeated until 1977, when two Black women were voted into aldermanic positions. William Speiser, the white male mayor of Pagedale during the 1970s, was arrested several times and involved in numerous physical altercations in and around city hall throughout his time in office. Fraud, fixing tickets, outbursts at meetings, and routinely firing anyone that disagreed with him were also common allegations against Speiser; however, he served as mayor for thirteen consecutive years.[15]

In 1982, Pagedale made national news by electing the first all-Black and all-woman city administration in the United States, which included the mayor, who ousted Speiser, and five alderpersons.[16] The positive notoriety did not last long, however. Two months later, the *Detroit Free Press* reported, "The meetings of the Board of Alderpersons sometimes resemble Latin American soccer matches with competing factions in the audience shouting loud approval or displeasure at the parliamentary play. Talk of impeachment is common and allegations of threats of physical violence against board members have been made at meetings (figure 5.1)."[17] What the report failed to mention was that this type of behavior was commonplace at city council meetings in Pagedale long before Black women were voted into office. Although Speiser had been engaging in fistfights during council meetings for years and was routinely antagonistic toward alderpersons, the media that began following Pagedale after it made national history with its all-Black and all-woman leadership assumed that political chaos in the city was due to an administration of "fighting Black women" who could not agree with each other on anything.[18]

The St. Louis media, which has a history of portraying the minutiae of local politics in North County municipalities as "a circus," had material to work with, since shortly after the election, Pagedale hired three contested police chiefs at one time due to infighting between the council and the mayor. The mayor and her appointed police chief were also arrested by one of the two additional police chiefs for assault, a charge they both disputed. The mayor accused the arresting police chief of fraud and holding her in a shoe store for five hours against her will, during which time she said he fired shots at her.[19] In comparison with previous white administrations, such events could be considered normal in Pagedale; however, white administrations had never been covered with the same scrutiny and certainly not with national attention. Three months after Black women took over leadership, a white man was elected to the one open seat on the council. Expressing her frustration with the constant focus on Black women in Pagedale, Darline Crawley, one of the first Black women elected in 1977 and a harsh critic of the mayor, dismissed race and gender as having any relevance, stating, "I hope to rectify this all female and all Black image. I'm supporting a white male in the election Tuesday. . . . Maybe if we break it up a little, some of the attention will go away and we can get back to running the city."[20] As of 2019, Darline Crawley continues to hold elected office in Pagedale and local media continues to cover controversies surrounding elected officials in the city.[21]

Pagedale has consistently elected all-Black and majority-women leadership since 1985, and many of the leaders across North St. Louis County identify as Black women. Throughout this time, Black women who hold elected office have continued to face much scrutiny in the press, and all the leaders I spoke with in Pagedale reported receiving threats against them or their families at one time or another. In the early 1990s, Mayor Mary Louise Carter and other elected officials in Pagedale were the targets of a series of car and fire bombings carried

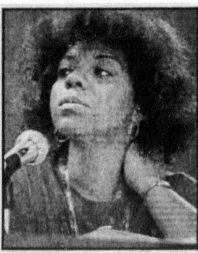

Photos by JIM BALMER

Pagedale Mayor Mary Hall (left) and her chief opponent, Alderperson Darline Crawley.

Government is a hot show in a small Missouri town

FIGURE 5.1 Front page of the *Detroit Free Press*, July 11, 1982. In spite of the fact Pagedale politics had long been a "hot show" under white male leadership, newspapers around the country featured local politics in Pagedale after it became the first city in the United States to elect all-Black, all-female leadership.

Detroit Free Press. Photo by Jim Balmer.

out in the city between 1989 and 1993. Although no one was seriously hurt and the people and motives behind the attacks were never definitively determined, several leaders stated they believed the attacks to be acts of intimidation against Black leadership.

Despite predictions made by researchers in the 1970s—that cities would embrace political mergers and approve tax increases and bond issues when Black leadership took over—cities that elected majority-Black officials did not become more open to consolidation measures, and Black leaders did not curb the trend toward funding municipal budgets through policing and the courts. Many Black women interviewed in the early 2000s regarding their experience of coming into municipal leadership in the 1980s and 1990s stated that they were very aware they would be scrutinized more than their white male predecessors and that nobody wanted to be at the helm of city leadership if, or when, it appeared that dissolution was the only option for their predominantly Black city. Most leaders who were interviewed defended the passing of ordinances aimed at property and behavior in their cities by stating they were continuing to run cities as they had been run previously and that the biggest challenges facing small cities were people who refused or did not know how to care for property—what they identified as essential for attracting investment and ensuring suburban success. Leaders generally framed their arguments by stating that Black suburban communities have the same rights as white suburbanites to expect a nice environment, stable home prices, and respectable behavior suitable for raising a family. Leaders in Pagedale (as well many leaders in other cities in North St. Louis County) routinely told me that people who do not care for their property or themselves do not belong in their cities and should go back to the projects in St. Louis city.[22]

It is clear from these interviews that actual class status does not necessarily determine residents' outlooks regarding power, subjectivity, or identity in Pagedale. Leaders consistently point out that they are all Black and all poor.[23] A middle-class identity does however shape many residents' outlook, in addition to differing generational attitudes and differing experiences of coming to live in Pagedale, including whether they own or rent their homes. A Black woman who moved to Pagedale from the housing projects in the city in the 1970s and owns her home (and has also held elected office), explained how middle-class identity in what is supposed to be a suburban area shapes the response of some residents toward others moving in, regardless of class, stating, "When I came to Pagedale I didn't know how to take care of property or how to act in the county. Someone had to tell me—you don't be doing that here. I didn't know it wasn't permissible. When people know what they're doing and why they're doing it they start to say, 'Well that's not bad at all, I got my barbecue in the backyard, I got my privacy and everything. I don't have to have all my kids in the street playing and be looking at my neighbor—all in their business.'"[24] This resident uses economistic logics of property to justify the policing of so-called urban behavior and indicates that the role of government is to teach people how to conduct their everyday lives in certain places. In light of the way this statement is framed, it can be understood that a desire for privacy is a respectable trait associated with suburban (white) culture, whereas barbequing in public or being "all in [other peoples'] business" is a problematic tendency within Black urban culture that requires reeducation upon individuals' moving to the suburbs. The attitudes expressed by this resident are shared by a number of people in Pagedale, including many in leadership, and municipal leaders maintain a *moral polity of blackness* defined and deployed paradoxically through the white suburban imaginary and an age-old politics of respectability.

Although many residents in Pagedale agree with these attitudes, many do not. The stories in chapter 3 told by Evelyn and Patrice echo the stories of Pagedale residents, especially those who identify as Black women. Interviews with residents as well as the available data regarding citations show that women in this area are more likely to be policed at home and for property violations, similar to those that Evelyn encountered, while men were more often policed in public space, although there are exceptions to the rule. Black men more often reported being pulled over for traffic violations when driving with other men in their car or stopped for "manner of walking," what many of them referred to as "walking while Black," which was the same infraction Michael Brown was initially stopped for in Ferguson. Individuals driving alone who were pulled over for traffic violations appeared to be more equally divided between Black men and women. Several women in Pagedale recounted that they had called the police to report incidences of domestic violence or fear of a domestic partner and ended up going to jail themselves when the police showed up and a warrant for outstanding property or traffic violations was discovered. In two of those instances, the domestic violence complaint was not investigated.

When interviewed, several municipal leaders in Pagedale spoke about gendered expectations they held, including their concern for teaching young women and girls about domestic skills, avoiding bad partners or baby daddies, learning good parenting, and dressing appropriately. Leaders complained that young men in their jurisdictions generally "passed through," but they did not regard them as residents if they did not take responsibility for heading a household. One leader stated that occupancy permit requirements were intended to allow inspectors to stop by any house at random for the purpose of ensuring boyfriends were not taking advantage of free housing in their city. Complaints by leaders about young men often focused on a need to "pull up their pants," "get a job," and take responsibility for their women and children. In this context, whether viewed through respectability politics or suburban norms, Black men who do not oversee women and hold full-time jobs with their pants pulled up, and Black women who engage in expressions of their sexuality or parent as the head of a household, fall outside the bounds (and rights) of gendered suburban citizenship. While this is a simplified assessment, these basic tenets give rise to multiple forms of cultural policing based on the "out-of-place" designation of Black residents. The visibility of out-of-place bodies works to control and exploit residents; however, it was also the basis by which women leading Ferguson resistance created alternative spaces of visibility and *appeared* as political actors. Furthermore, the Black women who assumed municipal leadership roles as early as 1978, many of whom still hold municipal office today and were interviewed for this research, have also struggled mightily with issues of visibility because of the fact that they are Black women, which calls for more nuanced considerations of the forces and motivations driving their rhetorical and literal practices.

Feminist scholars and urban historians have long written about the suburbs as the imagined space of domesticity and traditional gendered roles—wives and mothers who are responsible for the home and whose supposed purpose and fulfillment in life is the advancement and well-being of their husbands and children.[25] Whereas white single mothers have been able to push back against this cultural trope and establish themselves as liberal subjects, with varying degrees of success, Black women living in historically white suburbs still find themselves squarely judged against these standards, often by other Black women. As Roderick Ferguson observes, we are "in a historic moment in which minority middle classes ascend to power through appeals to normativity and thus become the regulators of working-class racial, gender, and sexual differences."[26]

Black women respondents living in Pagedale often reported that they felt disrespected by Black leaders and administrators because they, instead of men, were the heads of their households. By virtue of this fact, they stated that they felt judged by leaders and others as bad parents and undeserving citizens. They also felt that, as single mothers whose time and money were stretched across many demands, they were an easy target for cities looking to increase revenue through property-related violations. Those who had lived in the so-called urban core of St. Louis or other cities stated that being a single mother was more of an issue in the county than it was in the city, and they believed, on the basis of observations, that employed men who owned homes were more or less left alone whereas they (who were often employed and in many cases owned their homes) were held responsible for underemployed partners and adult children. Many women also stated that leaders and the police did not see their bodies as worthy of protection because their lack of gendered conformity was framed as the primary *problem* in the area, and they were therefore held responsible for anything that happened to them.

As discussed in chapter 3, many residents feel that Black leaders are able to more overtly say derogatory things about Black constituents because they are Black and that white leaders elsewhere could not make overt statements such as "Folks from the ghetto need to be taught how to live in the suburbs."[27] Many residents in Pagedale also voiced their perception that the majority-Black female leadership could "get away with" targeting gendered stereotypes and behavior, such as "promiscuous girls," young single mothers, and lesbian women, because they are women and that similar attitudes about girls and women would not be tolerated if they were men. Similarly, some respondents stated that the matriarchal image of many older Black female leaders in Pagedale allowed them to scold young Black men, telling them to "pull up their pants and get a job" without being accused of racialized or gendered biases. These types of admonitions of Black young people from an older generation of Black leadership fall squarely into long-theorized practices of respectability politics rooted in logics of assimilation and white heteronormative constructions of civil society. The way these logics play out in the historically white suburbs of St. Louis, however, sheds particular light on limits of suburban citizenship.

As described in preceding chapters, the suburbs have been a place where ethnic communities claim full citizenship through middle-class norms and space. Several scholars have described the quest for model-citizen status in and through the suburbs by various ethnic minorities, most often Asian Americans. Wendy Cheng describes how Asian and Latina/o Americans "had to either 'pass' as white . . . or evidence a 'proper' relationship to property as conceived as coextensive with a middle-class, white nuclear-family based vision of Americanness" in order to achieve provisional acceptance in the suburbs of Los Angeles.[28] In the case of African Americans, however, the specific and long history of antiblackness and their initial status *as property* in the United States denies Black suburban residents the necessary symbolic relationship *to property* and also requires that they make up for economic losses resulting from the risk attached to blackness.

Pagedale found itself at the center of a class action lawsuit in 2015 brought by the Institute for Justice, a libertarian public-interest law firm based in Arlington, Virginia, on behalf of Pagedale residents. Spurred by protests in Ferguson and the reports that followed, the complaint filed in the US District Court for the Eastern District of Missouri accuses the city of violating due process and excess-fines protections ensured in the US Constitution by turning its code enforcement and municipal court into "revenue-generating machines" to go after residents.[29] The complaint calls for an injunction against the city's reliance on such fines. The complaint focuses on property violations as well as both overt and veiled racialized prohibitions found in Pagedale city ordinances, such as "no sagging pants"; "no barbecuing in front of or next to a house"; "no congregating on a porch"; and so on.[30] According to the compliant, Pagedale residents could be, and were, ticketed for such things as not having curtains on their basement windows, having mismatched blinds, having more than three people at a barbeque, and having a basketball hoop in their driveway. The city prosecuted residents for conditions that were not forbidden by any applicable codes, such as having a crack in the driveway or not treating a fence, and many violations did not cite the reason the resident was receiving the violation.[31]

These restrictions are reminiscent of slave codes such as the Pennsylvania legislation listed at the end of W. E. B Du Bois's *The Philadelphia Negro*. Included in Du Bois's list are offenses punishable by whipping and fines such as "over four Negroes meeting together on Sundays or other days," and city ordinances to suppress "tumults" of slaves or disruptions by groups of "Negroes."[32] Pagedale leaders continue to claim that race has nothing to do with official practices in the city since both they and residents are Black; however, residents argue that similar ordinances are rarely tolerated in white communities. Referring to a majority-white suburb, one middle-aged Black resident of Pagedale stated, "Imagine if the city of Ladue told people they couldn't have more than three people at their backyard barbeque. The minute one person got a fine for that, everybody would be complaining and officials would have to listen. They don't listen to us here because they don't have to." When asked to clarify why officials don't have to listen to residents, she said, "because we're Black."[33]

Long before the Institute for Justice became involved in Pagedale in the aftermath of Ferguson protests, residents of Pagedale were sharing these stories with anyone who would listen, with little success at eliciting interest. The consistent story I heard over a ten-year period was of a city continuously fining, harassing, and sometimes jailing residents for minor traffic and nontraffic infractions. Residents routinely showed me the calendar handed out by the city that, in addition to providing information such as trash pickup days and holidays, included different laws and norms that residents were expected to follow (figure 5.2). Although these stories were in keeping with stories from other parts of North St. Louis County, accounts from Pagedale also involved the threat of demolition over non-safety-related code violations. Residents facing code violations, which include peeling paint, windows without screens or with a torn screen, loose siding, and mismatched curtains, are usually given thirty days to remedy issues. Properties that do not comply are cited again; owners with multiple citations can be jailed, and their homes may be placed on the demolition list. Many residents lack the resources to address repairs immediately and bear the added burden of fines and fees for violations, as well as jail time. One eighty-four-year-old

Black woman who has lived in Pagedale for forty-seven years and is part of the lawsuit received a letter ordering her to fix a dozen violations, none of which were safety issues and all of which were beyond her limited retirement income to address immediately. She was told that "all windows need screens and window treatment such as matching blinds and/or curtains, slats, etc.," and ordered to repaint her porch and paint her building foundation, as well as "touch up paint or repaint entire house, cut back weeds and treat fence line with brush killer," and trim an overgrown tree.[34] Much in the same way large urban areas became the front lines of the war on poverty through the criminalization of the poor and homeless (as discussed in chapter 1), Pagedale uses the concept of broken-windows policing to get rid of unbecoming properties the city claims bring down property values and, like many cities across St. Louis County, to fill budgetary gaps at the same time.

Property is a major theme in Pagedale. One leader stated, "If you don't know how to cut your grass then you shouldn't be living in a house."[35] When I relayed this statement to a resident who had received a violation for her grass being too long, she said, "If they don't know how to serve their residents and take care of the vacant lots they own where the houses are gone, then they shouldn't be running a city. They have vacant lots all over this city that they've taken away from people and they don't always cut the grass on those lots. Then they come out and measure my grass with a ruler."[36] In a deposition given by the mayor of Pagedale, the acting attorney for the lawsuit brought by the Institute of Justice, William Mauer, asked the mayor questions regarding ordinances aimed at property:

> Mr. Mauer: Why does Pagedale regulate the window treatments in a person's home?
>
> Mayor Carter: The reason that ordinance was passed was because we had some, I would say, I don't know if they were homeowners, renters or what, but they put Christmas paper up at the windows. They put sheets and hung them up in the night. I mean, and these are on, you know, major streets and stuff. That's why. That they would have to have some type of window treatment.
>
> Mr. Mauer: And so it was purely aesthetics?
>
> Mayor Carter: Exactly.
>
> Mr. Mauer: Okay. So they weren't actually harming anybody by having—
>
> Mayor Carter: Yeah, they're harming somebody. They're decreasing property value.
>
> Mr. Mauer: I see. . . . Does Pagedale regulate whether somebody has painted the foundation or not on their home?

MAYOR CARTER: Well, I don't know because we use St. Louis County ordinances also, we adopt their ordinances, and we also use the BOCA [Building Officials and Code Administrators] code. If, like I said, it's to keep the property values up. I mean, you going to have to paint it at some point.

MR. MAUER: Okay. So it's an aesthetic consideration?

MAYOR CARTER: Yes, it is.

MR. MAUER: Does the city regulate whether a house has chipped paint on it?

MAYOR CARTER: I don't know. If it just a couple of chips or something, but if the whole house is chipped, it's bad.

MR. MAUER: Okay. Also for aesthetic reasons?

MAYOR CARTER: Yes. And for property value.

MR. MAUER: So the property values follow good aesthetics?

MAYOR CARTER: Yes, it does.[37]

Although most cities in St. Louis County issue many more traffic violations than nontraffic violations, the opposite is true of Pagedale, where nontraffic

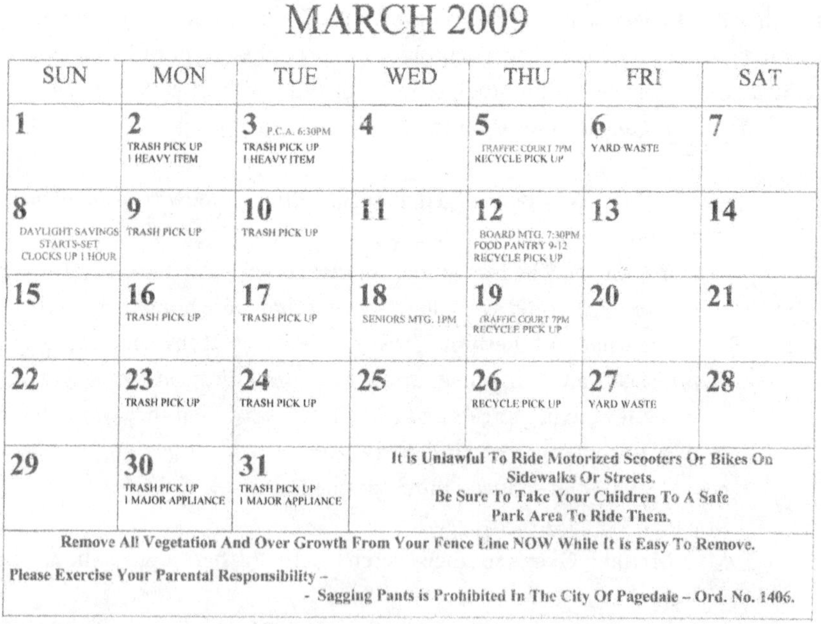

MARCH 2009

SUN	MON	TUE	WED	THU	FRI	SAT
1	2 TRASH PICK UP 1 HEAVY ITEM	3 P.C.A. 6:30PM TRASH PICK UP 1 HEAVY ITEM	4	5 TRAFFIC COURT 7PM RECYCLE PICK UP	6 YARD WASTE	7
8 DAYLIGHT SAVINGS STARTS–SET CLOCKS UP 1 HOUR	9 TRASH PICK UP	10 TRASH PICK UP	11	12 BOARD MTG. 7:30PM FOOD PANTRY 9-12 RECYCLE PICK UP	13	14
15	16 TRASH PICK UP	17 TRASH PICK UP	18 SENIORS MTG. 1PM	19 TRAFFIC COURT 7PM RECYCLE PICK UP	20	21
22	23 TRASH PICK UP	24 TRASH PICK UP	25	26 RECYCLE PICK UP	27 YARD WASTE	28
29	30 TRASH PICK UP 1 MAJOR APPLIANCE	31 TRASH PICK UP 1 MAJOR APPLIANCE	It is Uniawful To Ride Motorized Scooters Or Bikes On Sidewalks Or Streets. Be Sure To Take Your Children To A Safe Park Area To Ride Them.			

Remove All Vegetation And Over Growth From Your Fence Line NOW While It Is Easy To Remove.

Please Exercise Your Parental Responsibility –
- Sagging Pants is Prohibited In The City Of Pagedale – Ord. No. 1406.

FIGURE 5.2 Page from the City of Pagedale calendar. Each month features different city ordinances and reminders concerning property and behavior.

Collection of the author.

violations have been historically more numerous.[38] Several factors explain this phenomenon, but the most critical correlation is that Pagedale is effectively carrying out a land grab through the municipal court and through county and city liens on properties for unpaid taxes and unpaid fines and fees. Properties obtained by the city because of mounting citations or back taxes have often been turned over to the nonprofit housing and community-building organization, Beyond Housing, which builds new housing for low-income families participating in their home ownership and renters' programs. Through this process and with an ironic twist, poor people in the St. Louis region benefit from the circumstances of the very poor. Those who are consistently unable to keep up their property or pay property taxes subsequently lose their property and, as a result, "the more deserving poor" are able to find housing.[39] Leaders of Pagedale and others argue that turning "nuisance" properties, which bring down property values and scare away outside investment, into attractive new homes for low-income people participating in comprehensive programs through Beyond Housing benefits more people than it hurts because property values are brought up in the process and families are supported in areas that ensure their success.[40] These benefits have indeed proven to be great, and the programs offered through Beyond Housing take an important holistic approach to circumventing poverty in ways that most programs aimed at supporting families miss. The logic rhetorically promoted in this process, however, a process I later realized I had participated in, essentially justifies stripping very poor residents of their homes through the prioritization of the rights of property, good citizenship, and an aesthetics of suburban norms. In another ironic twist, this logic uses the rights of private property to deny the rights of private property, which is why a libertarian public interest law firm took notice of this case.

At the time of this writing, Beyond Housing has been focusing residential and commercial revitalization efforts in Pagedale for over twenty years. Gradually, the nonprofit agency added multiple family support services, in addition to their original mission to provide affordable housing, and has understandably become a national model for holistic antipoverty initiatives that go far beyond affordable housing. During the same period, the City of Pagedale, in an apparent effort to improve public perception, attract outside investment and partnerships, and boost economic stability in the city, implemented a zero-tolerance policy for "weak links" within the municipal boundaries. As one resident put it, "Your house could be falling down around you from the inside and your kids could be starving but as long as you put your last dime into new paint and matching curtains and cut your grass, the city don't care."[41] Another Pagedale resident stated, "They are putting so-called needy families in brand new homes but if you're really poor, the message is 'Get out.'"[42] This raises a question regarding how nonprofit organizations with sincere missions to address poverty and assist poor families can, in some instances, aid and abet oppressive practices and implement subjective interpretations of "highest and best use" that in turn impact the most vulnerable and marginalized members of society.

Similar to the ways in which E. Franklin Frazier's antiracist work, discussed in chapter 1, was used to draft the culture-of-poverty discourse that directed decades of racialized federal, state, and local policy afterward, this case illustrates how efforts that earnestly seek to alleviate oppression, and which have clearly helped many families, can also (directly and indirectly) reinforce messages of respectability and responsibility that determine and explain who succeeds and who fails within a model of community development. It also reveals the many complications and contradictions faced by those trying to transform communities and combat poverty. Beyond Housing's community participation approach relies on residents to be "engaged citizens," both discursively and in practice. Given the limitations of institutional structures and the democratic ideals behind this approach, responsibility for failures is inadvertently yet inherently placed on those who fall through the cracks and those who, for a multitude of reasons, do not participate. The difficulty in engaging an aggrieved population within a community while also partnering with entities viewed as oppressive and predatory tends to result in narrow outcomes of engagement.[43]

During the several years I spent working with the leadership of the City of Pagedale and Beyond Housing as a faculty representative of Washington University, I witnessed the contradictions that arise when forces align to "help residents," with varying definitions, methods, and metrics concerning that objective. Because the leadership of Pagedale is democratically elected and Black, the university categorically did not question whether leaders were acting in the best interest of their citizens. Moreover, because of the measurable impacts that Beyond Housing has had in this geography, its commitment to holistic intervention, and the recognition it has received for innovative practices, administrators at the university did not question specific methods or practices carried out by the nonprofit. Nor did I. Over the course of my extended time in the community and throughout the process of conducting a health impact assessment (HIA) of a Beyond Housing–initiated project in Pagedale,[44] it became evident that discursive representations of the community by people in charge were out of sync with the experiences of the most vulnerable residents. In fact, residents began to share many of the stories described throughout chapters 3 and 4, regarding constant harassment and what many felt were abuses of power by the city for the purpose of extracting money, obtaining property, and regulating behavior that supported development. By extension, many residents assumed Beyond Housing directly benefitted from these practices, which was often not the case. In spite of these discoveries, the HIA report promoted the discourses of healthy eating, active living, and even broken-windows policing, suggesting that if residents have access to healthy food and walkable streets, and maintain their property, the vast economic and health disparities found in their zip code would be greatly remediated. That is not to say that food security and walkable communities are not critically important issues; however, if residents are afraid to leave their houses for fear of being fined by the city and they must choose between fixing cosmetic issues with their property and buying healthy food, these factors will have no effect on their lives.

These conflicts were difficult to navigate personally yet paled in comparison to the difficulties residents articulated. As a principal investigator on the HIA, I found measurable positive impacts within the metrics of health, food security, and economic well-being that could result from the development proposed jointly by Beyond Housing and the City of Pagedale. At the same time, I observed veiled as well as explicit efforts to rid the city of the most economically and behaviorally "undesirable" residents, and experiences shared by residents reinforced these observations. While critiques of neoliberal urban practices, discussed in chapter 1, assume that cities will act in the interest of the few and not the many, such critiques become more complicated when cities are also connected to agencies like Beyond Housing, which earnestly seek to better the lives of many poor people. Beyond Housing's continued alignment with and vehement defense of the leadership of Pagedale, even as egregious practices of predatory policing were publicly exposed by the media post-Ferguson, were personally surprising, yet they reveal how the politics of community transformation can mirror the contradictions found in humanitarian discourse and practice. This is similar to what Jean Bricmont calls humanitarian imperialism, defined as helping individuals and families with one hand while (consciously or not) strengthening the structures that create underlying problems with the other.[45] My own experiences and relationships with leaders in Pagedale made it even more clear that sincere care and compassion can and does simultaneously exist with blatant forms of oppression.

Another frame I found helpful for understanding what is happening in Pagedale and other areas of North St. Louis County is triage. Conceptually developed within the medical field, triage refers to a decision-making hierarchy that dismisses those considered to be beyond hope, identifies those who can wait for help, and focuses resources on those who can be helped by immediate care. When I asked a friend who has worked as a social worker in North St. Louis County for many years whether nonprofits there help the poor at the expense of the very poor, her response was, "absolutely." She followed this statement up by lamenting that nonprofits, including those she worked for, are constantly trying to establish an evolutionary threshold separating those they can help from those who are beyond hope or refuse to conform to the stipulations of help that workers are required to enforce. In order to make and justify difficult decisions regarding limited resources, nonprofits also use well-established discourses and cultural politics to distinguish the worthy poor from the unworthy poor, or what Chandan Reddy calls "the dialectic of exceptionality and disposability."[46] This may explain why an organization with a clear mission and track record of assisting poor families would also be aligned with a government that stratifies its residents through cultural politics and racialized narratives of risk in order to bring up property values for those struggling toward the top of the spectrum. In this way, the nonprofit does not appear to compromise its values because the city establishes the metrics for differentiation and carries out punitive practices, thus revealing another double bind: in order to help residents, the nonprofit must be aligned with a structure that preys on residents.

Looking back at past research and documents from my time working in Pagedale, I came across a spreadsheet that one of my graduate students had created in 2008. It was produced at the request of Beyond Housing, which had asked for assistance with what was termed a "housing audit" in Pagedale. The list of ninety homes to be audited was provided by the mayor of Pagedale. Without questioning it much, I sent the student to meet with the person overseeing the request and tasked him with doing what was asked. When the spreadsheet was completed, I filed away a digital copy labeled "Pagedale Housing Audit." When looking at this document years later, I was dismayed to discover that I had assisted in carrying out the very practices I describe in chapter 2. The homes on the list were described as vacant, and the student was asked to perform a physical audit of each property and make recommendations concerning whether it should be demolished for a vacant lot, demolished and rebuilt as a Beyond Housing project, rehabbed as a Beyond Housing project, or remain as it was. The results of the audit showed that more than twenty of the properties listed as vacant had families living in them. The student color-coded the spreadsheet, making notes regarding the requested classifications. After rediscovering this document, I went back to look at the ownership history of the ninety properties and found that only eight of them were still in the same ownership as in 2008. Since 2008, Pagedale had taken over eighteen, Beyond Housing had been deeded six, and the St. Louis County land trust had gained control of two. Many of the remaining properties had been foreclosed on by lenders and sold at auction.

Narratives, as discussed at length in the preceding chapter, are important for justifying city practices, for carrying out development efforts, and for securing funding. In 2016, the Robert Wood Johnson Foundation, which funded the HIA in Pagedale described above, awarded the Culture of Health Award to the 24:1 Community in North St. Louis County. The website for the award describes 24:1 by stating,

> On a map, 24 contiguous municipalities just northwest of St. Louis resemble nothing more than a crazy quilt. And for decades, their governance and services were a patchwork, too. Each municipality—from the tiny, two-street Village of Glen Echo Park, population 160, to the neighborhood-sized City of Normandy, population 5,008—has its own government. That's two dozen mayors and city councils and almost as many police departments in an area that spans almost 11 square miles, is home to 36,250 people, and is served by one school district.[47]

This is an apt description, and the website goes on to justly praise the work of Beyond Housing and the leaders across this area for consolidating resources and coming together for the purpose of improving health and wellbeing and strengthening education across the twenty-four cities that make up the Normandy Schools Collaborative (formerly NSD). The narrative depicted on the website also reveals the complexities and contradictions that arise when agendas that support families trapped in poverty potentially collide with those that promote the priorities of economic development and the funding of city budgets. The website goes on to state,

> Banding together has enabled the cities to secure federal and state grants to begin widening streets, building sidewalks, and planting and trimming trees—efforts that make 24:1 safer, healthier, and more attractive for residents.
>
> To hold themselves accountable to their communities, the mayors wrote a set of 10 best practices, including having an annual budget, an annual audit, and police coverage. In a state that has come under intense scrutiny following the death two years ago of 18-year-old Michael Brown in a police shooting in Ferguson, a suburb just outside of 24:1, they were ahead of the curve. Last year, Missouri passed a statute that put in place 12 similar standards for municipalities across the state.[48]

What this narrative fails to mention is that the mayors credited as "ahead of the curve," in terms of best practices and accountability, are the same mayors who oversee cities with the highest degrees of policing for profit. The alliance also brought cities together to fight tooth and nail against state laws, including the one mentioned on the website, to regulate the percentage of city operating budgets that could be funded through predatory policing and the municipal courts. While there was a racialized outcome regarding which cities were most impacted by state laws stemming from Ferguson protests, as discussed in chapter 3, neither the white Republican lawmakers who sponsored the bills nor the Black mayors who opposed the laws were ultimately the people whose voices were underrepresented and erased through the various politics that were employed. Having used similar narratives to secure a significant amount of funding from the Robert Wood Johnson Foundation for research in and on this area, research that indeed contributed to this book, I have benefitted from similar politics of representation.

In 2018, after almost three years of litigation, residents of Pagedale won the class action lawsuit they had brought against the city in federal court. In May of 2018, the parties involved in the lawsuit agreed to a consent decree that was approved by the federal judge overseeing the case. The consent decree included dropping all pending cases where there was no good reason to proceed, eliminating several fines, fees, and laws in the municipal code that specifically punish poor residents and criminalize non-safety-related housing conditions, no longer writing citations that have no basis in municipal code, and providing residents with information regarding why they are being ticketed and how they can respond to the citation. After the consent decree was approved, Valarie Whitner, one of the lead plaintiffs in the case, was quoted in a press release from the Institute for Justice as saying, "Finally, my nightmare is over. Every morning I woke up worried that I'd get another ticket. Now I can sleep easy and get on with my life."[49] Longtime leaders of Pagedale continue to insist that they did nothing wrong, and many continue to be reelected. The consent decree makes Pagedale the second municipality in North St. Louis County to have outside oversight of its policing, administrative, and court practices, joining Ferguson, which agreed to a consent decree following the US Department of Justice report in the aftermath of Ferguson protests.

Throughout my work and research focused on Pagedale, a mix of contradictory (positive and negative) factors and outcomes emerged constantly, often simultaneously. This fact was further complicated by my personal relationships with residents, city leaders, and people from the nonprofit agency. I came to believe that city leaders and those working with Beyond Housing truly care about Pagedale and think they are doing the right thing, according to how they view the world and what is at stake. Many Pagedale residents have greatly benefitted from these efforts. Partnering with Beyond Housing and utilizing the tax increment financing structure described in chapter 3, Pagedale has gained a grocery store, a bank, a senior housing facility, a movie theater, a health clinic, and a coffee shop. This level of development in a low-income community that is not gentrifying is nonexistent elsewhere in Missouri and in most places across the country. Moreover, many Pagedale leaders have personally sacrificed much in order to dedicate their lives to public service. Black women who have served for decades overcame public slander and backlash specifically aimed at their gender and race. They did not back down to pipe bombs, car bombs, and threats to their families, and they have stood up to regional and state leaders of municipalities and agencies that have poached resources out of their cities and that they perceive as threats to their city and to local autonomy.

In spite of the many positive changes in recent years, the practices carried out by leaders in Pagedale devastate many residents, especially those who are the most economically vulnerable, and leaders have maintained this trajectory for a very long time. The fact that many contradictions exist at once and together is difficult to come to terms with personally and even more difficult analytically, but it speaks to what Avery Gordon, drawing on Patricia Williams, has simply stated: "Life is complicated." She goes on, "that life is complicated is a theoretical statement that guides efforts to treat race, class, and gender dynamics and con-sciousness as more dense and delicate than those categorical terms often imply." Gordon also reminds us that "all people possess a "complex personhood, . . . all people remember and forget, are beset by contradiction, and recognize and misrecognize themselves and others."[50] The same people who do much good can, and do, bring about much harm. This applies to all people, including those who are preyed upon by municipal officials and also have the capacity to act against their own self-interest and against each other. "Even those who live in the most dire circumstances possess a complex and often times contradictory humanity and subjectivity that is never adequately glimpsed by viewing them as victims or, on the other hand, as superhuman agents."[51] That life is complicated "is a theoretical statement that might guide a critique of privately purchased rights, of various forms of blindness and sanctioned denial; that might guide an attempt to drive a wedge into lives and visions of freedom ruled by the nexus of market exchange."[52] Wrestling with how to guide a critique of such things is where research gets messy, and it is where I have struggled not only to make sense of my findings but also, more importantly, to know when something is indeed "found" and how much it counts. In many ways this book reflects the contradictions that arise from the fact that people and places are messy and life is complicated.

The disparate politics of (now) older Black women who have been in leader-ship in North St. Louis County for more than thirty years and the young women and gender-nonconforming protesters who emerged after the death of Michael Brown illustrate the messy and often contrasting facets of gendered, generational, and sexual identity and the power of discourse and cultural politics in determin-ing regimes of truth. The "truths" put forward by the municipal leaders, who fought long and hard to gain and maintain positions of power, are very different from the "truths" of the young women and gender-nonconforming individuals leading resistance in North St. Louis County; however, the fact that these groups have all suffered the violence of illegibility brought about by their existence as Black women, or nonconforming Black people, is abundantly clear. As Brittany Cooper points out, laying claim to a public space from which to speak and be heard was a critical step for early Black women activists and intellectuals, and "respectability" provided such a space.[53] Cooper also points out that the Black women activists and intellectuals who were historically categorized as matriarchs of respectability politics pushed the limits placed on Black feminized bodies at critical junctures through intentional as well as embodied practices. Pagedale leaders in the 1970s and 1980s did indeed push the limits placed on their bodies at a critical time in Black political enfranchisement. Cooper brings an important dimension to other studies of Black women and respectability politics that developed during and after Black rural migration to cities like St. Louis after Reconstruction. She does so by contextualizing how "acceptable" public spaces and public personas were essential to visibility.[54] This visibility was crucial for the success of the first Black women elected to office in US cities like Pagedale. However, just as subjectification, subjectivity, and identity played out in complex and nuanced ways for Black women and gender-nonconforming people throughout history, a cultural politics rooted in tropes of respectability is both claimed and rejected by Black women in leadership positions as well as residents across North St. Louis County, often simultaneously. Black women leaders expressed over and over in this research that many of their actions stem from pushing back against the limitations placed not only on their own identities—as Black and female—but also against the representations of the places they have been elected to lead. This is a driving motivation behind their actions—to be perceived as worthy suburban communities by the larger region.

For multiple reasons explored in the next section, the space of death where Michael Brown's body lay did in fact open up spaces of visibility—a visibility of the realities of everyday life and death in this place—which is very different from the visibility sought by Black women in leadership in Pagedale. The Black queered ethics that protesters advance, particularly those identifying as women and queer, pushes beyond a demand for recognition and refuses to simply work within existing structures of governance—it requires an imagining beyond that which already is. The collective imagination, as argued in chapter 4, is a powerful thing, as is taking control of one's own narrative. As the young women who led protests in Ferguson pointed out in various ways, the emphasis placed on respectability politics by Black men and women throughout the post-Reconstruction era, during the 1960s and 1970s civil rights struggles, by Black women in cities across North St. Louis County, and even by those occupying the space of protest in Ferguson, did and does not result in the social, political, and spatial equity promised by the liberal state. According to one young woman I interviewed, the mistakes that Black women assuming leadership roles in the 1970s and 1980s made did not stem from their desire for visibility, or their tenacious insistence on being heard, or holding power, or a lack of care. Rather, these missteps stem from working within the system they inherited—a system they did not create and a system designed to equate blackness with risk. She explains,

> When we were protesting Kimberlee King's death in the Pagedale jail[55] I heard about all these things that were going on there and what people were saying about how the city was looking for all kinds of ways to put people in jail. Then later you told me about how Pagedale was the first city in America that had all Black female leadership and I was like "damn," I would never have known that because nobody ever talks about that. I want to be like proud of that fact but then you see how the leadership is still all Black women and you see what's happening there. They thought they could just move on out to the suburbs when the laws said they could and that would make them just like anybody else who lived there. When that didn't work out, when white people left because their daughter might date a Black guy, they thought they could get respect by making everybody else respectable and then I guess they thought, "Well I guess if we can't get respect we may as well make money."
>
> We're showing that Black women will never be respected so stop living as if you're going to get that. Black women need to stop living how they're told and ask themselves who they really are. Living outside of what you're told is protest. Clearly being the first all-Black women leadership in Pagedale didn't liberate women in Pagedale. But that's not the fault of the Black women—who they are—it's because they tried to do it in the structure that was already there.[56]

It is clear to residents of Pagedale, regardless of whether or not they support municipal leadership, that this system, which exploits and produces blackness-as-risk, is not broken. It is doing exactly what it was designed to do.

A DAY IN AUGUST

I wake up thinking about him just lyin' there. He was like the dog that's been hit that you gotta walk by to get to where you're going. It was over a hundred fucking degrees out there and you knew his body was decomposing fast right before your eyes but they just left him there. They didn't even cover him up for like over an hour.

—William, resident of Canfield Green Apartments

Eighteen-year-old Michael Brown Jr. walked with his friend, Dorian Johnson, down Canfield Drive on a hot and humid Saturday in August. He had spent most of his summer in school and had graduated days before from Normandy High School. It was just before noon and many residents of the surrounding Canfield Green Apartments were at home. Those without the comfort of air conditioning had their windows open, and some were on shaded balconies or front stoops as the temperature neared one hundred degrees. There was a bouncy castle set up nearby, and a few children played in and around it, their voices echoing off the three-story brick buildings on either side of Canfield Drive. At approximately noon, officer Darren Wilson drove his marked Ferguson police SUV down Canfield Drive and encountered the two walking in an otherwise empty street.

Darren Wilson

I see them walking down the middle of the street. And first thing that struck me was they're walking in the middle of the street. . . . And the next thing I noticed was the size of the individuals because either the first one was really small or the second one was really big.[1]

Wilson rolled down his window as he drove by the two and told them to get out of the street or be ticketed for a pedestrian infraction that was frequently cited by the Ferguson police department, described as "manner of walking."[2] The two were visibly irritated and responded that they had almost reached their destination and would soon be getting to the other side of the street. By all accounts, Wilson began to drive away but then stopped abruptly after twenty to thirty feet and backed up his vehicle to where Brown and Johnson were walking. Wilson testified later that he called for backup prior to reversing because he had "a sense about the situation." Brown approached the SUV as Wilson stopped next to them and is said to have closed Wilson's door or was in the way as the officer tried to open it. It is unclear from accounts which individual initiated physical contact. Wilson claims to have grabbed Brown's arm as he reached through the window and Johnson stated that Wilson reached out of his window and grabbed Brown.

Darren Wilson

And when I grabbed him, the only way I can describe it is I felt like a five-year-old holding onto Hulk Hogan. . . . Hulk Hogan, that's just how big he felt and how small I felt just from grasping his arm.[3]

Wilson fired his gun while Brown was near the vehicle, although witnesses' and Wilson's accounts differ regarding how that happened. Following the shot, Brown ran several steps away and then turned to face Wilson with his hands up.

Darren Wilson

When it went off, it shot through my door panel and my window was down and glass flew out of my door panel. I think that kind of startled him and me at the same time. . . .[4] He looked up at me and had the most intense aggressive face. The only way I can describe it, it looks like a demon. . . . He comes back towards me again with his hands up. I tried to pull the trigger again, nothing happened. . . . When I pulled the trigger again, it goes off. . . .[5] It went off twice in the car. Pull, click, click, went off, click, went off. . . . When I looked up after that, I see him start to run and I see a cloud of dust behind him. I then get out of my car.[6]

What happened in the next few seconds remains disputed by Wilson, Johnson, and other witnesses but ended with Brown, who was unarmed, dead and face down on the centerline of Canfield Drive with at least six bullet wounds, including two to the head. Witnesses, including Wilson, stated that less than a minute elapsed between the initial encounter and Brown's death. According to autopsies performed by both the state and the family, the first four shots that hit Brown were not thought to be life-threatening. The last bullets entered the top of his skull, indicating that he was leaning or falling forward at the time he was fatally shot. Several witnesses stated Brown was falling to his knees because he had already been shot multiple times when the last shots entered the top of his head from ten to fifteen feet away. Wilson claimed that Brown was empowered by being shot four times and had his head down because he was about to "run right through [him]."

Darren Wilson

I remember looking at my sights and firing, all I see is his head and that's what I shot. I don't know how many, I know at least once because I saw the last one go into him. And then when it went into him, the demeanor on his face went blank, the aggression was gone, I mean, I knew he stopped, the threat was stopped. . . . After that is when I got back on the radio and I said, "send me a supervisor and every car you have."[7]

According to Wilson, backup arrived soon after Brown fell to the ground, but he never called for medical assistance. The sergeant told Wilson to go sit in his car, which Wilson refused to do because he feared the crowd that was forming, so he gave Wilson the keys to a patrol car, and Wilson drove to the station alone.

Darren Wilson

I remember him saying, Darren, sit in the car. I said, "Sarge, I can't be singled out. It is already getting hostile, I can't be singled out in the car. . . .[8] I hear yelling, I hear screaming, as I'm walking back to my car. . . . It's just not a very well-liked community. . . .[9] That's not an area where you can't take anything lightly.[10]

People quickly came out into the street and the green spaces close to where Brown's body had fallen. As people tried to make sense of what had happened, police officers arriving at the scene were cordoning off the area. Several witnesses of the shooting told the congregating residents that Brown had had his hands above his head at the time he was shot.[11] Various accounts of what had happened circulated quickly through the crowd as well as on social media, and #Ferguson and #MikeBrown began trending on Twitter. For over an hour, Brown remained uncovered with an increasing trail of blood moving down the street as his body bled out (figure a.1).

The image was captured and uploaded to social media by countless cellphones. As time went on, more people began arriving from across the St. Louis region, as did law enforcement officials. The Ferguson and St. Louis County police departments struggled to secure the area, and many people later reported that it was unclear who was in charge. Bystanders reported that animosity between the

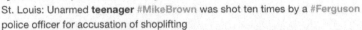

syndıcalıst @syndicalisms · 9 Aug 2014   ⌄

St. Louis: Unarmed **teenager** #MikeBrown was shot ten times by a #Ferguson police officer for accusation of shoplifting

  💬 97   ⟲ 2.1K   ♡ 517   ✉

FIGURE A.1   An image of Michael Brown's body on Canfield Drive taken by a bystander on August 9, 2014 and posted on Twitter the same day. The photo was downloaded and tweeted multiple times and retweeted thousands of times in the twenty-four hours following Brown's death.

Photographer and origin of the first tweet unknown.

police and the crowd was high and escalated as officials left the body exposed and threatened to arrest anyone asking for information.

Marlene

There was a lot of yelling going on between both sides. People wanted to know why this boy was lying in the street and the police acted like we had no right to be in our own front yard. Still, they wanted us to see it. There's hundreds of kids live in that area. Do you know how traumatic that was? He was out there the whole afternoon. This was a lynching, for real.

The arrival of Brown's father and later his mother added to the level of emotion and frustration in the crowd, and many people were shocked by what they described as a lack of empathy toward Brown's mother by police officers at the scene as she begged to be near her son. Some residents stated, "They treated her like a criminal."[12] People were increasingly agitated by the length of time Brown's body remained on the hot pavement, where, as one older man stated, "you could've fried an egg if you'd wanted."[13] It turned out to be four and half hours that Brown's body stayed on the pavement.

Cheyenne

We heard it on the radio that somebody was killed just down the street. So I guess that mother's instinct in me, I went down there and I was not prepared for what I saw. And, you know, I was not prepared for people's reactions either. Children crying, people just asking, "Why did this boy have to die?" And all that. Seeing the body lay there for all those hours. So that was a big deal, right then. And it just sparked something in me that I knew I had to come back. I didn't know what I was coming back for but I knew had to keep coming. I kept coming back each night. After a few days, we never went home.

Reverend Sekou

It was right before school started and there was a bouncy castle across the street from where he was lying. So there were five-year-olds saying, "Mike's laying in the street!" They brought out the police dogs before they brought out an ambulance. They tried to put his body in the trunk of a car. The community was like, "You put that body in the trunk of a car and ain't nobody leaving here alive." So they put his body in an SUV. That was undignified.[14]

Brown's family was not allowed to accompany his body when it was moved at around four thirty that afternoon. Left behind, his mother, Lezley McSpadden, dropped rose petals over the place where her son had died (soon driven over by patrol cars) after police tape was removed (figure a.2).

The crowd soon claimed the street again and constructed an improvised memorial of flowers and stuffed animals over Brown's blood, as an outpouring of grief and as a refusal to allow authorities to erase what had happened in that space. According to witnesses, police officers allowed their dogs to urinate on

FIGURE A.2   "Lezley McSpadden, center, drops rose petals on the blood stains from her 18-year-old son Michael Brown who was shot and killed by police in the middle of the street in Ferguson, Mo., near St. Louis on Saturday, Aug. 9, 2014."

Associated Press/*St. Louis Post-Dispatch*. Photo by Huy Mach.

the stuffed animals and attempted to dismantle the memorial that evening.[15] The memorial—as a site of memory, denigration, and resistance—would become a contentious symbol between residents and the city of Ferguson, as officials repeatedly ordered the police to take down the memorial, only to have residents rebuild it every time. Residents later spoke of the constant contestation of the memorial's right "to be in the street," and the disregard for what it represented, as a haunting reminder of how and why Michael Brown had died and the rights of residents to occupy the street in their everyday lives.

The police left Canfield Drive around ten on the night of August 9, and the crowd eventually dispersed. The next evening, a group estimated at around one hundred people attended a hastily organized candlelight vigil, including many who had witnessed Brown in the street the day before.

As night fell, a smaller group moved from the site of the shooting to nearby West Florissant Road, a commercial thoroughfare a few blocks away. Protesters blocked traffic, chanting, "Hands up, don't shoot," and isolated acts of looting by a few people took place, although the event was reported as "rioting in St. Louis suburbs."[16] The Ferguson and St. Louis County police departments responded by issuing a curfew and donning riot gear. Numerous tanks appeared in the street,

FIGURE A.3 "Police in riot gear watch protesters in Ferguson, Mo. on Wednesday, Aug. 13, 2014."

Associated Press. Photo by Jeff Roberson.

and the area was described as a war zone. Many people, including reporters, were arrested on the charge of unlawful assembly if they stopped moving. Continued protests, arrests, and militarized police responses, which included repeated use of tear gas and the firing of rubber bullets into the crowd, escalated over the following days (figure a.3). Meanwhile, the mayor of Ferguson insisted there were no racial tensions in Ferguson.

Many people who witnessed Brown in the street recalled specific ways in which the image of his body conveyed their own vulnerability—as people out of place. Almost all of them expressed feelings of being spoken to directly through the image of Brown's body and flesh, saying, "This could be you," for example. Most viewed his death as a lynching. "That will be you if you get out of line," a young Black man living in Canfield Green Apartments remembered feeling. Residents also spoke of a disturbing irony they had long felt but saw play out before them on that day: their experience of being targeted, harassed, and regarded as less than human by those who simultaneously practice a most extreme inhumanity. "I just finally woke up when I saw that," said one young woman said later as she stood in front of the Ferguson Police Department. She went on, "When people talk about police brutality, you think about the young Black men gettin' killed like Mike Brown. But I realized this is what I live every day."[17]

Part II
BLACKNESS AS FREEDOM

QUEERING PROTEST

Queer women in this movement are so unapologetically who they are
and so fiercely advocate for the recognition of all identities. They
don't accept anything less than liberation of all Black lives, and
I think they've made that very clear. They are very visibly leaders, and
I think you see that historically as well that queer and trans women
of color are always there leading. They're not always recognized and
they are very, very commonly erased.

—Kathryn (pseudonym)

The processes of mapping risk onto bodies and space reflect the historically
constituted practices of antiblackness that construct race and demarcate people
and geographies of freedom and unfreedom. These processes made the colonial
reordering of the modern world possible and built empires upon the labor and
bodies of enslaved Black people. As evidenced in St. Louis and beyond, a com-
monsense understanding of blackness-as-risk continues to operate as a structural
logic to order metropolitan space and determine the value of lives. In contrast
to this power *over* life, the resistance witnessed in Ferguson following the death
of Michael Brown represents the power *of* life, and it demonstrates how "the
biopolitical event is always a queer event—a subversive process of subjectiviza-
tion that, shattering ruling identities and norms, reveals the link between power
and freedom, and thereby inaugurates an alternative production of subjectivity."[1] The ability to imagine what could be in the face of what is emanates from
intimate spaces of trauma and is always already present within oppression itself.
The everyday spaces of extreme violence in this area coalesced with a collective trauma that transcends time and space. Although the specificity of extreme
violence in the St. Louis region fundamentally shaped the work of people leading resistance here, those who identify as women and queer drew upon their
experience of radical relationality that leverages an understanding of spatial and
temporal transcendence of antiblackness across registers.

It should be stated very clearly here that I have no authority to speak for this
movement. I participated in and observed many actions and events, and I spoke

to and heard from many people; however, it is not my story to tell, and that poses not only a limitation but a problem for writing these chapters. Yet I could not write a book about predatory policing in North St. Louis County without also foregrounding the extreme practices of freedom that emerged from this place, practices that profoundly shifted my own perspective regarding what it means to live as free and the inherent demands this concept places on those who claim to be on the side of freedom. I wrestled with how to represent what I discovered and what form it should take, and I never arrived at a perfect response. This section reflects this struggle, indeed the problem, that intrinsically results from even attempting to include these chapters in the book. Nevertheless, I believe it was a necessary problem to confront.

Black women and queer people of color were the unequivocal leaders of resistance following what amounted to a public lynching on August 9, 2014, in Ferguson. Through action, debate, and the narration of their own lives and collective Black flesh, the Black women and Black queer people who made up the core leadership of what came to be known as the Ferguson Protest Movement offered unwavering critiques of intersectional domination and racialized practices—in St. Louis County, across the country and the world, as well as within the Ferguson protest family itself.[2] The essential yet often overlooked work of Black women and queer of color activists and scholars, who have deeply felt both the oppressive and the liberatory capacities of inscribed flesh in their everyday lives, reveals the contradictory logics embedded within constitutional democracy as well as within the practices of people claiming to speak for Black, Brown, and queer communities. Through all forms of communicative acts, including the unapologetic presence and performance of now-visible bodies, these protesters took no prisoners in calling out actions and words that do not support *being human as praxis* and by pushing back against anything not in line with the unbounding of conferred identities, be it race, gender, sexuality, class, or anything else.[3] While this sounds like an individualistic approach rooted in liberal idealism—"I am who I am"—it is profoundly a collective philosophy. Blackness, as a lived expression of life, joy, and freedom in the face of death and unfreedom, is understood as a shared way of being and doing that, while it has everything to do with embracing the full spectrum of blackness, exceeds epidermal and cultural definitions. Indeed, it is the excess itself, which sits outside prevailing norms of sociality, that is ultimately powerful—a reconstructed self and collective mode of life that negates the dominant terms of identity and existence.[4]

Leaders of Ferguson resistance engaged in a queering of protest that not only revealed extreme violence practiced at multiple scales of governance in North St. Louis County, but also interrogated "how intersecting racial, gender, and sexual practices" within the culture of protest "antagonize and/or conspire with the normative investments of nation-states and capital."[5] Queer of color critique is most interested in understanding how social formations reproduce or trouble social imaginaries of homogeneity—most specifically within nationalist discourses. According to Roderick Ferguson, queer of color critique combines the intersectional interventions of Black feminism and queer politics—which names the liberal state as a problem—and probes the limits of historical materialism. Ferguson argues that the Marxist obsession with class and property obfuscates the impact of race and gender on the material world and has nurtured heteropatriarchy in past national liberation movements. Queer of color critique is concerned with exposing race and gender, and ultimately structures of gendered antiblackness, and countering heteropatriarchy within antiracist projects. The actions and conversations practiced by young Black women and queer leaders in response to the killing of Michael Brown and treatment of his body offered a queer of color critique that names intersectional oppression as violence executed by the state. This intervention made visible the implications of gender and sexuality *in material terms* and it vehemently rejected all forms of heteropatriarchy within Black resistance.

Many of the Black women and queer and trans individuals who emerged as leaders of Ferguson resistance view their work as a global emancipatory project essential to, and intersectional with, all efforts aimed at dismantling structural foundations and everyday practices of oppression, although the specificity of blackness and the terror inflicted on Black flesh remains central to their project.[6] These same Black women and Black queer protesters asserted themselves as always-already self-defined as deviant, a chosen location outside normative roles, scripts, and subjectivities. The very intentional and affective use of collective bodies—physical, fleshly, gendered, raced, sexualized, and exploited bodies— was critical to this work. This is the flesh that pushes and contests the inscripted lines found on gendered, sexualized, violated, and racialized bodies—the same bodies that Seyla Benhabib speaks of when she writes, "Women and their bodies are the symbolic-cultural site upon which human societies inscript their moral order."[7] This work was carried out upon what Katherine McKittrick describes as "demonic grounds"—the literal and figurative ground upon which inscribed flesh, past and present, is rejoined and becomes one.[8] The inscription of "demonic flesh" upon the body of Michael Brown became the demonic grounds, the territories of the soul,[9] upon which those inhabiting inscribed flesh, past and present, were brought together and where they staked their claims. Understanding the liberatory capacity of claiming and defining their own marked flesh, protesters identifying as women and queer used their collective bodies as placeholders of freedom. As Christina Sharpe writes, "Those black and blackened bodies become the bearers (through violence, regulation, transmission, etc.) of the knowledge of certain subjection as well as the placeholders of freedom for those who would claim freedom as their rightful yield."[10]

The curated visibility of bodies—bodies that love, bodies that fight, bodies that nurture, bodies that give birth, bodies that are violated and terrorized—shifted the discursive field of protest from symbolic life and identity (the claiming of rights, the recognition of personhood, and the fixing of identity) to a relentless praxis of *living* as fully human. In this way, freedom is a mode of everyday being and doing, a form of protest that has no need to work within conventional structures of power (and indeed no interest in doing so).

Chuck

This is very much a Black women-led movement, and I judge that based on who is getting arrested the most. We're in a place where we can get it right this time and we have to acknowledge the role of women. We have to fight patriarchy, and heterosexism. My growth has come through the women in this movement. The queer women in this movement. It's a matter of listening. The LGBTQ women have been incredible teachers.

Valerie (pseudonym)

From my experience, the women in the movement have been very strong. And a lot of times, the women have been the ones to "get it done." It didn't matter what the call was, they did it. As far as the men in the movement, I haven't seen anything like that. I don't see them doing much of anything other than making callouts to people. . . . Or they also like to make very private things public and glorify themselves.

Alisha

At every action there's always a Black woman leading it. And there's probably a Black woman on the bullhorn. And a Black woman planned it. That's definitely different from before. People are really challenging what humanity looks like, what leadership looks like, who can do what, and why. . . . Black women have been pushing back forever but in this movement they finally have their voice.

Ferguson resistance revealed a link between power and freedom, between terror and beauty, by disrupting, if not shattering, identities and norms conferred on residents of this area for over the past fifty years. This intervention not only linked the systemic violence practiced by municipalities in North St. Louis County to the physical death of Michael Brown and public desecration of his body, but also made decades of everyday political and physical violence visible. The tangible change that resulted from resistance in Ferguson, including whether and how it led to subsequent movements, is still up for debate. It is clear, however, that returning to an uncontested business as usual in this region is not possible, at least not without acknowledging that the choice to do nothing is the choice being made. It is also clear that a discernable shift occurred within national discourse regarding the nature and objectives of Black resistance in the twenty-first century, and that young Black female, queer, and trans protesters who showed up following the death of Brown continue to show up and haunt this region like a specter.

In writing the words *young, queer, Black, female, trans,* and *protester,* I might be characterizing leaders of the Ferguson Protest Movement, or I might simply be providing a list of marginalized subjectivities, each of which is accompanied by specific types of exclusion. To be represented as, and experience, all six descriptions at once (in many cases leaders also identified as poor) is to have intimate awareness of how it feels to be exempted from most recognitions and rights within society. When I spoke with these individuals, they read the killing of Michael Brown and the treatment of his body not as exceptional but as everyday, based on intimate experiences with multiple forms of violence directed at their bodies, and they stated that these experiences enabled them to carry out embodied and affective forms of protest in very specific terms. Yet, as everyone I spoke with conveyed in different ways, protest is not an individual endeavor, but a collective imagination of an alternative future, which is what Black struggle has always been about. Those who identified as queer, bi, or trans expressed that living their genuine identities and authentic lives occurred simultaneously with claiming blackness and that both were part of transformative and collective resistance. This is a particularly important point because it means that protest is not something special that one does at a certain time or as a reaction to a singular event. Rather, protest is "living the way you know you're supposed to live and being the person you know you're supposed to be in the face of someone telling you're supposed to be something different in order to get along in this world."[11]

Mary (pseudonym)

The most creative, passionate, talented, strongest individuals in the movement are lesbian, gay, trans, bi. The people that engaged me. That made me understand there was something I could do other than just watch. The people who speak across the spectrum. The people who understand how complex this issue really is. That it's really not about this single incident—that was just the catalyst for a much bigger platform.

And they do it in a way that is not polite. They have faced enormous pushback within the movement family. And they won't sit down. They won't shut up. They're like, "You know, you're gonna need to deal with us. You're gonna need to deal with all facets of blackness. You don't own it." I'm really grateful that they're forcing the conversation. They're refusing to walk away.

Alisha

I think queer women haven't just contributed to the movement. They are the movement. Literally, without them you do not have a movement. They are there in leadership, in numbers, in hard work. They contribute to the conversation in a way nobody else can, because they constantly remind you to check yourself.

Estell (pseudonym)

The queer women in the movement understand strategies that cut to the core of what is at issue. They are the ones that put their bodies in harm's way the most. They made white people feel the most uncomfortable because they are totally unapologetic about who they are, and they're going to get right up in your face and make you feel their presence there. Sometimes in intentionally shocking ways. It's a strategy thing they understand.

These women are the antithesis to Black patriarchy and honestly, that rubs a lot of the men in the movement the wrong way. This is one of the first times where race and queerness and transness and nonsexism have been front and center, and that makes it beautiful.

For many, a shift occurred in their thinking on August 9 regarding the nature of protest, from demanding equal rights through and under juridical law and social recognition to unapologetically embracing blackness as a force capable of liberating society *from itself*.[12] Echoing Aimé Césaire's recalibration of who is uncivilized in the colonial equation, one young woman recalled, "It's clear who the animals were that day," and several people reiterated her observation in various ways.[13] For many, struggle was no longer an effort to claim equal rights or be recognized as human. Rather, the struggle entailed revealing the inhumanity of normative culture in contrast to being human as praxis.[14]

Ms. Jones

They pick up raccoons that been hit by cars on West Florissant faster than they got that boy off the street. He was somebody's baby. His mama was coming unglued seein' him lying there behind the tape and they was just yelling at her to manage the crowd like it was her fault.

Those interviewed also stated that spaces were often shut down and foreclosed by those who believed that extending a focus beyond a narrowly defined police brutality aimed at young Black men would undermine efforts. Homophobia, sexism, and generational biases were the most obvious impediments people cited regarding a queered intersectional politics; however, experiences of class, racial mixing, intermarriage, faith, geography, and education, among others, were also cited as issues that created contradictions within the movement. What Ferguson protesters did overwhelmingly agree on was that politics of respectability, conformity, and assimilation were not viable modes of achieving freedom.

Tia (pseudonym)

The thing that made Ferguson different, as a sustained movement, is that people woke up to the fact that this is not about police brutality. The killing of young Black men is just a symptom of the disease that's always been there. Queer people, and especially queer women, have made people realize that conformity will never work. They bring a perspective that challenges all that.

Brianna

This is not a case of a bad apple or a boy that needed to pull up his pants to not get shot. The system did exactly what it was designed to do. When will they see changing the laws hasn't gotten us nowhere? We don't have to act like they tell us to act just so we can live. Black people gotta stop living their lives like that and stop apologizing for other Black people. I don't need to apologize for nothing. We're not the ones with the problem.

Angel

Some people don't want to change what they think or what they do in this movement. They think that by adding more Black politicians, or Black institutions, or Black businesspeople, that's radical. But it's not. We're pushing back by looking at history and saying, "Just slapping 'Black' on it does not make it radical." Trying to solve old problems with old solutions is not radical. Assimilating and conforming to a racist system does not get us anywhere. It doesn't work.

This is a Black queer ethics that moves beyond civil rights strategies and takes as its primary focus the practice of freedom, which casts a different light on the metrics of normativity established by traditional white middle-class heteronormativity. Ferguson protesters practiced an ethics of lived blackness that relied on unapologetically inhabiting their blackness and their bodies as an affective form of protest and performativity *in space*. The fact that the bodies doing affective work in the space of protest often identified and presented themselves as female and queer created a heightened effect since, as many stated, angry Black hetero men in the street are an expected stereotype.

A Black queer ethics is a political engagement. It does not, as Cathy Cohen describes, "focus on integration into dominant structures but instead seeks to transform the basic fabric and hierarchies that allow systems of oppression to persist and operate efficiently."[15] This queering of politics builds on iterations of "queer politics" that challenged persistent and invisible heteronormative attitudes and practices embedded in modern social structures.[16] Moving queer politics beyond the realm of sexual identity required the work and interventions of Black lesbian feminists who theorized the interconnected and interdependent relationships of systemic oppressions yet insisted on the centering of historically produced conditions of fungible Black life.[17] Queer, in this sense, moves beyond an identity linked to sexual orientations and subcultures and refers to a utopian and collective imagination of what could or should be in the world, while revealing what actually is. Queering politics occurs in, and is made visible by, the public sphere. The shift that mobilized radical imaginaries of what should be, in the face of what was, in North St. Louis County resonated because of the visible terror and aftermath inflicted on Brown's flesh in the public sphere and the implausibility of the modern state's representational claims.[18] In this case, it was the implausibility that the liberal state would deliver justice and equality under, and through, the law.

Brittany

If queer folks and the LGBTQ community were not involved in this movement it would look different. It just would. I don't know, man. It would just look completely different. A lot of times the LGBTQ folks out here are the heart and soul of the fight. It was an absolutely critical piece of gaining national attention in the way we did that. There was just a different tone because we were there. There was no backing down like in the past. We're beyond that.

Jonathan

You can't have a conversation about Ferguson and not talk about the LGBTQ community, the Black LGBTQ community specifically. . . . The ones doing the most daring actions, and the loudest ones that hold people accountable, and the ones actually doing the work—they're the LGBTQ leaders.

Beyond revealing contradictions that exist within state policy and normative practice, a transformative queer politics also reveals contradictions in the assumptions and practices of nonnormative antioppressive projects and highlights those things that are "not yet."[19] Cohen brings up an example, asking what would happen if queer activists considered the lives of women of color who are heterosexual but whose sexual choices fit outside what is considered acceptable or worthy of state support, such as prostitutes or "welfare queens."[20] To this point, the literal and figurative space of performativity, the space of angry, empowered, and visible eroticized queer Black feminized flesh practiced by some Ferguson protesters unsettles the frame of the pathologized Black hetero female epitomized by the image of the Black Jezebel or welfare queen.[21] The pathologized frame was used by many media outlets against Lezley McSpadden, the mother of Michael Brown. Quick to exploit the words of a bereaved Black mother at the scene of her son's death, some in the media used her statement "Do you know how hard I worked to keep that boy in school?" (among others) to represent McSpadden as a stereotypical young single mother (although she is married), struggling, and failing, to keep her son out of trouble in the chaotic streets of the Black ghetto, which happens to sit in the suburbs. Much of the support for Darren Wilson, and the police more generally, rhetorically blamed McSpadden for her son's fate, and public discourse largely focused on debating whether or not she was a good mother.[22] Brown's father and stepfather were largely credited, however, for remaining in his life.

Straight, queer, trans, and otherwise nonconforming protesters provided a very different image of Black women and Black visibility from the one conferred on Lezley McSpadden, although many protesters interviewed spoke of the trend of the media's interviewing and focusing their cameras on, in their words, "messed up" shirtless angry Black men as representative of the movement.[23] Black women leading resistance intimately understood the importance of pushing back against cultural representations of blackness and of themselves and their bodies in different types of spaces, and used their own voices and bodies to tell a very different story. Some expressed frustration with McSpadden and the Brown family for embracing what they viewed as a respectability politics similar to that of Black municipal leaders, which works within current systems of power and expectations of gender, sexuality, and blackness. Yet women and queer individuals leading Ferguson resistance were also vocally critical of all of the ways Black subjectivities are produced and demonized, including representations of McSpadden and Black women in municipal leadership.

The work that emerged from events in Ferguson ultimately revealed the limits placed on blackness and gender from both inside and outside the movement. Many Ferguson protest leaders refused to tolerate heteronormative and cisgendered assumptions and attitudes, especially attempts of Black masculinity to dominate the space of protest or speak for Black people as a whole. This core group continues to seek ways to destabilize all grounds upon which clear claims to identity are staked. In this way, a queering of protest was, and continues to be, lived out—not because many of the emergent leaders identify as queer, but by virtue of persistent and embodied critiques of power across scales that brings the continuum of violence, trauma, erasure, and shame, which precedes and exceeds the Black body, into view.

Diamond

Before anybody even knew about anybody's sexuality, we were out there, in front of the men. Making sure everybody was okay, standing our ground and making our voices heard. Putting our bodies in front of tanks and making people uncomfortable. But then we started pushing conversations about how this is not just about young Black men getting killed.

We were all hurt when [the men] didn't come out for the Black Women's march. Hurt, because we come out to lift up you guys, make sure you guys are okay, make sure you guys are loved on and supported, and stuff like that, but you guys don't do the same for us? That was hurtful. But we still come out fighting for you. . . . We're not going to pick and choose who to fight for. We're fighting for everybody.

Alisha

Queer and trans folks of color, particularly trans women, have, from my personal observation done the most to lift up the "No one's free until everybody's free" perspective. You have to ask yourself, Why are queer and trans Black women leading this movement? Because they get how toxic all forms of oppression are and they communicate that. Some of the most amazing and strongest leaders in this movement are Black trans folks.

Alexis

People are now having conversations about intersectionality, and that is really important because it means that we have to be inclusive of all Black life. When people say they love their LGBTQ brothers and sisters but [then they say], "they ate the food with poison in it that the straight people knew better than to eat," that's damaging to the whole concept of blackness. Because people started looking at us like we were toxic. Like we're spreading the poison. And that's dangerous, because it's actually violence against people even if they don't mean to hurt anybody.

Tia

Part of what puts people at intersections are the multiple oppressions so we are silenced and we are dismissed in certain settings, but we keep having these conversations. Being a Black person that sits at intersections really helps this work. It should not be persons-who-sit-at-intersections' responsibility to start these conversations but of course we're more likely to since we see the internal oppression.

"Sixela Yoccm"

I feel like queer people have been critical to this movement. . . . And I think it's because they tackle the issue of self-love. You shouldn't let people tell you how to be. You should be comfortable with who you are and let those that can't accept you be uncomfortable with that fact, not you. That's what queer people bring. Also challenging the straight Black men.

Jamell

[Queer leaders] not only helped to sustain the front line . . . , their life experience helped to redefine blackness. And in a movement where the unconditional love of blackness, and the right for blackness to be all that it can be, are most important, redefining what blackness is and what blackness includes has been an unfathomably tough job.

And that's one thing the LGBTQ community, I admire them for. Because it's not easy when you have to deal with oppression from the system and oppression and resentment from the people you are fighting with and for. They bring a more human side to the movement. A more inclusive and honest side, and it provides the door for every single Black person to feel connected and important.

Those who identified as women and queer were attacked from both outside and inside the movement. As discussed in greater detail in chapter 7, in addition to being targeted by law enforcement and social media threats, people with whom they stood side by side at protest actions also sought to silence their voices or felt entitled to their bodies, particularly those who claimed heteronormative and masculine identities. As Angel pointed out, "Black women are not only holding down the front lines, they are also maintaining jobs and parenting well at the same time." She added, "Women, like Brittany for example, are constantly being disrespected and dealing with comments from men. Brittany's got a lot of curves, you know what I mean? She's constantly dealing with men sexualizing her on top of everything else. . . . The men were frustrated because they wanted her to be available to them." There was also persistent pushback by men against conversations that expanded the terms of protest beyond a focus on straight Black men and their treatment by the police.

Diamond

Unfortunately, Black women are still trying to make our place. Oftentimes women are not really seen as people. And it's so ironic because the whole point is supposed to be claiming our humanness. The men are constantly putting themselves in front of cameras, in front of the media, in front of organizations. If it weren't for the women out here, this movement wouldn't be sustained. In fact, the women were the ones that stood out there and weren't moved. When the men ran, as tear gas was thrown, the women stood their ground, like we're going to protect the men, we're not going anywhere. We not only stood beside them, we stood in front of them. People seem to have amnesia and forget that. They don't want to admit their ass was saved by a lesbian because I will never be "their woman."

Antwan (pseudonym)

So, it's very frustrating to see how one side is saying, "You're trying to include far too many people and you're not focusing on those most important—young Black men getting killed by the police." And the other side is saying "No, we're trying to encompass as many people as there actually are. We're trying to show everybody that you don't have to leave one part of your identity at home." Narrowing Black identity is not helping anybody. Really that's the fundamental problem on both sides.

Cameron (pseudonym)

And Black women have been at the fore of this movement, but when it's time to talk about the work that's being done, it's revisionist history. I've seen Black men say stuff like, "Yeah being on the front lines and we had to get the women and children out of the way." To be honest, in many ways, in many cases, it was the opposite. Black women went up to young Black men and told them, "You need to go home." Because they were in the way of getting anything done. I've never been checked by so many Black women and I grew up in a house full of women. They'll say, "That's patriarchy running your mouth right now."

Brittany

As a woman, people think they can talk to you anytime they want. You need to do whatever they say right then. And your input matters very little because you're calling out certain toxic behaviors by a certain group of folks like men and they don't see a problem with themselves. They see it with you. They say, "Oh, well, if you are saying men are trash or men are treating women in a certain way maybe you should ask why we treatin' you that way." "If you hate us, why you here anyway?" Or, "Mike Brown was a man and that's why we are here."

Alexis

I've definitely had to carve out my own space and just claim my right to be here. I had to go and literally snatch the fucking bullhorn from the men. I literally had to stand up in meetings and say to dudes, "Shut the fuck up because you don't know what you're talking about." I really had to be assertive. I had to turn into the stereotypical strong Black sister in order to be considered a leader in this movement. Not because I wasn't leading before but because they didn't want to acknowledge what I was already doing.

These clowns go and post a photo on Instagram saying shit like, "Women has to act like queens in order to be treated like queens." Or to be respected you need to put yourself up on a pedestal that some Black man is gonna kick out from underneath your ass anyway. We're here because that shit has got to get put down if we're gonna get anywhere with this.

Alisha

The most frustrating thing about this whole experience is definitely Black men and their lack of understanding of Black women. Like you know what we're going through as a people but you still think you should be on top and keep me down. When it's time to put bodies on the line you're fine with me risking my life while you talk to a reporter. But outside of protest I should be subservient to you.

The affective environment of protest was something consistently brought up by protesters. As Diamond shared, "We make people uncomfortable by being very

FIGURE 6.1   Three women protesting in Ferguson. "Officers in riot gear and wielding smoke bombs confronted protesters as scores of people defied the state-issued curfew in protest of Michael Brown's death on Sunday, Aug. 17, 2014 in Ferguson, MO. The standoff came hours after Missouri Gov. Jay Nixon declared a state of emergency and announced the midnight curfew to quell rising unrest in the town."

New York Daily News. Photo by James Keivom.

comfortable with who we are."[24] In addition to consistently linking Brown's death to specific histories and cultures of predatory practices in North St. Louis County and insisting on repeated discussions within the field of protest regarding inter-sectional oppressions, protest leaders called out misogyny and homophobia within the movement and spoke at length in interviews about the importance of placing their bodies directly on the "front lines" of the war waged against them in ways that were intimately felt by those deployed to negate them and those indifferent to their experience.[25] While protesters maintained a commitment to nonviolence throughout the twenty-plus months of active protest after August 9, 2014, the very intentional and performative use of their bodies to create discomfort and disrupt the status quo of daily life in the St. Louis region were important factors in the specific affect of sustained resistance. This resistance was often carried out as the (intentional) spectacle of nonconforming bodies stopping flows of traffic in the street or on the highway. Other traditional locations of protest were uti-lized, such as shopping districts and malls, restaurants, sports venues, auditori-ums, and concert halls, where protesters created performative environments that were described as unapologetically Black as well as "in your face," not respectable,

FIGURE 6.2 "Ferguson protesters leave arm-in-arm from the St. Ann Police Department after being released from jail on Friday, Oct. 3, 2014. Protesters have been a constant presence in the St. Louis suburb in the nearly two months since Michael Brown was shot and killed by police officer Darren Wilson."

Associated Press/*St. Louis Post-Dispatch*. Photo by Robert Cohen.

FIGURE 6.3 "Ferguson tense after shootout on anniversary of Michael Brown's Death," August 9, 2015.

Getty Images. Photo by Scott Olson.

and, by people outside of the movement, "inappropriate." Often these spectacles of visible Black and nonconforming flesh were intuitively and courageously carried out "in the moment" in symbolic spaces of capitalist consumption where the effect of consumable yet unavailable bodies was heightened.[26] The consistent integration of performativity, confrontation, spectacle, intervention, visibility, and eroticism came to define ongoing protest in St. Louis.

Some thirty-five years after Audre Lorde delivered her paper titled "Uses of the Erotic: The Erotic as Power,"[27] Black women in Ferguson vividly demonstrated the uses and power of the erotic, which had long been used against them. Occupying the deepest margins as young, queer, Black, and feminized, these individuals claimed both leadership positions and the space of the street by relentlessly living Lorde's definition of erotic power—refusing to deny the full spectrum of "physical, emotional, and psychic expressions of what is deepest and strongest and richest" within them, which included refusing to deny who, and how, they love.[28] Whether on the front line of highly charged actions, speaking in public forums, or interacting within the protest family, these individuals embody the erotic as *work*, using their bodies, their language, their sexuality, their anger, and their passion as sources of disruption, power, desire, and knowledge in ways that shocked many politicians, officials, Black clergy, and those they described as "respectable Negros."[29] In the same way, they also challenged assumptions about Black identity within the movement. With the erotic knowledge that Lorde describes as a life force, these women leaders, both queer and straight, provide the lens through which to see and scrutinize *all* those things that do not lead to the freedom to live and love fully.

Quotidian expressions of the erotic, as Sharon Patricia Holland forcefully points out, are actually a useful place to study everyday antiblackness because they both trouble and reinforce the Black/white binary of racist practice in the most intimate registers of routine practice.[30] Recalling how Christina Sharpe conceptualizes monstrous intimacies, which include such things as shame, sexual violence, desire, and confinement, Holland likewise asserts that race and racism live within the space of everyday intimacies.[31] Working between critical race studies, queer theory, and feminism, Holland's project *The Erotic Life of Racism* works to show how racism, personal choice, and erotic pleasure can no longer be easily disaggregated, if they ever were. As Holland states, "we can't have our erotic life—a desiring life—without involving ourselves in the messy terrain of racist practice."[32] Holland subscribes to the possibility that blackness is not only the thingness of the thing—that which produces erotic value for whiteness, a body absent its own erotic life, the pornotrope that Hortense Spillers describes.[33] Holland seeks to free blackness from the theoretical frame of thingness and complicates blackness, as do the Ferguson protest leaders, as a fluid and dynamic dialectic of both subjectification and liberation that simultaneously and inherently reflects the lived realities of racial construction in the most basic and intimate ways. By insisting

Keith Rose
@KWRose

The power of Queer Women Of Color!!

#Ferguson #MoralMonday

6,519 views

3:25 PM · 8/10/15 · Twitter for iPhone

76 Retweets **52** Likes

FIGURE 6.4 Brittany Farrell in the midst of leading a highway shutdown on August 10, 2015. Alexis Templeton, also leading, is in the foreground. Posted on Twitter by Keith Rose.

that people confront all possibilities and iterations of lived blackness, Ferguson protesters release the uses of the erotic as Lorde imagined them. This shifts the meaning of the porno*topology* I theorize in the introduction from the space created at the intersection of terror and desire to a space inhabited by an erotic life rooted in blackness that refuses to be for others. Suffering may still be expected in North St. Louis County because an ethics of lived blackness has not been fully realized; however, suffering is now visible and no longer tolerated in the way that it once was.

Those leading Ferguson resistance took Lorde's definition of erotic work— the full habitation of psychic, emotional, and physical spaces that transcend "states of being that are not native to [oneself], such as resignation, despair, self-effacement, depression, self-denial"[34]—beyond the boundaries Lorde imagined, creating a site of visibility in which troubling visions of Black bodies, unmediated Black flesh, and queered blackness work to unsettle normative hierarchies of propriety, control, and power in the everyday lives of residents in North St. Louis County. For years, residents of this area had attempted to remain invisible lest they be targeted and fined through all manner of policing, which, as described in part I, capitalizes on discursively produced *urban* residents within historically produced *suburban* space. Women and queer protesters, however, used the tropes attached to their bodies to leverage visibility. These young queer women are well aware of what Nicole Fleetwood has articulated as "troubling vision," in which "the visible black body is always already troubling to the dominant visual field."[35] In fact, they very intentionally used the uncanny visibility of blackness deemed out of place as a critical component and affect of protest. Whereas Fleetwood looks at the specific work of Black women artists and cultural producers "whose work is reliant on the very problem their bodies pose as visible and corporal bodies,"[36] Black queer women who led in Ferguson resistance represent an ongoing praxis that similarly embraces and deploys the problem posed by the troubling presence of queered or feminized Black flesh in white space. In the case of these protesters, Fleetwood's theory of "excess flesh"—the strategic uses of the Black feminized (and queered) body as a form of resistance—goes beyond visual culture and is embodied through claims and expressions of sexuality and eroticism that resist objectification, including the pornotroping objectification of elicit desire within white culture and the objectification conferred by Black masculinity. The countervisibility that many Ferguson protesters practiced moved beyond a reworking of the Jezebel figure, understood as the antithesis of respectability. For many Black women leading resistance, choosing between an identity based on either sexual accessibility (the Black Jezebel) or asexual respectability (the Black mammy figure) is a false choice. Instead, the queering of gender, sexuality, and identity, which renders Black bodies less available to both white and Black heteronormative practices and constructs, reconfigures the parameters of such things as intimacy, pleasure, partnership, love, marriage, and family.[37]

Black women and girls have consistently reconfigured their identities outside the dialectical false choice throughout history, in less overt ways and with many differing outcomes. Aimee Meredith Cox makes this point in her work, focusing on the ways Black girls negotiate and critique the identities and stereotypes conferred on them, as well as the violences that accompany poverty, racism, and gendered subjectivities.[38] Using extensive ethnography of a homeless shelter in Detroit, Cox draws particular attention to how Black girls "choreograph" their own scripts in relationship to overarching narratives attached to race, gender, class, and sexuality—and also in response to everyday interactions with people in their lives. As Cox points out, while these countervisibility practices constitute powerful resistance, the choice to operate both within and outside normative scripts comes at a cost, especially for Black girls and young Black women, who are particularly vulnerable to the violence and surveillance of the state. Both power and vulnerability can be seen in the case of Ferguson resistance. While the work of young women and queer Black leaders was highly effective in revealing the violence of the state and shifting the means and objectives of Black protest, Black women, and especially Black queer and trans women, suffered the most severe consequences in the form of physical and political violence waged against them, from the expected formal institutions of power and, even more painfully, from within the Ferguson protest movement itself.

Protesters were not the only ones utilizing choreographed spectacle. In his article exploring practices of "choreopolicing," André Lepecki asks the question, "What are the relations between political demonstrations as expressions of freedom, and police counter-moves as implementations of obedience?"[39] Lepecki argues that the police assume the role of choreographing protest by controlling pathways of movement and establishing spaces of containment. Space is therefore, according to Lepecki, in the realm of the police. The traditional terms of so-called peaceful protest assume that bodies will conform within space and follow the choreography directed by the police. In contrast, Ferguson protesters followed their own choreography *in space* and intentionally located themselves "out of place" in an area where Black bodies had already been policed and choreographed as out of place for many decades. In both cases—the site of protest and the site of predatory policing—a consensual subjectivity was expected. The "policed dance of quotidian consensus" was the basis for policing residents in North St. Louis County; however, it was not what was practiced by protesters after the death of Michael Brown.[40] Rather, transformative resistance, as Jacques Rancière observes, "consists in transforming the space of moving along, of circulation, into the space for the appearance of a subject."[41] The pathways of circulation include literal space, such as streets, sidewalks, and highways, as well as spaces in which capital circulates, such as malls, shopping districts, and financial centers. These spaces can also be places in which culture and religion circulate, such as theaters, concert halls, and churches. At various times after August 9, all the spaces of circulation and conformity listed above were transformed by the *appearance* of the collective, the haunting of visible Black bodies—bodies that show up and continue to show up even after they are supposed to leave or recede. Transforming spaces of circulation and conformity into haunted spaces of bodily freedom and movement, albeit temporarily, was at the core of Ferguson resistance. The relationship between choreopolicing and choreopolitics, as outlined by Lepecki, illustrates the power/freedom dialectic of biopower, the power *over* life, and of biopolitics, the power *of* life. As Ferguson protesters insisted, the power of life to resist the power over one's life required the full habitation of one's body as well as a relentless haunting of space by bodies that never quite leave.

Mary (pseudonym)

Making people feel comfortable is not a priority for people in this movement. That's such a large piece of it. Other people call it anger but really it's not about anger. The entire movement is direct confrontation. Not violence, but confrontation. People are confronted with unapologetic blackness. Black bodies that come as they are. It could not be more confrontational.

Gloria (pseudonym)

The thing about Ferguson was it was so "in your face." We are going to make them feel the discomfort, see our pain and anger finally. We are not just a face in the crowd and we are not going to be moved. If they locked up fifteen of us, fifty more would show up the next night. We stayed in their faces, making them confront who we are. It wasn't just mass protest of people walking in the street like you see in other cities. It was that too, but what really defines this movement is the way we made everyone aware that we are unapologetically who we are and they've got to deal with that.

Vanessa (pseudonym)

All we have to use is our bodies, and we use them. Using our bodies unapologetically. Putting them in places they are not welcome. Making people feel the distance by putting our bodies where they are not supposed to be. Acting the way we're not supposed to act. Breaking all of the codes of conduct. Protest as performance of Black bodies. This is our blackness and we will not be contained. That's what it is.

Brittany

When I think of the Ferguson movement, I think of resistance. I think of people just doing away with the status quo, you know. It's just that, a lot of young unapologetic resistant young people and it was that resistance that, that got us to where we are today. It was that resistance. It was that rebellion . . . I mean we sparked the nation into resisting. It's not just Ferguson resisting anymore, it's the whole entire nation, young people.

Mary (pseudonym)

The Ferguson protesters are confrontational. More confrontational than anything I've seen in protest. Now or in the past. Ferguson is interruption. It was volcanic and it was not structured or organized. It was leaderless or leaderful, depending on how you look at it. Ferguson was and is completely flat out "We're done." "We're rejecting everything we've been told we're supposed to do or be."

I've learned from this movement that there is great value in making people uncomfortable and I'm learning to confront. I'm still a white grandmother but I'm now comfortable with diverse strategies and methods. There's a big difference between standing on a corner with a sign that you'll just drive right by than with saying, "Oh, you know what? I think we'll stop your car."

The emphasis placed on embodied experience, habitation, and spectacle by Ferguson protesters is directly linked to the experience and spectacle of embodied violence suffered by Brown, which initially sparked this movement. The desecration of Brown's body in the street, witnessed by hundreds in person and thousands through social media, could not be forgotten. The searing of an image onto a collective psyche is directly reminiscent of the embodied violence suffered by Emmett Till and witnessed by thousands who attended his funeral or saw highly circulated media photos of his terrorized body, which is credited as a catalyst of the Civil Rights Movement. In both cases, the image of a terrorized body held the power to mobilize people and emotions. In both cases, the words and actions of the mothers of the murdered boys were essential to initiating a response, which might otherwise have passed quickly, to unjust deaths. In both cases, the eventual acquittal of those who caused the deaths sparked renewed resistance and sustained national efforts and debates around Black struggle. The decision and the motives to create a spectacle of embodied violence, however, were quite different in each case. Demanding that the casket be left open and the media let in during the funeral for her son, "so all the world can see what they did to my boy," Mamie Till-Mobley understood, or at least hoped for, the power of the image to mobilize action.[42] Many people who saw Brown's body in the street or the image of the terror inflicted on him believed that Ferguson officials, like the murderers of Emmett Till, intended to send a specific message regarding what happens when Black people get out of line. Had officials in charge of the scene in Ferguson fully considered the power of the image to initiate action, as Mamie Till-Mobley had done, it is doubtful Brown's body would have remained on the hot pavement for four and a half hours. The power of the image, however, was not lost on Ferguson protesters and went far beyond the single image of Michael Brown's body.

The young women and queer of color leaders of Ferguson resistance also understand that seeking inclusion in, and through, modern state structures or discourses of freedom will not bring about the transformation they seek. As stated throughout this book, changing laws and policies that implicitly disadvantage people of color is important, but the more fundamental transformation sought by these protesters occurs in and through the orientation of the body—to itself, to other bodies, and to the world. As such, race is not an ideology to be debated but rather an embodied experience—a schema—that becomes part of body knowledge and the body itself. For those who are raced, the natural body schema is interrupted. Likewise, antiblackness is not so much a set of laws and regulations as it is the bodily response of people toward others and oneself that is felt at the core of one's being. Fanon argues that there exists a "historico-racial schema," which, for a nonwhite and especially a Black individual, bears the full weight of the white gaze.[43] He makes clear what all marked bodies understand— that the flesh of racialized bodies deeply feels and lives race. Sara Ahmed similarly observes that once race is "'in' bodies," it determines the proximities and distances of the body and what it can or cannot do.[44] The women and queer leaders of the Ferguson protest movement understand that transforming their experience in the world must occur at the level of corporal schema, the reorienting of bodies and a recalibration of proximities that determine what *their* bodies can and cannot do.

Enactments of excess flesh in the performative field of protest highlight power relations often obscured by, and through, the commodification of blackness—as something marked by difference.[45] The representation and subsequent claiming of bodies that exceed the norms of "proper corporeal containment," what Juana Maria Rodriguez calls "racialized excess," is already read as queer and beyond that which is viewed as useful or productive.[46] However, it is in the space that is created between the body and the boundaries prescribed and policed by the law—between performance and power—where the productive tensions reside. Black female and Black queered bodies produced a particularly visible tension within the boundaries that power seeks to define and maintain. This tension proves to be especially productive as a space of precarity and protest. Judith Butler argues that "performativity works within precarity and against its differential allocation. Or, rather, performativity names that unauthorized exercise of a right to existence that propels the precarious into political life."[47] The opportunities to propel the precarious into political life through embodied performance—highly visible unauthorized bodies—are also highlighted by Rodriguez when looking at queer Latinx sexual politics and how discomfort, politeness, and degrees of legibility appear on the spectrum between law and performance.[48] Again, this is the legibility that emerged with the appearance of bodies that showed up and haunted space, bodies that found and expanded the cracks within the boundaries of containment.

Angel

The movement was very much about the Black female body. First, because it was mostly Black female bodies that were out there. It just was. Black women's bodies were the ones in abundance. They were the visible bodies—the most powerful imagery was of the Black woman. . . . Black women who were historically denied their womanhood.

Kelly

What's unique about the Ferguson Protest Movement is it's in your face. Like, "Naw, we ain't goin' home. Like we're going to stay out here, and we're going to fight until everybody is free." And I feel like the Ferguson Movement is here to show the respectability part of how inequality and racism works today.

Mitchell

This movement is all about constant direct action. In your face direct action. Fuck the police direct action. I've gone to a lot of other protests in other cities because people invite me or send me a ticket and shit. But it's not like that in other cities. It's different here. Like we do not have the time to be sympathetic here.

Chuck

You know the reason why this movement is not polite? It's because white people's ignorance isn't polite. Everybody is done being polite. And that's what the queer women leaders do very intentionally. They make themselves heard regardless of whether people want to hear them. They know from their lived experience that you have to shut things down, shut people down, to get heard. People will say, "Until you speak and do things in this way we're not going to hear your message." And then they're saying, "Well fuck you, hear this message." . . .

Jon Swaine ✔
@jonswaine

`Following` ∨

Here is gas fired moments ago:

6:44 PM - 13 Aug 2014

591 Retweets **196** Likes

💬 47   ↺ 591   ♡ 196   ✉

FIGURE 6.5   Woman watching tear gas. Posted on Twitter by Jon Swaine, August 13, 2014.

Reproduced by permission from Jon Swaine.

People will also say things like "I don't think Mike Brown or Freddie Gray are the best messengers because of who they were." Fuck you and your messenger. I think they're perfect damn messengers. Well you know what? We tried data.

We tried polite reports. We tried writing books. We laid it all out nice and polite in ways that were clear as day. We tried every motherfucking polite way and you didn't motherfucking listen, okay?

Alisha

Like claiming really simple things become revolutionary. Simple things that are just supposed to be basic human things are revolutionary for a lot of Black people, and this movement is teaching me that I can be revolutionary in that respect. Like having a bank account is revolutionary. Self-care is revolutionary. Black Girl Magic is revolutionary. Going on vacation is revolutionary. Getting married can be revolutionary to some people. Like simple things but because they're Black, they're revolutionary. That's really part of this movement.

Embodied blackness is, upon becoming visible, a location of freedom. Blackness is the haunting of freedom in the face of unfreedom, living as fully human so as to reveal vast inhumanities. The insistence upon the visibility of unapologetic and unauthorized Black bodies is a queered practice when it shatters ruling identities and norms and reveals the link between power and freedom. In North St. Louis County, Black bodies—most especially Black queer bodies—became visible and mobilized radical imaginations of what should or could be in the face of what was. This visibility, which stemmed from the initial visibility of Michael Brown's body and the desecration of his flesh, exposed the unmet promises and false claims of the liberal state at multiple scales, including racialized practices carried out by Black leaders in tiny cities in the name of Black political autonomy. The power of bodies to become visible, to haunt, to show up unexpectedly, is the counterpoint to extreme violence, which, in its purest form, produces a life worse than death. While extreme violence was practiced out of view for decades in North St. Louis County, the possibility for bodies to resist was always already present in order for specific dynamics of power, containment, and violence to exist. This possibility to resist was literally made flesh by Black women and queer leaders of Ferguson resistance who used choreopolitics to invent, activate, and create alternative spaces of freedom.[49]

ONTOLOGIES OF RESISTANCE

So it's confusing if you don't know the history of how this movement
unfolded in Ferguson. Years from now when we're retelling the story
of what's come to be called BLM, I want people to say, "And then on
August 9th, 2014, people came out of their houses in St. Louis and
unyieldingly stood in the streets of Ferguson, and they did not back
down to the violence directed at them. And then more people came,
and more people came, and it turned into a nationwide movement."
You don't want to read, "August 9th came and then after that, the
organizers of Black Lives Matter started a movement." You know?

—Brittany Ferrell, as stated to Angel Carter

As the summer of 2014 turned to fall in St. Louis, Ferguson protesters maintained
steady pressure on the region. The reasons for coming out that were articulated
by protesters included pressuring the grand jury to indict Darren Wilson on
murder charges, but many were also focused on bringing national and global
attention to larger issues of Black vulnerability and shining a light on predatory
policing in North St. Louis County. A constant protest presence could be found
in the parking lot across the street from the Ferguson police station, where in
almost nightly clashes, lines of officers in riot gear taunted protesters and dared
them to set foot in the street, while protesters chanted back. Shared food and
other expressions of community also occurred nightly. On a weekly basis, protesters shut down local highways and major streets across the region. Cultural
and sports events in St. Louis, as well as county and municipal meetings, were
targeted by flash mobs. The St. Louis Cardinals baseball games and Rams football
games frequently included clashes between protesters and counterprotesters. On
October 6, a multiracial protest interrupted the St. Louis Symphony when over
fifty people who had purchased tickets and entered as members of the audience
gradually began singing "Which side are you on?" during the performance, with
many musicians joining in. Additionally, people from across the United States
and world traveled to St. Louis to show solidarity with local resistance, congregating at the makeshift memorial on Canfield Drive and in the parking lot across
from the police station. Counterprotesters, often with signs reading "Blue Lives
Matter," also frequented the area. Throughout the fall, tension and planning

on both sides continued in anticipation of the grand jury's decision regarding whether or not to indict Darren Wilson on charges of wrongfully killing Michael Brown, with growing signs that Wilson would not be charged.

A community that came to be called "the protest family" emerged from the sustained resistance and the shared trauma brought by events. Following the initial days of resistance and the militarized response by law enforcement, protesters stated that they spent their time almost exclusively with branches of the protest family, both inside and outside protest. A weekly meal was shared by the collective family in the parking lot adjacent to the police station and organized by Cathy Daniels, a respected elder and professional chef known to most as Mama Cat. The protest family meant different things to different people, but the experience of struggle did much to create bonds that held together in spite of vast disagreements and differing perspectives. As Angel recalled more than two years after the death of Michael Brown, "I have a community now. The respect and the love and support that people show—I am literally surrounded by people who would die for me." The bond of respect and love in the face of brutal disrespect and violence were and are an important dimension within this movement. In this way, Ferguson resistance represents a larger community that not only demands a better world but also provides a better way to survive in the one that currently exists.

Jonathan

The movement family is essentially like food in your stomach from people you don't necessarily know but can trust. Like Mama Cat. Early on she was out there providing meals and snacks for people who were exhausted and without nutrition. And the social time around meals that she provided was really important because those spaces were a rare thing. It was a space away from the trauma.

"Haiku Unsung"

There were people that fell out with their actual family because they didn't agree on either the message or the kinds of actions or both. But to be standing there side by side with somebody who's going to link arms with you and keep you from getting arrested or come and make sure that you're not sprayed or shot, that takes a tremendous amount of trust and love.

Brittany

We're able to laugh together, we're able to cry together, we fight together. And we see each other on the street and be like, "What's up?" You know if I got a dollar and you ain't got shit, we got fifty cents between us. Because there's not a lot of support doing this work. It's not honorable work to most folks, the ones willing to take the scraps they're given. So it's important to have the [protest] family there to support you and check you.

Ivy (pseudonym)

The Ferguson family to me is a sisterhood. The relationships I've created over these months are the best I've ever had. The people that are still around have a certain character. I don't know. It's just some dope ass people that I'm really glad to know. They will hold you to your word. They truly want to see the best for you. And you can just be honest with them no matter what.

Alexis

The family are the people that I met on the front lines in the very first days. I got gassed with them. I got shot at with them. I got arrested with them. I've set up organizational spaces with them. People I actually fucking like. We built it from there. We've just, you know, we have a bond and they are the people I ain't never got to ask if they're riding.

Kristina (pseudonym)

The movement family is like these people that some of them you can't stand but you still don't want the police to fuck them up. It's like when you don't really like all the people in your actual family but you still deal with them, and you don't want anybody else messing with them. That's exactly what it is. There are so many people I love and adore and there's people you don't speak to but you'll sit outside the jail and make sure the police don't kill them.

Mary (pseudonym)

I feel very fortunate to have the opportunity to participate in something so enormously significant. There is definitely a profound love. I mean, when you're in extraordinary situations, emergency situations, and there are people standing next to you that have your back. There is an enormous emotional support for one another, a depth of love and endurance. . . . It's a family. But it's a family built on the violence enacted in this society. It's a community of choice and I need to be here right now.

Many of those interviewed described the movement as leaderless and leaderful simultaneously. "People, especially the women, will step up when it really counts," one woman in her twenties said, "but at the end of the day, nobody is more important than anybody else in this movement." People also observed that nobody was beyond reproach. "The minute someone thinks they're all that, there's someone else lett'n 'em know they need to check themself," Gloria shared. While struggles for hierarchy clearly occurred, protesters often spoke about the organic nature of actions in contrast to formal organizational structures that emphasize planning, define strict parameters of execution, and identify consistent people in charge. Leaders emerged in and through actions; however, to many, protest was an act of everyday life. These actions often seemed to "just happen" in the heat of protest, without planning, and witnesses described how the performative and improvisational qualities of actions would organically emerge in particular ways at particular moments.

One such organic action took place on October 8, 2014. People who had been protesting the killing of Michael Brown were immediately outraged when an off-duty police officer working as a security guard in the City of St. Louis fired seventeen times on VonDerrit Myers, killing the Black teenager as he ran away. For several nights protesters shut down the major thoroughfare of Grand Avenue in South St. Louis city. A few days later, they marched across, and shut down, Interstate 44 and proceeded to enter the campus of nearby St. Louis University (SLU). There, they were joined by hundreds of university students. Coinciding with the Occupy movement, over a thousand people set up tents and occupied the campus for six days under the banner of Occupy SLU. SLU ultimately conceded to thirteen demands made by the Black Student Alliance, Tribe X—a newly formed organization of Ferguson protesters—and the established nongovernmental organization Metro St. Louis Coalition for Inclusion and Equity. In exchange, students disbanded and protesters agreed to leave the campus. Like many of the actions that characterize the Ferguson protest movement, Occupy SLU was not planned but unfolded minute by minute as a few individuals stepped up and were able to lead large crowds and determine strategy "on the fly." In fact, like Occupy SLU, the actions that were later viewed as having the most impact by protesters and people in the region alike were not planned but occurred in direct response to conditions on the ground. Alisha, a Ferguson protester and one of the coleaders of Occupy SLU (and a SLU student herself) described those days.

Alisha

Occupy SLU itself was never planned. We were planning to go to SLU, but we were never planning to stay at SLU, so none of the occupation, none of the demands, none of the accords were pre-planned. We literally just marched. I think it was a crowd of about two thousand people that started in Shaw. We had them as two separate groups, walking down Grand and, right by the Starbucks, we got met by a line of military police, geared up and blocking us.

And we stood there, in two lines, and I remember we had certain people who were supposed to talk to the police. Eventually, they had to move, because we made sure to keep everybody on the sidewalk, and legally, you can't block people from walking on the sidewalk. So they had to move out of our way. [The] DPS officers were trying to negotiate with us, because, we, myself, and some other school students were in the front, and they recognized us. And they were like, "Oh, don't do this, this is mid-terms week. These kids need to study, like, don't do this, this isn't the time for this. Then Jonathan pulled out his ID and then the DPS officer was like, "Well the school students can come in, but y'all can't, nobody else can come with y'all." So Jonathan said, "These are all my guests." And then, just like that, everybody just marched in, and went into the campus and chanted as we walked. And all the school students were holding up their IDs, and then we walked to the clock tower, and we stood out there.

And so a lot of people don't know that VonDerrit Myers's dad works at SLU, which is another reason why we felt like that should happen there. He worked at SLU so we felt SLU shouldn't get to be silent. First of all, you're St. Louis University, so these things are happening in your community. But, an employee is involved in this, and previous to that, I had gotten emails that were like, "Oh, don't worry, we're going to keep you safe," and I'm just like, "What does that mean, you're going to keep me safe? Because I'm a SLU student and I'm going to Ferguson every night."

And when we got there to the clock tower at SLU, the parents of VonDerrit Myers talked about their son, their loss, how they were feeling, how grateful they were, how they had never felt like this before, that they had any support from St. Louis University community. They kind of felt like nobody cared. And then there were different community members who came up and talked and spoke, so we must have been there for like a good thirty minutes before we posed the question, Do we want to keep marching or do we want to keep going?

I remember somebody saying, "Nah, we've been marching for like sixty days. We want to do something different. We don't want to just keep marching." So, to us, doing something different meant, okay, we're going to stay here. And that was the beginning of Occupy SLU and the encampment. We were there for six days. During those days, students brought food down and blankets, and other people came down to the campus and brought food and blankets. There were news cameras. And in the end, SLU's president had to sign a concession to our demands.

The organic action and seeming success of Occupy SLU coincided with a series of planned actions and resistance activities called Ferguson October, which were organized by several groups, some of which were established organizations in the region and others that had formed as part of Ferguson resistance. Advertised nationally on social media and attended by hundreds from outside the region throughout the month, the planning and execution of Ferguson October revealed many existing fissures between those who had been on the front lines since August 9 and those who were perceived to be riding a wave of local and national attention, especially with regard to how the resources that were pouring in from around the country would be collected and allocated. While those on the front lines perceived newly involved people as Johnny-come-latelies, those who considered themselves long-time radicals in the region were frustrated by young activists' reluctance to join well-established organizations and recognize the work of civil rights–era activists who had been organizing in St. Louis for decades. Many young protesters were frustrated with being dismissed by "old heads" as simply "street protesters," especially women, queer, and trans individuals who consistently criticized what they saw as histories of heteropatriarchy and respectability politics, and they pointed to what they considered as a lack of sustained progress in the region and the country. Protesters were particularly critical of nationally recognized activists who, to them, represented the respectability politics of municipal leaders and others they were struggling against and who they believed were exploiting the grief of Brown's family. This included the Reverend Al Sharpton who spoke at Brown's funeral, stating,

> Can you imagine [Michael Brown's parents] are heartbroken? Their son taken, discarded and marginalized. And they have to stop mourning to get you to control your anger, like you're more angry than they are? ... And now we get to the 21st century, we get to where we got some positions of power. And you decide it ain't Black no more to be successful. Now you want to be a nigga and call your woman a ho. You've lost where you've come from. We've got to clean up our community so we can clean up the United States of America.[1]

In response to criticisms that they were in engaging in angry, nonpeaceful protests, people like Mary responded this way: "They say this isn't peaceful because there are drums, and there's shouting, and things are getting interrupted. Because to them peaceful means quiet, and silence, while other people endure violence. It's like yeah, here's the thing, 'I'm not choking you right now. I'm not physically hurting you.' So this is peaceful."

There were particularly heightened tensions between protesters and the Organization for Black Struggle (OBS) and Missourians Organizing for Reform and Empowerment (MORE). OBS was founded in 1980 "to address, through a number of organizing strategies, quality of life issues affecting the black community."[2] The founding group was made up of seasoned Black activists, including Jamala Rogers and Percy Green III, who had a long history of putting their bodies on the line and targeting specific racist policies in St. Louis as members of the St. Louis chapter of the Congress of Racial Equity and Action Committee to Improve Opportunities for Negroes—which was later renamed as Action Committee to Improve Opportunities Now. The latter "used militant, nonviolent direct action to fight for more and better black employment at the city's major firms," as well as addressing police brutality and the connections between race and class during the 1960s and 1970s.[3] In fact, the ways in which Ferguson protesters used spectacle and made people in the region uncomfortably confront pain and privilege continued a long tradition of similar methods utilized by those struggling against a "culture of opposition" in St. Louis.[4] MORE, which was originally the St. Louis chapter of the Association for Community Organizations for Reform Now, focuses on community organizing around inequalities affecting low- and moderate-income people and has had a predominantly white leadership.

The connection of OBS with 1960s- and 1970s-era Black militant tactics and MORE's history as a predominately white liberal organization exposed one example of how generation and race played out when it came to organizing, supporting, and funding more recent protest efforts. Ferguson protesters' generation and knowledge, or as some argued, lack thereof, regarding the legacies of Black struggle in St. Louis became apparent in relation to interactions between emerging resistance efforts and the work of OBS and MORE. If, as Clarence Lang argues, "Civil Rights and Black Power were neither dichotomous nor seamless, but rather discernible phases in an ongoing Black Freedom Movement"[5] in St. Louis, then the Ferguson protesters could be understood as yet another "discernable phase," following a long history of embodied resistance. Yet many Ferguson protesters were frustrated with the correlation to OBS and what they interpreted as an attempted coopting by older activists who had, as many put it, "already had their moment." MORE, on the other hand, was viewed by many in Ferguson resistance as the classic predominantly white liberal organization capitalizing on Black struggle.[6]

Darwin (pseudonym)

So there were only two organizations that were already organized when Ferguson started. We didn't initially think about officially organizing ourselves because I guess we thought we'd only be out there two or three days. Once it got into weeks and then months, we realized really fast that was a huge mistake we made entrusting the financial and organizational stuff to OBS and MORE.

Brittany

You got the organization MORE, that is predominantly white teaming up with OBS, a predominantly Black organization that hasn't had any status in like twenty years. No one's heard of them except those directly involved in community organizing. MORE, because it's white, has the resources, so there was a benefit for OBS to team up with them. Any money that came into Ferguson was funneled through MORE to get to where the money was needed. The problem was white folks go home at the end of the day, and they're not directly affected. They didn't know where the money was needed because they weren't out there. And OBS had to agree to a lot of stuff because people thought MORE was more legitimate. So there you have it, a white organization controlling and profiting from Black work.

Diamond

So in late August I was scouted by OBS because they wanted people from the front lines. But they didn't have the funds so I got traded to MORE with some other protesters. We started working for MORE and we were supposed to come up with proposals of what people actually wanted to see happen in the community. When we did, it was all, "No, no, no, we can't do that." And I was like, "I thought you guys were about doing stuff out here with all the resources you collected. You pulled us away from active protest to help you, and now you're saying no to everything that we're bringing you from the community."

They actually told us we couldn't protest while working for them. Then they said doing things like working on neighborhood restoration, creating safe spaces, helping kids—that's not what they're about. So we felt like we got tricked. And we were promised money for housing and things like that in return, and then they said, "Yeah, no. Never mind. We actually don't have it for you."

Jonathan

So a lot of the frustration has been with MORE and OBS. And "Cut the Check" will always be symbolic of that issue. Tribe X has had issues with not just them but other organizations that haven't stepped up or made themselves accountable. Better Family Life, Urban League, United Way, all these organizations are using Ferguson to fund their service work but they're not being held accountable to the people that brought the attention and funding to them.

Ultimately, the tensions that arose between young protesters, who were accustomed to spontaneously responding to conditions in front of them, and older organizers with decades of strategic planning experience and established institutionalized structures, resulted in failed collaboration on multiple levels. While some examples of coming together were seen, what transpired during Ferguson October revealed that established and revered organizations and donors were reluctant to relinquish substantial control and resources to the more organic forms of resistance, and young leaders placed little trust in institutional and organizational structures.

This schism, as well as what occurs when voices demand to be heard, was particularly evident at the Ferguson October interfaith event for clergy and activists on October 12, called "Mass Meeting on Ferguson," which was attended by more than a thousand people. Organized by local clergy, established organizations, and selected protesters—most of whom were men—the event began with a march of clergy ending at the Chaifetz Arena on the SLU campus. Speakers were to include local and national clergy such as Cornel West and Jim Wallis. About an hour into the event, young people in the audience began to speak out during the speech of Cornell William Brooks, the president of the NAACP. Several stood up and began chanting, "Let them speak," referring to activists in the audience. The speakers seated on the podium joined in and several young activists approached the stage. After a few minutes, Traci Blackmon, a local pastor who was moderating the event, came to the podium and announced, "The next voice we will hear will be a word from the streets." Representing somewhat divergent lines of the protest family, Tef Poe and Ashley Yates were allowed to speak at that point on behalf of activists. Poe, an outspoken St. Louis rap artist who helped lead a Ferguson delegation to the United Nations, called out academics, clergy, and other artists for not showing up in the initial and sustained days of protest, stating, among other things, "This ain't your grandparents' civil rights movement."[7] Yates, challenging notions of peaceful protest, focused much of what she said on righteous anger and the links between affective rage and expressions of humanity. She passionately drew parallels between the association of blackness with risk and inhuman practices that place property above life, stating,

> I sat in a closed-council meeting with some Ferguson representatives. There were a lot of business owners there. One of the things they talked about was the fear of riots. They talked about the fear of property values decreasing and customers decreasing and what their home value would look like after "Ferguson" was said and done. I looked each and every one of them in the eyes and I asked them what the value of their house was and what it had been. Each of them was able to tell me a number. Then I looked them in the eyes and I said, "What's the value of a life that was born in 1996?"

What was very apparent was that the "Mass Meeting on Ferguson" had suddenly shifted from a planned event to a spontaneous and organic expression that is the essence of Ferguson resistance.[8]

As protesters entered their third month of actions, the differences between protest leaders like Poe and Yates and the people each represented at the "Mass Meeting" continued to emerge in the space of protest. The women who had been leading protests since mid-August continued to be alienated by the attention and resources given to male activists, especially local celebrities and music artists who claimed to speak for the movement as a whole but who many felt were promoting their careers through activist activities. While women made up the majority of consistent protesters, both men and women observed that the media regularly interviewed and had cameras on men, either because they sought men out or because men were inserting themselves in those spaces. They also observed that money and resources that eventually made it to the so-called street protesters were funneled to, and distributed by, organizations and institutions largely led by men, including Black churches. Some protesters also expressed frustration with older Black women, who they felt did not hold Black men accountable and granted them special privileges, revealing more generational and respectability politics. Protesters identified class and educational distinctions regarding who got to speak on behalf of the movement and who was recognized nationally as a leader. On the other hand, people and organizations that to many represented male patriarchy, such as Louis Farrakhan and the Million Man March, were using iconography and images associated with Black women leaders to promote causes without their permission.

Brittany

Louis Farrakhan and the Nation of Islam are promoting their march on October 10th using my image, and I was so upset because I'm a proud gay woman and I've had to carve out my own space being a Black gay woman in a Black liberation movement. Because oftentimes people don't really know how to accept the fact that if you're fighting for Black liberation you're fighting for all people not just straight cisgendered Black folks. And I was like, "No, you're not about to use me to promote your march because I'm not comin' to your march because I don't feel safe at your march." I don't think it is okay to be openly against gay people and then have an openly gay person on your flier just to promote your event. I'm going to be consistent with my message. I'm not going to be used. I'm not going to be anybody's Black women's face. I'm not doing that.[9]

Nell (pseudonym)

During Ferguson October, the people coming in from outside to organize wanted to deal with the orgs and groups headed by men. I'm not saying all those guys didn't mean well most of the time, but they became the focus of attention when things were more mainstream.

"Unsung Haiku"

There was this one night at the PD when some rapper pulled up in one of his vans that had his name and all his social media stuff on the side. He parked it so media cameras had it in the background. I was like, "Man, you going to have to move this truck or we're flipping it." There were a lot of artists who came out there for the sake of getting footage. They'd put revolutionary lyrics in their songs but I know, as an artist who was actually out there every day, they were only out there to show face. No chanting, no sign, no nothing. Just taking lots of selfies.

Kristina (pseudonym)

And you're not supposed to tell them [hetero men] anything either. Within the movement we were being suppressed as Black women, and if we tried to do anything nice for ourselves, watch out. A select few [hetero men] were benefitting from the movement. Getting money from orgs and stuff while we could barely eat. And they were the ones telling us to love and support each other but not helping anybody out. Or telling us to go clean somebody's house for money while they're just getting checks for showing up. Why would I go scream at the police but then remain silent about y'all's stuff. They just really starting to resemble my oppressor, and I've liberated myself from that shit.

Mary (pseudonym)

It's also about generation because a lot of the older Black women still hold up the men, and support them. They don't think Black men should be challenged in public. And I find that really interesting. I think, "Are you really gonna put up with that?" Because there was a time when I would have too, but I've been changed by these young women leaders. Like some of the older women think men should not have to do work like mopping, sweeping, and cooking. There's also not nearly as many men in the movement as women. When the men are there they will try to take charge and when they're not, things will get done. There are few men who respect the work and do important stuff, but I can count them on one hand.

Brittany

Lately I've been holding men to the same expectation that I hold white people. I refuse to do the work for them. You know, I will be damned if in fifty years from now Tef Poe is painted as the pinnacle leader of the movement, you know. Or if any cisgendered man is because he fits the narrative people want to tell. We need to get this history right.

Darwin (pseudonym)

The one thing I would say is that if a real problem comes up at an action, people go get a man before they go get a female. That has happened a whole lot. And I've been one of those chosen people. Like just the presence of a man settles things down. And I would say that even though this is a women's led movement, they have the control but none of the power in the form of money or resources. So they can't actually steer the larger movement and get the results they want because the money gets given to the men. Either directly or to their organizations that they lead.

Every time we need a space, the women have to go talk to a man. Like, "Hey, can we meet at your church?" Then we get there, and the women lead. But they don't get money or anything else. And that's the truth. The donors look at organizations, and every time they give to the one that's led by a man. The media, the politicians, the officials, they always go to the men first. The access to money and the distribution of funds have really been glossed over when people talk about this movement. I'm sorry, it just has.

Alisha

You have so many people profiting from Ferguson. Building their careers and their platforms on Ferguson, but they've never even gone to an action. It happens all the time. So many people are supposed to be more qualified to talk about this than the people on the streets. People who never put their bodies on the line are getting on planes that other people paid for. Staying in hotels that other people paid for. And the people in the streets are the people at the bottom, a lot of them. Like I'm just trying to get groceries for next week.

Similar conflicts rooted in patriarchy and heteronormativity arose around issues of intersectional oppressions. While many of those interviewed repeatedly stated their appreciation for intersectional conversations and the way difficult discussions shaped the movement, some people, mostly men, expressed dislike for these conversations and were frustrated by the issues women and queer protesters relentlessly brought up. Several protesters who identified as straight Black men complained at length that discussions among protesters veered too far away from a focus on Mike Brown and police brutality specifically against young Black men. These interviews highlighted many of the issues and contradictions brought up by women regarding oppressive attitudes and practices within the movement and foregrounded how multiple processes of identity formation and experience are always at work within groups that are historically and politically misrecognized and portrayed as a single unified group. These differences and tensions—which can be viewed as inherent within, and productive to, the spaces of struggle— consistently came up.

E. J.

So the LGBT and the rest of whatever letter they keep adding, community, they definitely did their part in the beginning. Because, you know, they're Black. In the beginning, it was like, as long as you're Black, that's all that matters because this is about Black liberation. But once you're like trying to make this more than a Black thing, like where are you going with that? Like we're all just doing the work. I was never down on no LGBT, or whatever those letters are, that was actually doing work. You're doing this because you're Black. Like you could get killed because you're Black. All these other identities and shit ain't gonna get you any more killed.

The interviews with men who identified as straight and cisgendered were consistently twice as long (at least) as all other interviews conducted with protesters, although the same questions were asked. In several of these interviews the men spent much of the time making a case that their work was underappreciated. The same men insisted that tensions between men and women, or between straight and queer people, "were just never an issue." These interviews, however, are full of contradictions similar to the contradictions that queer theory aims to reveal. The vulnerability of Black bodies was a central theme in all the interviews, but it was approached from completely different vantage points for people identifying as straight men versus queer women. The assumed availability and therefore vulnerability of the women's bodies, for instance, was consistently challenged by young women protesters and was a consistent theme of frustration in interviews with women. Queer Black women stated over and over that straight men were constantly offended by the "unavailability" of queer feminized bodies, which they said provoked hostility toward them. Many straight men, however, claimed to respect all women, straight or otherwise, yet also indicated that women were supposed to act in a certain way in order for respect to be earned. Men complained that queer women did not appreciate the hypervulnerability of young

Black straight men's bodies, like that of Michael Brown, and that, by expanding the focus beyond young Black men targeted by the police, women were putting the most vulnerable lives—those of young Black men—at even more risk. The ways by which protesters across the spectrums of age, gender, and sexuality experienced vulnerability, risk, and attachment (of and to their own bodies and the bodies of others) ultimately determined how they imagined the world and the work of resistance. These factors also shaped how they viewed their own participation in the spaces of protests.

Darwin (pseudonym)

I don't think queer people added anything to the conversations. You know, that was just never part of it. Why should I care who you sleep with? We don't need to talk about that. But I guess they brought more leadership because, you know, that community is already organized. They've been protesting for years. I guess because their leadership has been the most stable, they're important in that way.

But there's never been any dynamics between the queer people and the straight people. You know, I think I have the best perspective on this because I'm one of the few males that been out there the whole time. I mean, in the beginning there were a bunch of males out there. Now there's a limited amount. And I'm here to tell you that being involved in it together with women was never an issue. Not one time did someone come up to me and say, "Man, I ain't doing this because a woman said it." It just never came up.

The only time a problem arose was when a woman thought she was being disrespected but they weren't actually. Not one guy ever complained about taking orders from a woman. Sometimes they thought the women were a little mean about the way they said things. But never about their ability to lead. Like I'm the first one who ever said this is a woman-led movement. No one said it before I did. No one. I was telling the media when they were constantly interviewing me on camera, I said, "Well, the women are smarter, they're stronger, and they're sober." And that's the truth.

And then people come down here and they see us fighting and they see girls holding hands and they see guys at meetings talkin' bout their boyfriends. They like, "What's going on here? I thought people were out here protesting for Black folks." You gotta think about that.

Mitchell

Some people think gays get treated differently where honestly I don't think they do at all. Before all this shit happened I had never even talked to a gay person.

I'd never even met one I knew was gay. So when I would see gay people they would think I had a problem with them because I didn't talk to them. I just don't have anything to say to them. I don't have a problem with them.

Like Charles Wade and DeRay McKessen, they're openly gay and I've talked to them plenty. I went to eat with them even. But that doesn't make me gay. I don't have no problem sharing that I'm not gay. I don't see why people bring all that extra shit in because that's when you start confusing people. We're gonna confuse the kids. They ain't gonna turn this into "Gay Lives Matter." What the hell. Now you're putting something on them they didn't even come here for. For you to do that to a kid? That's fucked up because you're taking advantage of them. You're confusing them. We should be leading kids in the direction we want them to go. And that's not the direction.

My mom did it right. But I have a gay cousin so I'm like more open to this stuff. Like I'll talk to gay people. I've got friends that won't even talk to them. I was kind of like exposed to it comin' up so I feel more comfortable talking to them. But you still got people that's not going to be as open as I am. You're not going to see no straight guy go talk to a lesbian. That's just not going to happen. They're not going to go up to a lesbian and be like, "Hey how 'bout that Royals game last night?" We've got bigger issues than gay rights. We've got young Black men dyin' for no reason.

E. J.

But then they started talkin' 'bout all this intersectionality and whatever shit. Like there's different kinds of oppression. Like what happened with the Civil Rights Movement when people started forgetting what it's actually about. Like the energy started shifting over to like the LGBT shit. And the feminists and all, they started sayin' like we got to recognize all this other stuff. I thought I was out here for Mike Brown. Who is paying you all to say that? Because they gotta be paying you. Because you weren't saying that shit in the beginning. Okay, you are what you are, but don't derail the movement trying to shift this to some other shit that it's not actually about. I am fully against that. I don't need to listen to this feminist shit. Did you know feminism was started by white women? And white women and Asian women ain't got no respect for Black women. Black women have a way different struggle so don't be usin' all this feminist talk.

I'm still learnin' how to not to say "bitch" or "ho" too much when I talk 'bout a woman because you're not supposed to say that nowadays. They get offended. This is a new world. Nobody really taught us how to work together. I definitely have had numerous conversations with many feminists that say, "Hey, don't call us bitch, don't say female. Call us women." But when they're doin' wrong and I call 'em on it, I say, "Woman, get your ass back over here." And they're like, see, that's misogyny. I'm like, "No it isn't." Or like a female decides she wants to be promiscuous. If she's a feminist, I can't call her a ho. As long as she claims feminism, she can do whatever she wants. What's that about? That's why I can't go along with the feminist thing. They just make shit up as they go along. That's what the police do too. That's what the government does. They act like the government.

Roderick Ferguson points out that scholars also perpetuate tropes of Black gendered deviance. He argues that this is done by using a feminist frame to identify the detachment of (white) women from a male head as *agency* while framing Black single mothers and gender-nonconforming individuals as dependent, deviant, and/or pathological. Citing William Julius Wilson specifically, Ferguson argues that Wilson's book *The Truly Disadvantaged* "implies that black women function to consummate black men as liberal subjects, arguing for the universalization of black men through access to black women's bodies."[10] Certainly the viewpoints shared by women and men concerning Black women's bodies and the universalization of Black men, as expressed in excerpts above, support Ferguson's observations. The use of the words *female* and *the females* as nouns was a particularly common practice of the men interviewed. Many of the women cited this usage as further evidence of how Black men were using feminism as an additional way to objectify women's bodies and minds. For these men, feminism only applied to females who claimed a sexual identity apart from men and, by calling them "the females," hetero men shifted the focus from claimed identities to conferred subjectivities attached to specific anatomies.

People across gender identification, age, and sexual orientation who made up Ferguson resistance did coalesce around a commonly stated frustration— that their efforts were consistently conflated with, or dismissed as, just another manifestation of the Black Lives Matter movement. To many people who are unfamiliar with the specific events and people that came to make up the Ferguson Protest Movement, Ferguson is synonymous with what is today understood as the Black Lives Matter movement, or evolving iterations such as the Movement for Black Lives. Most Ferguson protesters, however, reported exasperation regarding this perception. Many, in fact, went as far as to say that Black Lives Matter, which is an organization founded by queer Black women following the death of Trayvon Martin, unrightfully capitalized on and conveniently coopted the work of Ferguson resistance. While some leaders did specifically identify with the Black Lives Matter organization, as cohesively working in a similar direction as Ferguson protesters, many felt that the Black Lives Matter organization had exploited the sacrifices of Ferguson protesters and the visibility of events that had traumatized people in the St. Louis region. This frustration regarding important distinctions between the Ferguson Protest Movement and Black Lives Matter (the organization and the subsequent movement) transcended many of the differences between the multiple identities represented across Ferguson resistance.

Brittany

I did not know about the Black Lives Matter organization until they came here last August. They made their first bus ride here. That's when I was introduced [to the founders]. It's confusing to people because there is this organization called Black Lives Matter that is said to have started the slogan and then you have this movement that would not have happened had it not been for the people in St. Louis and Ferguson standing up. . . .

I feel like it takes away from the effort folks in this city put into this movement. The whole movement is now credited to an organization somewhere else rather than the people that stood up here. And folks at the organization are not willing to clarify that the movement and the organization are two separate things. They've claimed that recognition.

E. J.

The Ferguson situation after Mike Brown was like a storm at sea. And Black Lives Matter was like a surfer that was able to ride that wave, to make it look like they were at the center of it. Most people did not know that the Black Lives Matter organization existed until after Mike Brown got killed. Most people don't even know it's an organization now. It's a trendy little chant and hashtag that ties together the work of a lot of people in a lot of places, but Ferguson put it on the map.

Cassandra (pseudonym)

I think the most troubling organization to me is Black Lives Matter. I think about this a lot and I'm going to think about it until somebody actually says something. I remember when we first took to the streets in August. And I remember when I first met Alicia and Patrisse and Diana weeks later at Starsky's church and they wanted to interview us for an article Alicia was writing about the Bay Area. And at the time I didn't know what Black Lives Matter was. Nobody did.

I didn't know what was unfolding. I thought everyone that came on their freedom bus just wanted to help. I didn't know they were coming to build a brand and capitalize on the backs of people that sacrificed and continue to sacrifice their lives. Like just yesterday someone on Facebook was commenting, "Alicia

Garza was invited to the State of the Union and she deserves to be there because she started this movement." And I was like, "No, she was the founder of an organization." And he was like, "What's the difference, it's just semantics." There's actually a big difference. They refuse to denounce that narrative. This is erasure. It's revisionist history. It's queer Black women erasing queer Black women.

Alexis

Black Lives Matter was not a movement before Ferguson, it was solely an organization. If it were not for the Ferguson protesters there would be no Black Lives Matter movement. Period.

Mama Cat

We decided Diamond was going to be the one to articulate [to the founders of the Black Lives Matter organization] how we were feeling. So I was standing there and [one of the founders] looks into Diamond's eyes and says, "I see you. I hear you. I, I do, I do, I hear you." And we had a meeting right after that and [another Ferguson protester] said to Diamond, "She's going to grab you by the shoulders and say, 'I see you. I hear you.'" And Diamond says, "She already did that."

Many people interviewed also stated that they were frustrated with how they perceived the Black Lives Matter organization and other organizations that claimed to speak for the movement had reduced the struggle to a set of demands. They stated that asking for body cameras and more police training suggested that such things were sufficient to make Black lives nondisposable. Many Ferguson protesters argued, however, that this approach does not address the antiblackness they experienced daily and, by appealing to technologies of the liberal state, it reduces the saliency and potential for radical Black flesh to effectively disrupt systems rooted in white supremacy. The counterargument made by organizers such as those who started Campaign Zero is that a step in the right direction is still a step and that unapologetic protest and policy changes must occur together. Although there were many specific criticisms of Black Lives Matter as an organization, especially in the early days of protest, responses were more mixed regarding whether or not a conflation of Ferguson resistance with variations of Black Lives Matter as a national movement was a good or bad thing from a long-term perspective.

Kristina (pseudonym)

Black Lives Matter has nothing to do with St. Louis. They've been here but did they meet with the community? No. They met with people they wanted to meet with. That's how they entered the community. I've spoken to all three of the founding members in person but I've never organized with them. They organize with an elite group of hand-selected people. This has got to be confusing to people that don't actually know the history and what's been happening. Like if you weren't in Ferguson you just believe what the media tells you about Black Lives Matter. Why wouldn't you?

Jonathan

The amount of focus that has been put on Black struggle because of Ferguson is amazing. I never thought there would be such national and international attention put back on that struggle at this time. People credit BLM with doing that, but it was Ferguson that made these conversations possible. I think when you say "Black Lives Matter," it ends up putting a blanket over the whole character and color of people in Ferguson. I'm fine with it being used as long as you clarify what you're talking about.

Mr. Moff

Last year [Lost Voices] hosted a Stop the Violence march. It was huge. We reached out to everyone we could think of—priests, pastors, aldermen, and we reached out to Black Lives Matter. Instead of helping us, they decided to hold their own march instead. And theirs was not successful because they were too busy making themselves look good and we had all the people.

Ongoing discussions and disagreements between core leaders continue to pose important questions regarding the relationship between the Ferguson protest family, the Black Lives Matter organization, and Black struggle more generally.[11] Many of those who prioritized local issues and continue to focus attention on reform in the St. Louis region are publicly critical of Ferguson leaders who gained a national spotlight and are now indistinguishable from Black Lives Matter platforms.[12] The divisions discussed above with regard to those who do not support intersectional politics are fully evident as well. The execution-style murder of protester Darren Seals (aka King D Seals) on September 6, 2016, brought many of these disagreements and hard feelings into public view through social media. While there was shared animosity toward the police and consensus that the investigation of Seals's death would not be carried out in a just manner, those within Seals's network of activists redirected much of their anger and grief toward the women and queer of color leaders. Some alluded that protesters at odds with Seals within the movement were indirectly responsible for his death. Those who were not in Seals's circle of activists attempted to walk a line between acknowledging disagreements with Seals and showing respect for his passion for the movement.

As discussed previously with regard to the gendered oppressions experienced within the movement, the generational and racial conflicts that arose between Ferguson protesters and established organizations such as OBS and MORE, and the misrecognitions concerning relationships to, and between, the Black Lives Matter organization and movement are constitutive of the history and conditions of organizing around shared struggle. These contestations of meaning, belonging, territory, and imagination, as well as concerns regarding who may speak for whom, reveal the multivalent and fluid conditions of Black identity and the shared yet differing experiences of blackness, which include traumas, loss, and displacements as well as magnificent expressions of life and freedom. For Stuart Hall, "imaginative rediscoveries" require the acknowledgment of difference and rupture while remembering that "what we share is precisely the experience of a profound discontinuity."[13] Robin D. G. Kelley describes the imaginative capacity of Black radicalism as "freedom dreams," recognizing that "things are not what they seem and that the desires, hopes, and intentions of the people who fought [and fight] for change cannot be easily categorized, contained, or explained."[14] It is tempting to try to put each group or individual that appears in this story in a box with a label, and in some ways analysis does exactly that as a means to provide a level of understanding. It is important to at least state, however, that the desires, hopes, and intentions of all the people represented consistently move across boundaries that are themselves in flux.

In contrast to Black respectability politics, which many people associate with the leaders of the Civil Rights Movement (and Black municipal leaders in the St. Louis region), and to the heteropatriarchy embedded within past Black liberation organizations and activities in the 1950s through 1970s,[15] the resistance that emerged in Ferguson pushes and interrogates the boundaries of Black intelligibility. This is a queer of color intervention in the praxis of protest in the same way queer of color critique intervenes in the historical and theoretical frameworks of liberation theory.[16] The bodies and voices of Ferguson protesters call into question the myriad ways previously invisible people fundamentally shaped the history of resistance against racialized violence and oppression. By specifically emphasizing a love of blackness and themselves, an unapologetic and unwavering visibility, and the multiplicity of intersecting identities, Ferguson resistance activates an always-already-present capacity for blackness to imagine freedom in response to violence. The work of Ferguson

resistance can be viewed as a continuum of Black feminist praxis that empha-
sizes the relationship between intersecting oppressions yet recognizes gendered
antiblackness as fundamental to structures of oppression. Ula Taylor reminds
us, "the ultimate goal of black feminism is to create a political movement that
not only struggles against exploitative capitalism . . . but that also seeks to
develop institutions to protect what the dominant culture has little respect and
value for—black women's minds and bodies."[17]

Coda

ARCHIPELAGOES OF LIFE

This is about rejecting everything people say we have to be in order to be recognized, to be citizens, to be humans.

—Alexis Templeton

What we're doing is creating something different. For me, it's a different way of viewing myself, a different way of living, a different way of loving my blackness.

—Kristina (pseudonym)

A cultural politics of race and space relies on the logics of antiblackness as described in disturbing detail throughout the preceding chapters of this book. As a fundamental technique of biopower, power *over* life, this politics deploys culture to produce and police disposable yet profitable bodies in North St. Louis County. But to theorize the experience of living under the "racial state of municipal governance" as solely a form of social death denies how relations of power are dependent upon possibilities for resistance. Michel Foucault makes this point when he states that "if there were no possibility of resistance, there would be no power relations at all."[1] The paradoxically liberating capacity of lived flesh to resist and the ability of embodied knowledge of suffering to move beyond discursive enclosures of rights and personhood lie at the core of Alexander Weheliye's powerful critique of the limits of biopolitics, bare life, and related theories of modern political violence. Lived flesh and embodied knowledge are especially important with regard to theorizing modern racial projects. As Weheliye argues, "the existence of alternative modes of life [occurs] alongside the violence, subjection, exploitation, and racialization that define the modern human."[2] This argument asserts the possibility of fully inhabited flesh, including its capacity to experience such things as pleasure, desire, pain, and even death, to redefine living as human in ways that transcend the limits of both biopolitical and liberal humanism critiques, especially the conceptualization of bare life, which leaves the body suspended in a condition of utter abjection. When people who are designated as those who "could die" *appear* within spaces imagined as protected (the spaces of life and flourishing), suffering is made visible and spatial dissonance results.

Haunting, at its most basic level, occurs when something that is supposed to be invisible, or is said to not exist, can suddenly be seen. Seeing people who should not be seen, especially when their personhood is said to be in question in the first place, is an uncanny experience, and a choice must be made to either see or to deny those who haunt. Through haunting, time and space are collapsed such that past, present, and future are not a continuum but must be sorted out. Avery Gordon explains,

> Haunting raises specters, and it alters the experience of being in linear time, alters the way we normally separate and sequence the past, the present and the future. These specters or ghosts appear when the trouble they represent and symptomize is no longer being contained or repressed or blocked from view. . . . The whole essence, if you can use that word, of a ghost is that it has a real presence and demands its due, demands your attention. Haunting and the appearance of specters or ghosts is one way, I tried to suggest, we're notified that what's been suppressed or concealed is very much alive and present, messing or interfering precisely with those always incomplete forms of containment and repression ceaselessly directed towards us.[3]

This statement provides a productive and provocative way to think about the queering of protest presented in part II of this book. Ferguson protesters demanded their due, revealed that they are not only alive but living their blackness fully, and strategically messed with the forms of containment and repression that are ceaselessly directed toward them. Women and queer individuals leading Ferguson resistance also illustrated how the performance of visibility leverages the power that embodied blackness holds—revealing the inhuman and reconfiguring the metrics of what it means to live as fully human. This living as fully human is similar to what Fred Moten has described as a social poetics that is "enthralled by generativity."[4] The choreopolitics of bodies in space employed by nonconforming protesters joined with the uncanny experience of bodies that show up in places where they are not supposed to be seen, and demanded that the terms of visibility and generativity be set by people practicing a sociality that exists outside, and beyond, the normative social world.[5]

Disrupting the static Look!—the gaze that attempts to inscribe a fixed identity onto Black bodies—a sensate *praxis* of blackness, now as flesh, supersedes and exceeds the human and thus resituates blackness outside abjection, outside enduring distinctions regarding degrees of the human that construct and constrain bodies, indeed outside an ontological ordering of the world.[6] In so doing, the degrees of the inhuman practiced against inscribed flesh also becomes visible. This reconfiguration (of the body) and resituation (in space) is the ethics of lived blackness. The ethics of lived blackness reveals itself as an always-already-present site of freedom with "poetic access to what it is of the other world that remains unheard, unnoted, unrecognized in this one."[7]

The ephemeral space of violence evidenced through the inscribed flesh of Michael Brown and the space of resistance that was opened up by differently inscribed Black flesh in Ferguson became a worldwide symbol of how profane and sacred spaces can exist within the same place. In this way, the haunting of a space connected diaspora subjects in both beautiful and horrific terms, linking Black experience and Black flesh across time and space—what Nadia Ellis has described as a "territory of the soul."[8] Haunting, however, is more than just a connection to the past. Haunting is very much about the future. As Gordon has argued, haunting reveals the something-to-be-done; it is "one way in which abusive systems of power make themselves known and their impacts felt in everyday life."[9] Until 2014, the abusive systems of power that had been operating in North St. Louis County for decades at extreme scales were invisible to some and conveniently ignored by others, except those who experienced them daily. Although these defuturing systems have not been dismantled in any permanent way, they continue to emerge as visible and call for something to be done, which does not necessarily lead to futuring practices.

Sending a militarized police force to Ferguson and deciding not to indict Darren Wilson were two responses to the something-to-be-done. Passing legislation limiting predatory policing practices in North St. Louis County that was subsequently fought and overturned by Black municipal leadership or forcing largely unenforced consent decrees on the cities of Ferguson and Pagedale that do not address the other twenty-nine municipalities in this geography were other responses. Ousting Bob McCulloch, the white St. Louis County prosecutor who handled the investigation of Brown's death and held the office for twenty-seven years, and electing Wesley Bell, the Black challenger (and a municipal judge and prosecutor in North St. Louis County who was part of the predatory system) were additional reactions to protests. The momentum to initiate yet another effort to reunite the city and county of St. Louis after 143 years of separation and to restructure redundant and abusive municipal jurisdictions (which failed due to corruption and questionable motives) was also attributed to awareness raised by Ferguson resistance.

The one step forward, one step back pattern of redressing state-sanctioned racialized violence through policy reforms *is not* what emergent leaders in Ferguson were and are fighting for. Rather, the legacy of "Ferguson" in response to what amounts to a public lynching and which continues a long history of the Black radical imagination, is a call to confront blackness itself as a way that affords different calculations and imaginations of what it means to live and practice freedom. Just as Black political autonomy has been shown to be a hollow prize within prevailing systems of power, remediating inequality predicated on the violent and historical differentiation of people and space through mechanisms of the liberal state simply perpetuates this cycle. But "what if blackness is the name that has been given to the social field and social life of an illicit alternative capacity to desire?"[10] While blackness cannot be separated from Black people without violence resulting, what I believe Moten is suggesting by posing this question is that blackness holds the possibility to usher in a world with a future—something none of us currently can claim.

What this book has tried to convey in part is that the stakes surrounding how we respond to the something-to-be-done do not just apply to people who live in places like North St. Louis County. The modalities and uses of antiblackness that produce invisible, precarious and profitable people and populations across the globe through the denial of personhood and attachments of blackness to risk, in fact deny the possibility for anyone to experience the full potential of living as human. These modalities are also unsustainable, as they undergird the gradual destruction of life-sustaining resources, which will ultimately deny a future for all life. For these reasons, we all live in a precarious state of existence, which is not to deny the fact that precarity is experienced in vastly different degrees or that privilege renders precariousness illegible.[11]

Bodies continue to show up and haunt St. Louis and elsewhere in ways that rework "the human" as a powerful act of protest against defuturing systems and actions. Although no longer at the top of national news feeds (at least as I write this), the work of those who were ignited in the days after Michael Brown's death continues, in various ways, to show how "in this very violence something rotten in the law is revealed."[12] "Justice for Mike Brown" brought people to the street, but young emergent leaders pushed people in the region and beyond to confront the afterlife of slavery in the everyday lives of people all around them, even if they subsequently chose to look away. While most people outside the protest family consider the Ferguson Protest Movement to be over, those whose lives were transformed across space and time are committed to fight in registers that go beyond those recognized by the liberal state. This resistance and the capacity to imagine other worlds crop up across the globe and are connected through a radical relationality that not only multiplies "the reals" but maps that which is currently unimaginable.[13] Together these outcroppings create, as Arturo Escobar beautifully describes, archipelagoes of life that sit within the sea of unsustainable ways of being and doing.[14]

"Until everyone can answer the question, 'What is the value of a life born in 1996?' . . . . we don't stop" (Ashley Yates).

Notes

INTRODUCTION

1. "North St. Louis County" and "North County" are both locally understood designations for roughly the northern third of St. Louis County, Missouri (see maps 2.2 and 2.3), but this is not a legally defined entity.

2. The concept of spatial imaginaries used throughout this book draws from the fields of social philosophy and human geography and asserts that the lived experience of place includes physical, social, political, and symbolic space. See, for example, Henri Lefebvre, *The Production of Space*, trans. Donald Nicholson-Smith (Malden, MA: Wiley-Blackwell, 1992); Derek Gregory, *Geographical Imaginations* (Malden, MA: Wiley-Blackwell, 1994); and Doreen Massey, *For Space* (Thousand Oaks, CA: Sage, 2005). George Lipsitz developed the concept of the white spatial imaginary, which is the historically specific understanding of white space in the United States as separate and distinct from Black space. Lipsitz makes the point that while formal laws and policies intended to oppress, exclude, and segregate Black citizens in the United States have been removed, a residual and powerful imagination of space, and specifically the definition and separateness of white space in contradistinction from Black space, remains firmly in place. *How Racism Takes Place* (Philadelphia: Temple University Press, 2011).

3. The analytical frame of fungibility—as fundamental to the construction of blackness through slavery—proved critical for understanding phenomena found in North St. Louis County. This conceptualization views blackness as an ontological status that maintains the imprint of slavery on Black bodies in order for current organizations and hierarchies of society to remain in place. Beyond creating the capacity to exploit gendered Black bodies, the discursively produced symbolic value of fungible blackness—that which can be made and remade, changed and exchanged—provides unending possibilities to benefit and expand dominant social, economic, and political structures. See, for example, Orlando Patterson, *Slavery and Social Death* (Cambridge, MA: Harvard University Press, 1982); Saidiya Hartman, *Scenes of Subjection: Terror, Slavery, and Self-Making in Nineteenth-Century America* (Oxford: Oxford University Press, 1997); Jered Sexton, *Amalgamation Schemes: Antiblackness and the Critique of Multiculturalism* (Minneapolis, MN: University of Minnesota Press, 2008); Frank B. Wilderson, III, *Red, White, and Black: Cinema and the Structure of U.S. Antagonisms* (Durham, NC: Duke University Press, 2010); Christina Sharpe, *In the Wake: On Blackness and Being* (Durham, NC: Duke University Press, 2016); and Tiffany Lethabo King, "Humans Involved: Lurking in the Lines of Posthumanist Flight," *Critical Ethnic Studies* 3, no. 1 (2017): 162–85.

4. This list is based on a review of municipal ordinances in the cities that occupy St. Louis County.

5. Resident interviews. Additionally, over fifty media articles have been written on this subject. See, for example, Radley Balko, "Why We Need to Fix St. Louis County," *Washington Post*, October 16, 2014; Campbell Robertson et al., "Ferguson Became Symbol, but Bias Knows No Borders," *New York Times*, March 7, 2015; Jennifer Mann, "Municipalities Ticket for Trees and Toys as Traffic Revenue Declines," *St. Louis Post-Dispatch*, May 24, 2015.

6. This observation is based on interviews with residents, documents obtained from the City of Pagedale, Missouri, documents obtained from a class action lawsuit against the City of Pagedale, and media attention documenting practices in Pagedale. See, for example, Jennifer Mann, "After Code Violation Crackdown, Pagedale Officials Now Threaten to Demolish Homes," *St. Louis Post-Dispatch*, August 10, 2015.

7. Broken-windows policing links space to crime and claims that lower-order markers of disorder such as broken windows or misdemeanor infractions like littering lead to more serious crime. George Kelling and James Q. Wilson, "Broken Windows: The Police and Neighborhood Safety," *Atlantic*, March 1982, 29–38.

8. David Theo Goldberg has theorized modern racial states as places "where states of being and states of governance meet." "Racial States," in *A Companion to Racial and Ethnic Studies*, ed. David Theo Goldberg and John Solomos (Malden, MA: Blackwell, 2002), 236.

9. Neil Brenner and Nik Theodore, "Cities and the Geographies of 'Actually Existing Neoliberalism,'" *Antipode* 34, no. 3 (July 2002): 349–79.

10. Kimberlé Crenshaw, "Color Blindness, History and the Law," in *The House that Race Built*, ed. Wahneema Lubiano (New York: Vintage Press, 1998), 280–89. Crenshaw, among others, has shown how formal and informal practices rooted in racialized distinctions coalesce in the public and private spheres, resulting in both blatant and obscured forms of racial discrimination.

11. See, for example, Jodi Rios, "Flesh in the Street," *Kalfou* 3, no. 1 (2016): 63.

12. Audre Lorde, "The Master's Tools Will Never Dismantle the Master's House," *Sister Outsider: Essays and Speeches by Audre Lorde* (Berkeley, CA: Crossing Press, 2007): 110–14.

13. Mayors interviewed for this work and quoted in the local media consistently refer to local autonomy as the most important issue surrounding any reform measures. The concept of minority mayors winning a "hollow prize" comes from H. Paul Friesema's "Black Control of Central Cities: The Hollow Prize," *American Institute of Planners Journal* 35 (March 1969): 75–79. Friesema observed that by the time a member of a minority finally rises to the position of mayor, his or her city is very likely to be in decline—and legislatures are unlikely to assist minority municipalities.

14. Nadia Ellis explores these themes in *Territories of the Soul: Queered Belonging in the Black Diaspora* (Durham, NC: Duke University Press, 2015). See specifically the chapter "Burning Spear and Nathaniel Mackey at Large," 147–76.

15. Ellis, *Territories of the Soul*.

16. The references to haunting, bodies that show up, and a something-to-be-done that are found throughout this book draw specifically from the work of Avery Gordon. See, for example, *Ghostly Matters: Haunting and the Sociological Imagination* (Minneapolis: University of Minnesota Press, 1997); "Some Thoughts on Haunting and Futurity," *Borderlands* 10, no. 2 (2011).

17. Achille Mbembe, "Necropolitics," trans. Libby Meintjes, *Public Culture* 15, no. 1 (2003): 11–40.

18. Hortense Spillers, "Mama's Baby, Papa's Maybe: An American Grammar Book," *Diacritics* 17, no. 2 (Summer 1987): 65–81.

19. Saidiya Hartman writes, "This is the afterlife of slavery—skewed life chances, limited access to health and education, premature death, incarceration, and impoverishment. I, too, am the afterlife of slavery." *Lose Your Mother: A Journey along the Atlantic Slave Route* (New York: Farrar, Straus and Giroux, 2008), 6.

20. In the field of geography, topology has come to be understood as abstract, nonrepresentational, and relational space, whereas topography represents or refers to actual

physical space. I use *topology* (*pornotopology*) as opposed to *topography* very intentionally to signify the abstracted and relational nature of Black space.

21. Hartman, *Scenes of Subjection*, 85.

22. Hartman, 3–4.

23. Hartman, 4.

24. Jodi Rios, "Reconsidering the Margin: Relationships of Difference and Transformative Education," in *Service-Learning in Design and Planning: Educating at the Boundaries*, ed. Tom Agnotti, Cheryl Doble, and Paula Horrigan (Oakland, CA: New Village Press, 2011): 39–54; Christine Hoehner et al., "Page Avenue HIA: Building on Diverse Partnerships and Evidence to Promote a Healthy Community," *Health and Place* 18, no. 1 (January 2012): 85–95.

25. Arturo Escobar, *Designs for the Pluriverse: Radical Interdependence, Autonomy, and the Making of Worlds* (Durham, NC: Duke University Press, 2017), 226. In 1967, Horst Rittel was the first to describe design thinking as a multifaceted approach to tackling "wicked problems," defined by the fundamental indeterminacy inherent within the problems faced by design. See, for example, C. West Churchman, "Wicked Problems," *Management Science* 4, no. 14 (December 1967): B-141–42. Design thinking was soon picked up by other disciplines and the business sector as a methodology for problem solving. J. Christopher Jones, *Design Methods: Seeds of Human Futures* (New York: John Wiley & Sons, 1981); Horst W. J. Rittel and Melvin M. Webber, "Dilemmas in a General Theory of Planning" (working paper, Institute of Urban and Regional Development, University of California, Berkeley, November 1972); Richard Buchanan, "Wicked Problems in Design Thinking," *Design Issues* 8, no. 2 (Spring 1992): 5–21; Panagiotis Louridas, "Design as Bricolage: Anthropology Meets Design Thinking," *Design Studies* 20, no. 6 (October 1999): 517–35; Anne Rylander, "Design Thinking as Knowledge Work: Epistemological Foundations and Practical Implications," *Design Management Journal* (Fall 2009): 7–19; V. P. Turnbull Hocking, "Designerly Ways of Knowing: What Does Design Have to Offer?," in *Tackling Wicked Problems through the Transdisciplinary Imagination*, ed. Valerie Brown et al. (London: Earthscan, 2010), 242–50.

26. This trend includes the report issued by the US Department of Justice, Civil Rights Division, titled *The Ferguson Report: Department of Justice Investigation of the Ferguson Police Department* (New York: New Press, 2015). This report was released online by the Department of Justice on March 4, 2015, https://www.justice.gov/sites/default/files/opa/pressreleases/attachments/2015/03/04/ferguson_police_department_report.pdf.

27. This conclusion is based on a review of the data regarding demographics and municipal court citations between 2004 and 2014.

28. Saidiya Hartman, *Venus in Two Acts* (Bloomington: Indiana University Press, 2008), 4.

29. See the discussion of choreopolitics in chapter 6, which borrows from André Lepecki's "Choreopolice and Choreopolitics: Or, the Task of the Dancer," *TDR: The Drama Review* 57, no. 4 (Winter 2013): 13–27.

30. Fred Moten, "Blackness and Nothingness: (Mysticism in the Flesh)," *South Atlantic Quarterly* 112, no. 4 (Fall 2013): 737–80.

31. Cedric J. Robinson, *Black Marxism: The Making of the Black Radical Tradition* (Chapel Hill: University of North Carolina Press, 2000), 171.

32. Hartman, *Scenes of Subjection*.

33. Frank B. Wilderson III, "The Prison Slave as Hegemony's (Silent) Scandal," *Social Justice* 30, no. 2 (2003): 18.

34. Wilderson, 18.

35. Wilderson, 32.

36. Raúl Fornet-Betancourt et al., "The Ethic of Care for the Self as a Practice of Freedom: An Interview with Michel Foucault on January 20, 1984," *Philosophy & Social Criticism* 12, no. 2–3 (July 1987): 112–31.

1. RACE AND SPACE

1. Saidya Hartman, *Scenes of Subjection: Terror, Slavery, and Self-Making in Nineteenth-Century America* (New York: Oxford University Press, 1997), 116.

2. Emmanuel Chukwudi Eze, ed., *Race and the Enlightenment: A Reader* (Malden, MA: Blackwell, 1999).

3. Georg Wilhelm Friedrich Hegel, "Geographical Basis of World History," in Eze, 110–49.

4. Eze, 142.

5. Hanna Arendt writes about the rightless condition of belonging nowhere in the world in *The Origins of Totalitarianism* (New York: Harcourt, Brace, Jovanovich, 1973). Georgio Agamben has further theorized political violence in its extreme as the total exclusion from legal protections and thus from personhood. *Homo Sacer: Sovereign Power and Bare Life*, trans. Daniel Heller-Roazen (Palo Alto, CA: Stanford University Press, 1998).

6. This phenomenon is discussed later in the chapter.

7. Sylvia Wynter, "Unsettling the Coloniality of Being/Power/Truth/Freedom: Towards the Human, after Man, Its Overrepresentation—an Argument," *CR: The New Centennial Review* 3, no. 3 (2003): 287–88.

8. Interview with city official, April 10, 2008.

9. Immediately following the Civil War, the federal government under a Republican-led Congress helped to establish coalition governance in the South in order to amend state constitutions and pass legislation ensuring civil rights for all Black citizens as part of the terms of reentry into the Union by southern states, a process known as Reconstruction. White backlash, including lynchings carried out by the Ku Klux Klan, led to legislative takeover by the Democratic Party and the passage of segregationist policies known as Jim Crow laws in the South. The removal of federal troops from the South through the Compromise of 1877 solidified the defeat of abolition democracy. Black migration to northern cities following the war also led to formal and informal policies and practices in the North that confined Black residents to crowded and subpar urban spaces.

10. Loïc Wacquant discusses the emergence of the Black American ghetto of the Fordist United States in relationship to histories of the ghetto as a space of ethnic containment in "A Janus-Faced Institution of Ethnoracial Closure: A Sociological Specification of the Ghetto," in *The Ghetto: Contemporary Global Issues and Controversies*, ed. Ray Hutchison and Bruce D. Haynes (Boulder, CO: Westview Press, 2012), 1–32.

11. Lee D. Baker, *Anthropology and the Racial Politics of Culture* (Durham, NC: Duke University Press, 2010), 4.

12. An in-depth analysis of the influence and consequences of the work of Franz Boas can be found in Baker, *Anthropology*.

13. Ruth Benedict, *Race: Science and Politics* (New York: Modern Age Books, 1940), 154.

14. W. E. B. Du Bois delivered his speech "The Conservation of Races" to the organizational meeting of the American Negro Academy on March 5, 1897. The speech reinforced his support of Alexander Crummell as the first president of the academy and was a refutation of Frederick Douglass's assimilationist discourse. The speech echoed Crummell's belief that a return to the culture of preslavery African civilization would uplift the entire race with the help of an elite group of leaders. Du Bois would formalize his notion of the "talented tenth" in an essay of the same name in 1903. W. E. B. Du Bois, "The Conservation of Races," in *Oxford W. E. B. Du Bois Reader*, ed. Eric J. Sundquist

(Oxford: Oxford University Press, 1996), 38–47; W. E. B. Du Bois, "The Talented Tenth," in *The Negro Problem: A Series of Articles by Representative American Negroes of To-day* (New York: J. Pott, 1903), 33–75.

15. Anne McClintock, *Imperial Leather: Race, Gender, and Sexuality in the Colonial Contest* (New York: Routledge, 1995).

16. W. E. B. Du Bois, *The Philadelphia Negro: A Social Study* (Philadelphia: University of Pennsylvania Press, 1996).

17. Du Bois.

18. Robert E. Park, Ernest W. Burgess, and Roderick D. McKenzie, *The City: Suggestions for Investigation of Human Behavior in the Urban Environment* (Chicago: Chicago University Press, 1925).

19. Scholars such as David Roediger and George Lipsitz have traced how ethnic European and Jewish immigrants to the United States became part of white society in the nineteenth and twentieth centuries through spatial means and in contrast to the racialization of Black space. See, for example, David Roediger, *The Wages of Whiteness: Race and the Making of the American Working Class* (New York: Verso, 1991); David Roediger, *Working toward Whiteness: How America's Immigrants Became White* (New York: Basic Books, 2006); George Lipsitz, *The Possessive Investment in Whiteness: How White People Benefit from Identity Politics* (Philadelphia: Temple University Press, 2006.

20. Ernest W. Burgess, "The Growth of the City: An Introduction to a Research Project," in Park, Burgess, and McKenzie, *The City*, 56.

21. Lewis Mumford, "What Is a City?," in *The City Reader*, ed. Richard T. LeGates and Frederick Stout (New York: Routledge, 1996), 183–96. The maxim "form follows function" is credited to the early modernist architect Louis Sullivan.

22. The urban planning policies carried out by Robert Moses in the tri-borough area of New York City are a good example of this approach. For discussions regarding the politics behind differing views of urban planning in New York City during the Moses era, see Hilary Ballon and Kenneth T. Jackson, eds., *Robert Moses and the Modern City: The Transformation of New York* (New York: W. W. Norton, 2008).

23. Louis Wirth, "Urbanism as a Way of Life," *American Journal of Sociology* 44, no. 1 (1938): 1–24.

24. Sir Ebenezer Howard published *To-morrow: A Peaceful Path to Real Reform* in 1898 in the United Kingdom, initiating his theory of the garden city—a cluster of low-density radiating plans that incorporated housing, industry, and agriculture. The Garden City movement that followed Howard's ideas influenced planning in the United States at the turn of the twentieth century and contributed to what was a growing disdain for urban space and people throughout the century to come.

25. For a discussion of how nature came to signify whiteness (against the urban setting and its dark-complected peoples) in the nineteenth and twentieth centuries, see Iyko Day, *Alien Capital: Asian Racialization and the Logic of Settler Colonial Capital* (Durham, NC: Duke University Press, 2016).

26. E. Franklin Frazier, *The Negro Family in the United States* (Notre Dame, IN: University of Notre Dame, 1939).

27. For an in-depth discussion regarding the contributions of Frazier's work, see Anthony M. Platt, *E. Franklin Frazier Reconsidered* (New Brunswick, NJ: Rutgers University Press, 1991).

28. Oliver C. Cox, *Caste, Class and Race: A Study in Social Dynamics* (New York: Monthly Review Press, 1959), xxxi.

29. W. E. B. Du Bois, "The Concept of Race," in *Dusk of Dawn* (New Brunswick, NJ: Transaction, 2011).

30. Aimé Césaire, *Discourse on Colonialism*, trans. Joan Pinkham (New York: Monthly Review Press, 2000), 89.

31. Frantz Fanon, "On National Culture," in *The Wretched of the Earth*, trans. C. Farrington (New York: Grove Weidenfeld Press, 1991).

32. Fanon, 233.

33. Anna Julia Cooper, *A Voice from the South* (Mineola, NY: Dover Publications, 2016).

34. Ula Y. Taylor, *The Veiled Garvey: The Life and Times of Amy Jacques Garvey* (Chapel Hill: University of North Carolina Press, 2003), 2.

35. Oscar Lewis's ethnography *Five Families: Mexican Case Studies in the Culture of Poverty* was published in 1959 and argued that generations of poverty create cultural distinctions that preclude individuals and groups from escaping the underclass. Lewis later wrote on Puerto Rican culture in Puerto Rico and New York, arguing essentially the same point. See also Oscar Lewis, "The Culture of Poverty," *Scientific American* 215, no. 4 (October 1966): 19–25. For Moynihan's report, see Office of Policy, Planning, and Research, US Department of Labor, *The Negro Family: The Case For National Action* (Washington, DC: US Government Printing Office, 1965).

36. In his State of the Union address of 1964, Lyndon Johnson declared a "war on poverty," which was intended to introduce his platform for broad legislation aimed at "curing and preventing" the causes of poverty rather than responding to its effects.

37. Moynihan lays out this argument in chapter 4 of the report, titled "The Tangle of Pathology," which begins with a section on the problems of Negro "Matriarchy."

38. Office of Policy, Planning, and Research, US Department of Labor, *Negro Family*, 18.

39. Jonathan Metzl, *The Protest Psychosis: How Schizophrenia Became a Black Disease* (Boston: Beacon Press, 2011).

40. Four pieces of legislation are considered to be the major policies passed as part of the Johnson administration's war on poverty: (1) the Social Security Act Amendments of 1965, which created Medicare and Medicaid and expanded Social Security benefits for several vulnerable groups; (2) the Food Stamp Act of 1964, which formalized the temporary food stamp program already in place; (3) the Economic Opportunity Act of 1964, establishing the Job Corps, VISTA program, and several other programs including federal work-study for college students and Head Start for children in pre-K; (4) the Elementary and Secondary Education Act of 1965, which created Title I subsidies for school districts educating impoverished students and other education-focused programs.

41. Dan Baum, "Legalize It All: How to Win the War on Drugs," *Harper's Magazine*, April 2016, 1, http://harpers.org/archive/2016/04/legalize-it-all/1/. The epigraph is from Dan Baum's 1994 interview with John Ehrlichman, one of Nixon's top advisors. Baum interviewed Ehrlichman in 1994 while researching his book *Smoke and Mirrors: The War on Drugs and the Politics of Failure* (Boston: Little, Brown and Company, 1996).

42. Ruth Wilson Gilmore, *Golden Gulag: Prisons, Surplus, Crisis, and Opposition in Globalizing California* (Berkeley: University of California Press, 2007). See also Jordan Camp, *Incarcerating the Crisis: Freedom Struggles and the Rise of the Neoliberal State* (Berkeley: University of California Press, 2016); Naomi Murakawa, *The First Civil Right: How Liberals Built Prison America* (Oxford: Oxford University Press, 2016); Elizabeth Hinton, *From the War on Poverty to the War on Crime: The Making of Mass Incarceration in America* (Cambridge, MA: Harvard University Press, 2016).

43. First credited to Orlando Patterson, the concept of social death operates as an important frame for many scholars who study processes of racialization and the intelligibility of personhood. Orlando Patterson, *Slavery and Social Death: A Comparative Study* (Cambridge, MA: Harvard University Press, 1982); Sharon Patricia Holland, *Raising the Dead: Readings of Death and (Black) Subjectivity* (Durham, NC: Duke University Press, 2000); Ruth Wilson Gilmore, "Fatal Couplings of Power and Difference: Notes on Racism

and Geography," *Professional Geographer* 54, no. 1 (February 2002): 15–24; Lisa Marie Cacho, *Social Death: Racialized Rightlessness and the Criminalization of the Unprotected* (New York: New York University Press, 2012).

44. Cited in Hinton, *From the War on Poverty to the War on Crime*, 308.

45. The term *prison industrial complex* is derived from, and related to, the earlier term *military industrial complex*, famously used by President Eisenhower to describe the link between corporate interests and government policy in expanding military presence and spending. Angela Davis states that "taking into account the structural similarities of business-government linkages in the realms of military production and public punishment, the expanding penal system can now be characterized as a 'prison industrial complex.'" "Masked Racism: Reflections on the Prison Industrial Complex," *Color Lines*, September 10, 1998.

46. For an in-depth discussion of the criminalization of Black women and welfare reform discourse, see Ange-Marie Hancock, *The Politics of Disgust: The Public Identity of the Welfare Queen* (New York: New York University Press, 2004).

47. The most important funding sources that community development agencies could tap were the Community Development Block Grant (1974), the Low Income Housing Tax Credit (1986), and funds from the National Affordable Housing Act (1990). These and other tools were also misused to aid developers, with little impact on low-income communities. The tax increment financing incentive is one example of a tool that can easily be redirected away from its intended use.

48. Mary C. Comerio, "Pruitt-Igoe and Other Stories," *Journal of Architectural Education* 34, no. 4 (1981): 26–31; Katharine G. Bristol, "The Pruitt-Igoe Myth," *Journal of Architectural Education* 44, no. 3 (1991): 163–71.

49. Matthew Lassiter and Christopher Niedt argue this point regarding actual suburban diversity in "Suburban Diversity in Postwar America," introduction to special issue, *Journal of Urban History* 39, no. 1 (January 2013): 3–14.

50. Sheryll D. Cashin argues that Black suburbs cannot live up to the suburban ideal, and many Black suburbanites may give up more than they gain by moving to the suburbs. "Middle-Class Black Suburbs and the State of Integration: A Post-integrationist Vision for Metropolitan America," *Cornell Law Review* 86 (2001): 755–67, 771–74. Interviews with Black residents who moved to North St. Louis County in the 1960s and 1970s and a review of St. Louis County property assessment records and US Census tract data reveal that property values and income have steadily fallen when adjusted for inflation over the past forty years.

51. See, for example, William Julius Wilson, *The Truly Disadvantaged: The Inner City, Underclass, and Public Policy* (Chicago: University of Chicago Press, 1987); Elijah Anderson, *Code of the Street: Decency, Violence, and the Moral Life of the Inner City* (New York: Norton, 1999).

52. Michael Omi and Howard Winant, *Racial Formation in the United States: From the 1960's to the 1980's* (New York: Routledge, 1995).

53. P. Khalil Saucier and Tyron P. Woods, "Racial Optimism and the Drag of Thymotics," in *Conceptual Aphasia in Black: Displacing Racial Formation*, ed. P. Khalil Saucier and Tyron P. Woods (Lanham, MD: Lexington Books, 2016), 1–34.

54. Daniel HoSang, Oneka LaBennett, and Laura Pulido, eds., *Racial Formation in the Twenty-First Century* (Berkeley: University of California Press, 2012); Eduardo Bonilla-Silva, "More than Prejudice: Restatement, Reflections, and New Directions in Critical Race Theory," *Sociology of Race and Ethnicity* 1, no. 1 (2015): 75–89; Eduardo Bonilla-Silva, "Rethinking Racism: Toward a Structural Interpretation," *American Sociological Review* 63, no. 3 (1997): 465–80; E. San Juan, *Racial Formations/Critical Transformations: Articulations of Power in Ethnic and Racial Studies in the United States*

(Amherst, NY: Humanity Books, 1994); João H. Costa Vargas, *The Denial of Antiblackness: Multiracial Redemption and Black Suffering* (Minneapolis: University of Minnesota Press, 2018); Joe Feagin and Sean Elias, "Rethinking Racial Formation Theory: A Systemic Racism Critique," *Ethnic and Racial Studies* 36, no. 6 (2013): 931–60; James Thomas, "Affect and the Sociology of Race: A Program for Critical Inquiry," *Ethnicities* 14, no. 1 (February 2014): 74.

55. See, for example, Barnor Hesse, "Counter-racial Formation Theory" (vii–xii), Greg Thomas, "No Reprieve: The 'Racial Formation' of the United States as a Settler-Colonial Empire (Black Power, White-Sociology and Omi and Winant, Revisited)" (35–50), and Tamara K. Nopper, "Strangers to the Economy: Black Work and the Wages of Non-blackness" (87–102), in Saucier and Woods, *Conceptual Aphasia in Black*.

56. Saucier and Woods, "Racial Optimism and the Drag of Thymotics," 10.

57. Saucier and Woods, "Racial Optimism and the Drag of Thymotics," 13.

58. Saucier and Woods, "Racial Optimism and the Drag of Thymotics," 12.

59. See, for example, Kim Moody, *Workers in a Lean World* (New York: Verso, 1997), 119–20; James Ferguson and Akhil Gupta, "Spatializing States: Toward an Ethnography of Neoliberal Governmentality," *American Ethnologist* 29, no. 4 (November 2002): 981–1002; David Harvey, *A Brief History of Neoliberalism* (Oxford: Oxford University Press, 2007).

60. See, for example, David Harvey, *The Condition of Postmodernity* (Malden, MA: Blackwell, 1990); Fredric Jameson, *Postmodernism, or, The Cultural Logic of Late Capitalism* (Durham, NC: Duke University Press, 1992); Michael Hardt and Antonio Negri, *Labor of Dionysus: A Critique of the State-Form* (Minneapolis: University of Minnesota Press, 1994).

61. See, for example, Neil Smith, *The Urban Frontier: Gentrification and the Revanchist City* (New York: Routledge, 1996); Manuel Castells and Alan Sheridan, *The Urban Question: A Marxist Approach* (Oxford: Oxford University Press, 1981); David Harvey, "From Managerialism to Entrepreneurialism: The Transformation in Urban Governance in Late Capitalism," *Human Geography* 71, no. 1 (1989): 3–17; Mike Davis, *Beyond Blade Runner: Urban Control and the Ecology of Fear* (Vancouver: Open Media, 1992); Edward Soja, *Postmodern Geographies: The Reassertion of Space in Critical Social Theory* (London: Verso Press, 1989); Stuart Hall, et al., *Policing the Crisis: Mugging, the State and Law and Order* (London: Palgrave Macmillan, 2013); Paul Gilroy, *There Ain't No Black in the Union Jack: The Cultural Politics of Race and Nation* (Chicago: University of Chicago Press, 1987).

62. Cedric J. Robinson, *Black Marxism: The Making of the Black Radical Tradition* (Chapel Hill: University of North Carolina Press, 2000).

63. See, for example, Edward Said, *Orientalism* (New York: Vintage Books, 1979); Homi Bhaba, *The Location of Culture* (New York: Routledge, 1994); Gayatri Spivak, *In Other Worlds: Essays in Cultural Politics* (York, UK: Methuen Books, 1987); Ngũgĩ wa Thiong'o, *Decolonizing the Mind: The Politics of Language in African Literature* (Portsmouth, NH: Heinemann Press, 1987); Achille Mbembe, "Provisional Notes on the Postcolony," *Journal of the International African Institute* 62, no. 1 (1992): 3–37.

64. For example, Patricia Hill Collins conceptualized the "matrix of domination"—comprising race, class, and gender—as interlocking systems of oppression. *Black Feminist Thought: Knowledge, Consciousness, and the Politics of Empowerment* (Boston: Unwin Hyman, 1990).

65. David Theo Goldberg, *The Threat of Race: Reflections on Racial Neoliberalism* (Oxford: Wiley-Blackwell, 2009).

66. Costa Vargas, *Denial of Antiblackness*.

67. Charles Tiebout has been cited as theorizing the far end of the spectrum of localism in the 1950s. He first laid out his public choice model in "A Pure Theory of Local Expenditures," in which he argues that citizens are actually consumers who vote with their feet and force municipalities into a healthy competition for ideal residents who choose among various packages of taxes and services. *Journal of Political Economy* 64, no. 5 (October 1956): 416–24. The legal scholar Gerald Frug is largely credited with reframing the localism debate in the 1990s, arguing that increased democratic participation, community building, and efficiency occur when local governments are given more, rather than less, power. Gerald Frug and David J. Barron, *City Bound: How States Stifle Urban Innovation* (Ithaca, NY: Cornell University Press, 2013).

68. Richard Briffault is viewed as one of the major framers of the regionalist argument in the mid-1990s, when he waged a searing critique of localism. Briffault claims that the reason proponents of localism refuse to consider the possibility of a regional scale is purely in order to protect special interests and maintain the status quo for the privileged few at the expense of the many. "Localism and Regionalism" (Columbia Law School, Public Law and Legal Theory Working Paper No. 1, August 1999), http://ssrn.com/abstract=198822. Sheryll Cashin also takes this angle, attacking the arguments for localism point by point and arguing through data that roughly 25 percent of the wealthiest municipalities benefit from, and have power in, fragmented governance, while the other 75 percent are milked of their resources. "Localism, Self-Interest, and the Tyranny of the Favored Quarter: Addressing the Barriers to New Regionalism," *Georgetown Law Review* 88 (2000): 1985–2048.

69. Kelling and Wilson's 1982 article on broken-windows policing, mentioned in the introduction, directly linked space to crime and claimed that lower-order markers of disorder, such as broken windows and trash in vacant lots, lead to more serious crime. This fed into an increase in the passing of local ordinances and zero-tolerance policing, which aggressively ticketed or arrested people for creating spatial disorder. The convergence of broken-windows policy, federal and state government retrenchment, and disinvestment has resulted in cities passing laws making it illegal to do some of the most basic things, such as sleeping, eating, or playing in public. Many laws are aimed at particular groups and cultures. Using George Kelling's extension of the broken-windows theory, the New York City police chief William Bratton, in coordination with then mayor Rudy Giuliani, formalized the most famous example of stop-and-frisk policing policy. The policy took a broad interpretation of *Terry v. Ohio* (1968), in which the US Supreme Court ruled that individuals' Fourth Amendment rights are not violated when a police officer stops them without probable cause if he or she suspects them of past, present, or future criminal activity. While most associated with post-1990s New York City, the practice was not new and became common across the United States, resulting in well-known coinages regarding the criminalization of basic activities carried out by people of color, such as "driving while Black" or "walking while Brown."

70. NAACP, Criminal Justice Fact Sheet, http://www.naacp.org/pages/criminal-justice-fact-sheet. The 1994 crime bill, or Violent Crime Control and Law Enforcement Act, reinforced the popular "tough on crime" idea that the solution to crime is stricter policing and harsher punishments. Two years later, the Clinton administration passed the Personal Responsibility and Work Opportunity Reconciliation Act, which, as its title suggests, promoted the idea that poverty is caused by lack of personal responsibility. The bipartisan rhetoric around the legislation used tropes of the Black welfare queen to build support for the bill and represented thirty years of discourse around the culture-of-poverty thesis.

71. Hinton, *From the War on Poverty to the War on Crime*, 25; Michelle Alexander, *The New Jim Crow: Mass Incarceration in the Age of Colorblindness* (New York: New

224   NOTES TO PAGES 41–42

Press, 2012). Elizabeth Hinton's quote challenges Alexander's claim that the current era of mass incarceration in a colorblind society is a return to the old Jim Crow era. Instead, Hinton claims that a new era of "urban insecurity" has entered the global stage and that despite its historical background, this era must be understood in its own terms.

72. John R. Logan and Harvey L. Molotch lay out the factors and processes for understanding the political economy of place based on Marxist political economy in *Urban Fortunes: The Political Economy of Place* (Berkeley: University of California Press, 1987). Logan and Molotch build on David Harvey's reading of the city as a contested site of labor and capital that produces real and imagined social and physical spaces. David Harvey, *Social Justice and the City* (London: Edward Arnold, 1973). For a discussion regarding processes of environmental racism, see Rob Nixon, *Slow Violence and the Environmentalism of the Poor* (Cambridge, MA: Harvard University Press, 2011).

2. CONFLUENCE AND CONTESTATION

1. The research that went into this chapter made use of many historical archives cited throughout the text; however, I also relied on an extensive analysis of the many histories already written about St. Louis. Some of the secondary sources are more reliable and respected than others; nevertheless, a comparative use of these histories, taking into account when they were written and how they were framed, proved very helpful to this narrative. The secondary sources I consulted for this chapter include the following: Adam Arenson, *The Great Heart of the Republic: St. Louis and the Cultural Civil War* (Cambridge, MA: Harvard University Press, 2011); Thomas Barclay, *The St. Louis Home Rule Charter of 1876: Its Framing and Adoption* (Columbia: University of Missouri Press, 1962); Henry W. Berger, *St. Louis and Empire: 250 Years of Imperial Quest and Urban Crisis* (Carbondale: Southern Illinois University Press, 2015); Shirley Christian, *Before Lewis and Clark: The Story of the Chouteaus, the French Dynasty That Ruled America's Frontier* (Lincoln: University of Nebraska Press, 2004); Cyprian Clamorgan, *The Colored Aristocracy of St. Louis*, ed. Julie Winch (Columbia: University of Missouri Press, 1999); Patricia Cleary, *The World, the Flesh, and the Devil: A History of Colonial St. Louis* (Columbia: University of Missouri Press, 2011); Robert A. Cohn, *The History and Growth of St. Louis County*, 6th ed. (St. Louis: St. Louis County Office of Public Information, 1974); J. Frederick Fausz, *Founding St. Louis: First City of the New West* (Charleston, SC: History Press, 2011); Louis S. Gerteis, *Civil War St. Louis* (Lawrence: University of Kansas Press, 2001); McCune Gill, *The St. Louis Story* (St. Louis: Historical Record Association, 1952); Colin Gordon, *Mapping Decline: St. Louis and the Fate of the American City* (Philadelphia: University of Philadelphia Press, 2008); Nini Harris, *A Most Unsettled State: First-Person Accounts of St. Louis during the Civil War* (St. Louis: Reedy Press, 2013); Walter Johnson, *River of Dark Dreams: Slavery and Empire in the Cotton Kingdom* (Cambridge, MA: Harvard University Press, 2013); E. Terrence Jones, *Fragmented by Design: Why St. Louis Has So Many Governments* (St. Louis: Palmerston and Reed, 2000); Elizabeth Keckley, *Behind the Scenes: Or, Thirty Years a Slave and Four Years in the White House* (Rockville, MD: Wildside Press, 2015); Gary R. Kremer, *Race and Meaning: The African American Experience in Missouri* (Columbia: University of Missouri Press, 2014); Clarence Lang, *Grassroots at the Gateway: Class Politics and Black Freedom Struggle in St. Louis 1936–1975* (Ann Arbor: University of Michigan Press, 2009); George Lipsitz, *The Sidewalks of St. Louis: Places, People, and Politics in an American City* (Columbia: University of Missouri, 1991); John Francis McDermott, ed., *The Early Histories of St. Louis* (St. Louis: St. Louis Historical Documents Foundation, 1952); John Francis McDermott, ed., *The Spanish in the Mississippi Valley, 1762–1804* (Edwardsville: Southern Illinois University Press, 1974); Charles E. Peterson, *Colonial St. Louis: Building a Creole Capital* (Tucson, AZ: Patrice Press, 1993); James Neal

Primm, *Lion of the Valley: St. Louis Missouri* (Boulder, CO: Pruett, 1981); Eric Sandweiss, *St. Louis: The Evolution of an American Urban Landscape* (Philadelphia: Temple University Press, 2001); Lee Ann Sandweiss, ed., *Seeking St. Louis: Voices from a River City, 1670–2000* (St. Louis: Missouri Historical Society Press, 2000); Thomas M. Spencer, ed., *The Other Missouri History: Populists, Prostitutes, and Regular Folk* (Columbia: University of Missouri Press, 2004); Amos Stoddard, *Sketches of Louisiana: Historical and Descriptive* (Carlisle, MA: Applewood Books, 2010); Solomon Sutker and Sara Smith Sutker, *Racial Transition in the Inner Suburb: Studies of the St. Louis Area* (New York: Praeger Press, 1974); William L. Thomas, *The History of St. Louis County Missouri: The Story Told 100 Years Ago* (Clayton, MO: County Living, 2011); Jo Ann Trogdon, *The Unknown Travels and Dubious Pursuits of William Clark* (Columbia: University of Missouri, 2015); Julie Winch, *The Clamorgans: One Family's History of Race in America* (New York: Hill and Wang, 2011); John A. Wright Sr., *St. Louis: Disappearing Black Communities* (Charleston, SC: Arcadia, 2004); John A. Wright Sr., *Kinloch: Missouri's First Black City* (Charleston, SC: Arcadia, 2000).

2. Auguste Chouteau, "Testimony before the Recorder of Land Titles, St. Louis, 1825," in McDermott, *Early Histories of St. Louis*, 91–93.

3. The territory directly across the Mississippi River from St. Louis, which had also been held by France, was ceded to Great Britain at the same time.

4. John Francis McDermott, "The Myth of the 'Imbecile Governor': Captain Fernando de Leyba and the Defense of St. Louis in 1780," in McDermott, *The Spanish in the Mississippi Valley*, 328.

5. "Census," website of the St. Louis Genealogical Society, last modified June 30, 2016, http://stlgs.org/research-2/government/census.

6. Luis de Unzaga to Pedro Piernas, 1770, in Lawrence Kinnaird, ed., *Spain in the Mississippi Valley, 1765–1794, Annual Report of the American Historical Association for the Year 1945* (Washington, DC: US Government Printing Office, 1946), 190.

7. Amos Stoddard, "State of Slavery in St. Louis," in *Sketches of Louisiana*, 331–43.

8. Stoddard, 332.

9. Stoddard.

10. Stoddard, 333.

11. Eric Sandweiss, *St. Louis*.

12. McDermott, *Early Histories of St. Louis*.

13. Stuart Banner, "Written Law and Unwritten Norms in Colonial St. Louis," *Law and History Review* 14, no. 1 (1996): 38.

14. Banner.

15. Banner.

16. Fausz, *Founding St. Louis*, 148–50.

17. Fausz, 188.

18. See, for example, Johnson, *River of Dark Dreams*.

19. Hereafter, I refer to John Baptiste Lucas as J. B. C. Lucas, which is how he is known in this region today.

20. Eric Sandweiss, *St. Louis*, 30.

21. Eric Sandweiss, 31.

22. *St. Louis County, Missouri Fact Book, St. Louis County Research and Statistics Division* (Clayton, MO: St. Louis County Planning Department, 2012), ii.

23. Amos Stoddard, "Address to the People of Upper Louisiana: March 10, 1804," in Lee Anne Sandweiss, *Seeking St. Louis*, 36.

24. Peter S. Onuf, "Empire for Liberty," in Christine Daniels and Michael V. Kennedy, *Negotiated Empires* (Philadelphia: Routledge, 2002), 302, quoted in Fausz, *Founding St. Louis*, 189.

25. William E. Foley, "Slave Freedom Suits before Dred Scott: The Case of Marie Jean Scypion's Descendants," *Missouri Historical Review* 79, no. 1 (October 1984): 1–23. See also J. B. C. Lucas 1806 Notes, box 3, Lucas Papers, Missouri Historical Society.

26. Foley, "Slave Freedom Suits before Dred Scott."

27. Foley.

28. I will return to this discussion in chapters 3 and 4.

29. Foley, "Slave Freedom Suits before Dred Scott."

30. Thomas Jefferson to John Holmes, April 22, 1820, in *Thomas Jefferson*, online exhibition, Library of Congress, https://www.loc.gov/exhibits/jefferson/159.html.

31. This account is based on historical narratives in box 14, folders 1–18, Normandy Area Historical Association Archives, including "A History of Normandy"; "A History of Greendale"; "Capsules of Normandy History"; Pine Lawn (History)"; "A Tribute to Bellerive Acres"; Robert Hereford, "History of Normandy," February 23, 1946; Ward Barnes, "The Story of Normandy"; "Normandy History Has Colorful Background," *Community Journal*, August 3, 1966.

32. Box 14, folders 1–18, Normandy Area Historical Association Archives.

33. Box 14, folders 1–18, Normandy Area Historical Association Archives.

34. Box 14, folders 1–18, Normandy Area Historical Association Archives.

35. Dred Scott v. Sanford, 60 U.S. 393 (1857).

36. Plessy v. Ferguson, 163 U.S. 537 (1896).

37. Quoted in Berger, *St. Louis and Empire*, 29.

38. Clamorgan, *Colored Aristocracy of St. Louis*, 45–46.

39. Clamorgan, 47.

40. William W. Brown, *Narrative of William W. Brown, a Fugitive Slave* (Boston: Anti-Slavery Office, 1847).

41. Brown, 83.

42. Janet S. Herman, "The McIntosh Affair," Missouri Historical Society Bulletin 26 (January 1970), 126, quoted in Harriet C. Frazier, *Lynchings in Missouri, 1803–1981* (Jefferson, NC: McFarland, 2009), 24.

43. Abraham Lincoln, "The Perpetuation of Our Political Institutions: Address before the Young Men's Lyceum of Springfield, Illinois," January 27, 1838, Abraham Lincoln Online, accessed April 18, 2019, http://www.abrahamlincolnonline.org/lincoln/speeches/lyceum.htm.

44. See, for example, Charles Lumpkins, *American Pogrom: The East St. Louis Race Riot and Black Politics* (Athens: Ohio University Press, 2008).

45. Mary E. Seematter, "Trials and Confessions: Race and Justice in Antebellum St. Louis," *Gateway Heritage* 12 (1991): 36; Harriet C. Frazier, *Slavery and Crime in Missouri, 1773–1865* (Jefferson, NC: McFarland, 2001), 219–22.

46. Emily August provides a detailed account of these hangings and insightful analysis regarding the spectacular nature of Black suffering that simultaneously obscures the Black body, in "Cadaver Poetics: Surgical Medicine and the Reinvention of the Body in the Nineteenth Century" (PhD diss., Vanderbilt University, 2014).

47. US Census Bureau, *1870 Census: The Statistics of the Population of the United States,* Missouri, table 3 (Washington, DC: Government Printing Office, 1872), 194.

48. St. Louis Home Rule Charter of 1876, *Missouri Republican*, August 6, 1876, 2.

49. The 1870s saw a series of labor strikes and agreements across the United States that, to some extent, brought Black and white workers together against industrial management. The Great Southwest Strike of 1876 was a railroad strike involving the Knights of Labor against Jay Gould's railroad empire in Texas, Arkansas, Missouri, Kansas, and Illinois. The following year, the Great Railroad Strike of 1877 culminated in the 1877 St. Louis general strike, which galvanized workers across the city. It was ended when an

estimated eight thousand troops and police killed at least eighteen people and imprisoned the leaders. Cumulatively, these strikes resulted in a considerable backlash against organized labor and renewed efforts to racialize labor organizing.

50. The character of the Veiled Prophet of Khorassan comes from the Irish poet Thomas Moore, who wrote a poem by the same name published in his book, *Lalla Rookh* (1817), which depicts a Persian romance.

51. See, for example, Lucy Ferriss, *Unveiling the Prophet* (Columbia: University of Missouri Press, 2005); Thomas M. Spencer, *The St. Louis Veiled Prophet Celebration: Power on Parade* (Columbia: University of Missouri Press, 2000).

52. Ferriss, *Unveiling the Prophet.*

53. Lang, *Grassroots at the Gateway,* 241. Civic Progress, to which Lang refers, is an exclusive organization composed solely of executives from the city's top corporations whose mission is to achieve "world status" for the city of St. Louis. It has been criticized as prioritizing the needs of the city's most privileged residents.

54. In an article based on interviews with representatives from Missourians Organizing for Reform and Empowerment, *Feministing* reported, "[MORE] is targeting the Veiled Prophet Organization in its inaugural #UnveilTheProfitweek of action to expose the 'power behind the police'—the corporate executives, developers, bankers, and others who shape (and profit from) people's lives in Ferguson and beyond." Dana Bolger, "Removing the Mask: Ferguson Organizers Expose Veiled Profit in St. Louis," *Feministing,* 2015, http://feministing.com/2015/07/02/removing-the-mask-ferguson-organizers-expose-veiled-profit-in-st-louis/.

55. Henry J. Schmandt, "Municipal Home Rule in Missouri," *Washington University Law Quarterly,* vol. 4 (1953): 385–412.

56. Mo. Const. of 1945, art. VI, § 19(a). This is Missouri's fourth and current constitution.

57. The city has unsuccessfully attempted to rejoin the county four times since 1876. For a discussion of merger plans, see Peter W. Salsich Jr. and Samantha Caluori, "Can St. Louis City and County Get Back Together? (Do Municipal Boundaries Matter Today?)," *St. Louis University Public Law Review* 34, no. 13 (2014): 13–50.

58. Annie L. Y. Orff, "From City to Suburb: A Glimpse of the Beautiful Spot in the Shadow of St. Louis," *Chaperone Magazine* (1893): 69–71.

59. Wright, *St. Louis.*

60. "Lots White Men Buy Doubled in Price to Negroes," *St. Louis Post-Dispatch,* January 24, 1917.

61. "Lots White Men Buy Doubled in Price to Negroes."

62. *Argus,* circa 1915, Missouri Historical Society Library.

63. Harold M. Rose, "The All-Negro Town: Its Evolution and Function," in *Black America: Geographic Perspectives,* ed. Robert Ernst and Lawrence Hugg (Garden City, NY: Anchor Press, 1976), 352–67.

64. *1960 Census of Population, Advance Report,* Missouri, table 3, (US Census Bureau: December 2, 1960), 23; *2010 Census of Population and Housing Units: 1990 to 2010,* Missouri, table 9, (US Census Bureau: September 2012), 72.

65. Wm. K. Bixby to unnamed neighbors, February 5, 1915, http://mappingdecline. lib.uiowa.edu/_includes/documents/rp_doc6.pdf. This letter can be found in the documents section of the website for Colin Gordon's book *Mapping Decline.*

66. Buchanan v. Warley, 245 U.S. 60 (1916), ruling November 5, 1917.

67. Shelley v. Kraemer, 334 U.S. 1 (1948). This Supreme Court ruling, which originated in St. Louis, rendered racially restrictive housing covenants unenforceable in state courts.

68. Gordon, *Mapping Decline.*

69. I discuss this process in Jodi Rios, "Everyday Racialization: Contesting Space and Identity in Suburban St. Louis," in *Making Suburbia: New Histories of Everyday America*, ed. John Archer, Paul J. P. Sandul, and Katherine Solomonson (Ann Arbor: University of Michigan Press, 2015), 185–207.

70. See David R. Roediger's study regarding the formation of white working-class racism in the United States and specifically his discussion of Irish-American white racial formation in David Roediger, *The Wages of Whiteness: Race and the Making of the American Working Class* (New York: Verso, 1991), 133–66. See also George Lipsitz's discussion of labor politics and the relationality of identities in *The Possessive Investment in Whiteness: How White People Benefit from Identity Politics* (Philadelphia: Temple University Press, 2006), 48–69.

71. John Keaser, "The Town That Started from Scratch: How City Fathers of Bellefontaine Neighbors Guided It from Dormant Village of 766 Persons to Population of 5200 in 18 Short Months," *St. Louis Post-Dispatch*, April 20, 1952.

72. This observation is based on interviews with St. Louis residents and my own experience of living in the region for twenty years.

73. E. Terrence Jones looks at this phenomenon in *Fragmented by Design*.

74. "Warnings on Sales of Jennings Homes in Panic," *St. Louis Post-Dispatch*, January 10, 1964.

75. "Warnings on Sales of Jennings Homes in Panic."

76. "Negro Guarded in Bomb Threats," *Philadelphia Inquirer*, January 9, 1964.

77. "Normandy's Black History," oral history, Normandy Historical Society Archives, Missouri Historical Society Library.

78. Section 235 of the Fair Housing Act shifted funding from public housing projects to subsidies in the private housing market. Studies have shown that white homebuyers were able to use subsidies to buy new housing in the outer suburbs while Black homebuyers were limited to buying older housing stock in the inner-ring suburbs. See, for example, Kevin Fox Gotham, "Separate and Unequal: The Housing Act of 1968 and the Section 235 Program," *Sociological Forum* 15, no. 1 (2000): 13–37.

79. Rick Corry and Tom Dyer, University of Missouri–St. Louis report, *Factors in Suburban Blight: A Study of Housing in Northwoods, Pine Lawn, and Hillsdale* (June 1973); Normandy Municipal Council report, *Citizens' GOALS Project*, Don Moschenross, director (November 1973); University of Missouri–St. Louis study report, *Households in the Normandy School District*, supervised by Sarah Boggs and E. Terrence Jones (November 1974); Sutker and Sutker, *Racial Transition in the Inner Suburb*; University of Missouri–St. Louis Study report, *Local Government Intervention in the Face of Mortgage Disinvestment: The Case of Normandy*, conducted by Bryan Downes, Joan Saunders, and John Collins, revised working draft, January 1976, box 14, folder 11, archives of the Normandy Municipal Council, Missouri Historical Society Library.

80. See, for example, "Normandy High Gets Tough," *St. Louis Post-Dispatch*, November 28, 1970; Normandy Calm after Warning," *St. Louis Post-Dispatch*, November 30, 1970; "Classes Resume at Normandy High," *St. Louis Globe Democrat*, November 30, 1970; "Normandy High Reopens—Police Patrol Campus," *St. Louis Globe Democrat*, December 1, 1970; "Parents of Blacks at Normandy Meet," *St. Louis Post-Dispatch*, December 7, 1970.

81. Eric L. Zoeckler, "Split on Ending Blockbusting," *St. Louis Post-Dispatch*, November 29, 1973.

82. This account is based on statistics published by the Normandy Municipal Council in a report titled *A Look at the Normandy Area: A Study Compiled for the Normandy Residential Services* (July 1975).

83. Downes, Saunders, and Collins, "Local Government Intervention."

84. See, for example, D. D. Obika, "Beverly Hills Woman Says Realtor Lied about House," *St. Louis Post-Dispatch*, May 7, 1976.

85. For discussions of discrimination practices in mortgage lending, including higher requirements for nonwhite borrowers of Federal Housing Administration and Home Owner's Lending Corporation loans, see Douglas S. Massey et al., "Riding the Stagecoach to Hell: A Qualitative Analysis of Racial Discrimination in Mortgage Lending," *City & Community* 15, no. 2 (June 2016): 118–36; Amy Hillier, "Redlining and the Homeowners' Loan Corporation," *Journal of Urban History* 29, no. 4 (2003): 394–420.

86. Downes, Saunders, and Collins, "Local Government Intervention."

87. Downes, Saunders, and Collins.

88. Tim Fischesser, interview by author, March 10, 2010.

89. Courtney Barrett, "An Alliance of Diversity," *St. Louis Post-Dispatch*, November 30, 1981.

90. Barrett.

91. Barrett.

92. See Sidney Plotkin and William E. Scheuerman, *Private Interest, Public Spending: Balanced-Budget Conservatism and the Fiscal Crisis* (New York: Black Rose, 1994), for a discussion of how every subunit of government has been pitted against every other subunit in response to vase decreases in public funding from federal and state revenues.

93. Better Together report, The Will to Change: Why Does a Region with World-Class Resources Struggle to Thrive? (May 2016), 5, https://static1.squarespace.com/static/59790f03a5790abd8c698c9c/t/5c49665b4fa51a8e6ec61a4a/1548314246674/BT-Will-to-Change-Final.pdf.

94. This overview is based on resident interviews and a review of municipal property tax rates for St. Louis County. Adding to the fierce competition between jurisdictions and the creative measures to raise revenue was the passage of the 1980 Hancock Amendment to the Missouri Constitution, which limits the tax revenue the state can collect from personal income, prevents the state from imposing laws on local governments without funding them, and bars local governments from levying or increasing any tax without voter approval.

95. TIF is the ability to capture and use most of the increased local property tax (and, in Missouri, sales tax) revenues from new development in a defined district for a defined period of time. The cost of the development is paid back after the project is built, making it an attractive development tool. The intended uses of TIF are for the revitalization of depressed areas, to build affordable housing, create jobs, and remediate areas with environmental issues, although these uses are often liberally interpreted.

96. Better Together St. Louis, *Will to Change*, 5.

97. Better Together, Tax Increment Financing Map, accessed January 6, 2017, http://www.bettertogetherstl.com/tax-incremental-financing-map.

98. This conclusion is based on a comparative data analysis of sales tax revenue and revenue generated by court fines and fees, 2005–10.

99. T. E. Lauer, "Prolegomenon to Municipal Court Reform in Missouri," *Missouri Law Review* 31, no. 1 (Winter 1966): 69–97.

100. Lauer, 91.

101. Lauer, 75.

102. Lauer, 77.

103. This conclusion is based on analysis of court records for municipalities in North St. Louis County that show a disproportionate number of citations issued to Black individuals and numerous media articles and segments since the death of Michael Brown Jr., focused on the racial implications of policing in North St. Louis County.

104. Analysis of municipal court records across St. Louis County and the state looking at arrests with jail time and the percent of municipal budget funded through court fines and fees between 1970 and 2015. It should be noted that, although there is a state-wide decrease in these two factors, some small cities across Missouri continue to implement jail time for minor offenses and use predatory policing practices for the funding of municipal budgets.

105. Analysis of St. Louis County municipal court records.

106. These statements are based on a review of municipal ordinances in North St. Louis County, an interview with a municipal alderperson on March 12, 2010, media and witness accounts of the day Michael Brown Jr. died in Ferguson, and the court transcript of the grand jury testimony of Darren Wilson, the police officer who shot Brown.

107. US Department of Justice, Civil Rights Division, *The Ferguson Report: Department of Justice Investigation of the Ferguson Police Department* (New York: New Press, 2015). This report was released online by the Department of Justice on March 4, 2015, https://www.justice.gov/sites/default/files/opa/pressreleases/attachments/2015/03/04/ferguson_police_department_report.pdf.

108. The data and circumstances regarding these practices are discussed in chapter 3.

109. Depending on the source and how boundaries are drawn, the St. Louis region is said to include twelve to seventeen counties. The fifteen counties included in map 2.1 have economies that are highly dependent upon the St. Louis metropolitan area.

110. US Census Bureau, *2012 US Census of Federal, State, and Local Governments*, "Government Facts," accessed January 29, 2019, https://www.census.gov/govs/.

111. US Census Bureau, *2013–2017 American Community Survey 5-Year Estimates—St. Louis City*, "Community Facts," accessed January 29, 2019, https://factfinder.census.gov/faces/nav/jsf/pages/community_facts.xhtml.

112. The numbers in this paragraph were updated in 2019; however, municipal disincorporations and the merging of cities and services continue to occur.

113. US Census Bureau, *2010 Demographic Profile—St. Louis County*, "Community Facts," accessed January 29, 2019, https://factfinder.census.gov/faces/nav/jsf/pages/community_facts.xhtml.

114. US Census Bureau, *1960 Census of Population, Advance Report*, Missouri—Table 3 (December 2, 1960), 23; US Census Bureau, *1980 Census of Population and Housing, Census Tracts, St. Louis, MO.-Ill*—Section1: Table P-7 (July 1983), 140–153.

115. Stated by Thomas Harvey in an interview with the author on November 4, 2014. Harvey was relaying his experience of explaining predatory policing practices in North St. Louis County to leaders at the Southern Poverty Law Center and the responses he received.

3. RACIAL STATES AND LOCAL GOVERNANCE

1. These differences are discussed later in the chapter.

2. See, for example, Walter Johnson, "Ferguson's Fortune 500 Company," *Atlantic*, April 25, 2015.

3. George Lipsitz developed the concept of white and Black spatial imaginaries, which are the historically specific understanding of white space in the United States as separate and distinct from Black space. *How Racism Takes Place* (Philadelphia: Temple University Press, 2011).

4. Michel Foucault, "Michel Foucault: La Justice et la Police," video interview (1977), accessed November 10, 2019, http://www.ina.fr/video/I06277669/michel-foucault-la-justice-et-la-police-video.html, cited in Lepecki, "Choreopolice and Choreopolitics," *The Drama Review* 57, no. 4 (2013): 19.

5. Of the more than one hundred people interviewed randomly over the course of eight years, more than half had been stopped more than eight times for traffic violations, and 40 percent had received a property violation citation. Of those receiving property violations, 90 percent had received between five and ten violations in one year. Of the more than one hundred people interviewed at court nights in sixteen municipalities, more than half had been stopped more than five times while driving in North St. Louis County.

6. Multiple people being held for minor traffic offenses in the last ten years have died by hanging themselves in municipal jails in St. Louis County, including in the towns of Jennings, Pine Lawn, and Pagedale.

7. Interview with North St. Louis County resident.

8. Interview with North St. Louis County resident.

9. Interview with North St. Louis County resident.

10. Interview with municipal judge who spoke on condition of anonymity, August 10, 2015.

11. The original Macks Creek Law (302.241.2 RSMo) set the limit for the amount Missouri cities could collect from fines and fees to 35 percent of the annual general operating revenue of the municipality. A reform bill, House Bill 103, became effective in August 2013 and lowered the amount to 30 percent of the annual general operation revenue.

12. Interview with John Amman, March 13, 2015.

13. Ryan J. Reilly and Mariah Stewart, "How Municipalities in StL County Use Police as Armed Tax Collectors," *St. Louis American*, April 2, 2015.

14. Hall et al. use a Marxist theorization of wagelessness, or the wageless class, as the necessary production of a disposable reserve labor force inherent to capitalist societies. The wageless class, or Black subproletariat, is tied to both the history of slavery and the history of labor in the United States—where surplus labor intersects with racialized rationalizations of wageless labor within slave society. This combination of race and class, which Hall et al. describe as "secondariness," is acutely visible in North St. Louis County, where Black residents experienced few economic advantages in the era of economic growth in the 1990s and early 2000s and have significantly added to the wageless class in the wake of recent economic downturns. Stuart Hall et al., *Policing the Crisis: Mugging, the State and Law and Order* (London: Palgrave Macmillan, 2013).

15. Interviews with North St. Louis County residents.

16. See, for example, Better Together, *Public Safety—Municipal Courts Report* (October 2014); Editorial Board, "The Problem is Bigger than Ferguson," *New York Times*, March 12, 2015; Jennifer Mann, "Municipal Courts Operate in Secret and Work Hard to Keep It That Way," *St. Louis Post-Dispatch*, March 15, 2015; Erica Hellerstein, "'It's racist as hell': Inside St. Louis County's Predatory Night Courts," *ThinkProgress*, April 10, 2015.

17. Missouri Courts, traffic and nontraffic ordinance filings, 2005–15; see, for example, "Annual Judicial and Statistical Reports," accessed May 3, 2019, http://www.courts.mo.gov/page.jsp?id=296.

18. US Department of Justice, Civil Rights Division, *The Ferguson Report: Department of Justice Investigation of the Ferguson Police Department* (New York: New Press, 2015). This report was released online by the Department of Justice on March 4, 2015, https://www.justice.gov/sites/default/files/opa/pressreleases/attachments/2015/03/04/ferguson_police_department_report.pdf.

19. US Department of Justice, 32.

20. US Department of Justice, 20.

21. US Department of Justice. See also Campbell Roberts, "A City Where Policing, Discrimination and Raising Revenue Went Hand in Hand," *New York Times*, March 4, 2015.

22. Data reported to the Missouri state courts by the municipal court of Pine Lawn for 2014 and analyzed by author.

23. Data reported to the Missouri state courts by the municipal court of Ferguson for 2014 and analyzed by author.

24. In 1983, the US Supreme Court ruled that it was unconstitutional to jail someone claiming the inability to pay fines and court fees without holding a hearing to investigate such claims. Bearden v. Georgia, 461 U.S. 660 (1983).

25. This observation is based on court records and interviews with residents of North St. Louis County.

26. Jennifer Mann and Jeremy Kohler, *Municipal Courts: Progress Report*, special publication, *St. Louis Post-Dispatch*, June 20, 2015, http://graphics.stltoday.com/apps/muni-courts/.

27. Thomas v. City of St. Ann, Eastern District of MO (U.S.) 4:16-cv-01302, 78 (2016).

28. Thomas v. City of St. Ann.

29. Interview with North St. Louis County resident.

30. Michael McLaughlin, "St. Louis County Police Fatally Shoot Man Carrying Knife, Bible in Jennings," *Huffington Post*, April 18, 2015.

31. Interviews with North St. Louis County residents.

32. Interview with North St. Louis County resident.

33. Interviews with North St. Louis County residents.

34. Interview with North St. Louis County resident.

35. See, for example, Eyder Peralta and Cheryl Corley, "The Driving Life and Death of Philando Castile," National Public Radio, July 15, 2016, http://www.npr.org/sections/thetwo-way/2016/07/15/485835272/the-driving-life-and-death-of-philando-castile.

36. Interviews with North St. Louis County residents.

37. Interviews with North St. Louis County residents.

38. Interviews with North St. Louis County residents.

39. Interviews with North St. Louis County residents.

40. Interviews with North St. Louis County residents.

41. Review of municipal court dockets, 2013–14.

42. Interviews with North St. Louis County residents.

43. This conclusion is based on a review of the data reported to the Missouri Attorney General's Office.

44. Analysis of municipal records from 2015 reported to the Missouri Attorney General's Office.

45. The Missouri legislature voted on May 12, 2016, to limit the fines cities can charge residents for nontraffic ordinance violations. The new bill also added fines and fees collected from nontraffic violations to the total amount that was capped by Senate Bill 5.

46. This statement, or something similar, was made by more than twenty residents of North St. Louis County during resident interviews.

47. The International Code Council publishes the International Property Maintenance Code for adoption as legally enforced codes by municipalities and associations.

48. The data in this paragraph concerning the city of Normandy were obtained by the author from the Regional Justice Information Service using the Missouri Sunshine Law. The Revised Statutes of Missouri Chapter 610 were signed into the Missouri Constitution in 1973, following the passage of the Freedom of Information Act by the US Congress in 1966. The law expressly states that meetings, records, votes, actions, and deliberations of public governmental bodies are to be open to the public.

49. Interview with municipal leader, April 9, 2012.

50. The information in this paragraph pertaining to population and race is based on data from the US Census Bureau, American Fact Finder, Community Facts, 2010 Demographic Profile, accessed for each city on November 5, 2019, https://factfinder.census.gov/faces/nav/jsf/pages/index.xhtml; the information in this paragraph regarding the percentage of nontraffic violations issued to Black residents is based on my analysis of data requested from the city of Bellerive, which I obtained from the Regional Justice Information Service through invocation of the Missouri Sunshine Law.

51. Hall et al., *Policing the Crisis*.

52. Hall et al., 54.

53. Interviews with public officials and statements made by officials at public meetings between August 2014 and November 2015.

54. Whitner v. City of Pagedale, Eastern District of MO (U.S.) 4:15-cv-01655-RWS (2016), "Deposition of the Honorable Mary Louise Carter," on behalf of the plaintiffs, July 24, 2017.

55. In an interview, the mayor of Normandy, Patrick Green, repeatedly spoke about the right of his city to secure the level of economic advantages and order enjoyed by its more well-to-do counterparts by policing behavior in public space and protecting the value of private property. In independent interviews, Mayor Green of Normandy, Mayor Mary Louise Carter of Pagedale, and Mayor Viola Murphy of Cool Valley all argued that the seemingly excessive amount of fines collected in their cities, as reported in the media, was due to residents' inability to follow the law.

56. On the criminalization of poverty, see, for example, Kaaryn Gustafson, "The Criminalization of Poverty," *Journal of Criminal Law and Criminology* 99, no. 3 (2009): 643–716; Priscilla A. Ocen, "The New Racially Restrictive Covenant: Race, Welfare, and the Policing of Black Women in Subsidized Housing," *UCLA Law Review* 59 (2012): 1565; Suzanne Allen, Chris Flaherty, and Gretchen Ely, "Throwaway Moms: Maternal Incarceration and the Criminalization of Female Poverty," *Affilia* 25, no. 2 (2010): 160–72; Jackie Esmonde, "Criminalizing Poverty: The Criminal Law Power and the Safe Streets Act," *Journal of Law and Social Policy* 17 (2002): 63–86. On the prison industrial complex, see, for example, Ruth Wilson Gilmore, *Golden Gulag: Prisons, Surplus, Crisis, and Opposition in Globalizing California* (Berkeley: University of California Press, 2007); and Michelle Alexander, *The New Jim Crow: Mass Incarceration in the Age of Colorblindness* (New York: New Press, 2012).

57. Thomas v. St. Ann.

58. Although the conventional understanding of property refers to "things" owned by persons, and the rights of individuals with regard to these things, the concept of property has evolved to include intangible rights as protected by legal ruling. As Cheryl Harris theorizes, property is in this case a right, not a thing, and is metaphysical, not physical. Whiteness therefore includes multiple forms and interpretations of rights and is not just an identity but also a property with inherent, as opposed to explicit, legal status and legal rights. The right to move, the right to exclude, and the right to prosper at the expense of others are all part of the possessive rights of, and investment in, whiteness—itself a defensible property—that have created the physical, social, and political conditions in North St. Louis County. Cheryl Harris, "Whiteness as Property," *Harvard Law Review* 106, no. 8 (1993): 1707–91. Associations between blackness and risk have been theorized by several scholars, including Shona Jackson, "Risk, Blackness, and Postcolonial Studies: An Introduction," *Callaloo* 37, no. 1 (Winter 2014): 63–68, and Rashad Shabazz, *Spatializing Blackness: Architectures of Confinement and Black Masculinity in Chicago* (Urbana: University of Illinois Press, 2015). In this case, I am linking associations between blackness and risk as the antithesis to Cheryl Harris's conceptualization of whiteness-as-property.

59. Harris, "Whiteness as Property."

60. For example, Guy Stuart traces the racialized social factors that impacted risk assessment by mortgage lenders throughout the twentieth century with a particular focus on mortgage lending practices in Chicago in the 1990s, showing how embedded racialized discriminations continue to produce the spaces of the American city. *Discriminating Risk: The U.S. Mortgage Lending Industry in the 20th Century* (Ithaca, NY: Cornell University Press, 2003).

61. According to data collected by the organization Mapping Police Violence, 102 unarmed Black persons were killed by police in the United States in 2015. Following those incidents, charges were brought against ten police officers, and two officers were convicted of crimes. "Police Killed More than 100 Unarmed Black People in 2015," accessed December 6, 2016, http://mappingpoliceviolence.org/unarmed/.

62. Michel Foucault, *The Punitive Society: Lectures at the Collège de France, 1972–73*, ed. Bernard E. Harcourt, trans. Graham Burchell (New York: Palgrave MacMillan, 2015).

63. Interview with Patrick Green, mayor of Normandy, November 30, 2015. Interview conducted by research assistant Daniel Sachs. Suburban citizenship is discussed in chapter 4.

64. Foucault, 13.

65. Foucault, 12.

66. Governor Jay Nixon commissioned a cross-sectional panel (the Ferguson Commission) to investigate the causes of the Ferguson uprisings. The commission delivered its report, *Forward through Ferguson*, on September 21, 2015.

67. Ferguson Commission, *Forward through Ferguson*, 6.

68. Ferguson Commission, 7.

69. Ferguson Commission, 9.

70. Ferguson Commission, 10.

71. *Report of the Municipal Division Work Group to the Supreme Court of Missouri* (March 1, 2016), https://www.courts.mo.gov/file.jsp?id=9809. With regard to the excessive and inequitable use of municipal fines and fees, the report blames state laws that allow municipalities to fund budgets through the courts and incompetence within the municipal courts.

72. Municipal leaders cited the sovereign right of their cities to exist multiple times in interviews. Mayor Patrick Green of Normandy and Mayor Mary Louise Carter of Pagedale are especially vocal regarding this claim.

73. See, for example, Schmandt, "Municipal Home Rule in Missouri." In 1868, Judge John Dillon of Iowa ruled in federal court that cities exist at the pleasure of the state. In 1875, Missouri became the first state to establish municipal home rule in St. Louis by constitutional grant. Missouri later extended home rule provisions to smaller cities in the state.

74. Twelve North County municipalities filed a lawsuit in Cole County Circuit Court challenging the constitutionality of Senate Bill 5. The plaintiffs include the cities of Normandy, Cool Valley, Velda Village Hills, Village of Glen Echo Park, Bel-Ridge, Bel-Nor, Pagedale, Moline Acres, Village of Uplands Park, Vinita Park, Northwoods, and Wellston. In the lawsuit, the municipalities claim that Senate Bill 5 imposed unconstitutional and unfunded mandates on the St. Louis County municipalities. It also claims that the new law does not apply equally to all municipalities in the state and unfairly targets majority-Black municipalities in St. Louis County. See City of Normandy v. Greitens, supreme court of Missouri sc95624 (May 16, 2016), available at https://www.courts.mo.gov/file.jsp?id=112954.

75. Jennifer Mann and Jeremy Kohler, "Judge Sides with St. Louis County Cities That Claimed Municipal Court Reform Law Is Unfair," *St. Louis Post-Dispatch*, March 28, 2016. The state has appealed the ruling, and the state auditor and attorney general are attempting to enforce the provisions of Senate Bill 5.

76. The issues and decisions facing cities in financial distress as well as the racialized factors impacting municipal dissolution are addressed in Michelle Wilde Anderson, "The New Minimal Cities," *Yale Law Journal* 123 (2014): 1118, and Michelle Wilde Anderson, "Cities Inside Out: Race, Poverty, and Exclusion at the Urban Fringe," *UCLA Law Review* 55 (2008): 1095.

77. John A. Wright Sr., *St. Louis: Disappearing Black Communities* (Charleston, SC: Arcadia, 2004).

78. These observations are based on interviews with leaders at Better Together and Arch City Defenders, as well as the author's attendance at multiple meetings on court reform between October 2014 and December 2015.

79. See, for example, Jason Rosenbaum, "5 Takeaways From a City-County Merger Plan That Never Got to Voters," *St. Louis Public Radio*, May 7, 2019, https://news.stlpub licradio.org/post/5-takeaways-city-county-merger-plan-never-got-voters?utm_source= newsletter&utm_medium=email&utm_content=5%20Takeaways%20From%20A%20 City-County%20Merger%20Plan%20That%20Never%20Got%20To%20Voters&utm_ campaign=newsletter_LRL#stream/0.

80. See, for example, Jeremy Kohler, "North County Cities Sue to Block Law That Limits Revenue from Traffic Cases," *St. Louis Post-Dispatch*, November 19, 2015.

81. Sheryll Cashin describes "the tyranny of the favored quarter" as a phenomenon whereby well-resourced areas within metropolitan regions create externalities that are then shifted to areas without resources. Poorer neighbors are burdened by their more affluent neighbors' ability to capture valuable assets and push out waste, or "unwelcome" types of people and entities that require outside assistance. "Localism, Self-Interest, and the Tyranny of the Favored Quarter: Addressing the Barriers to New Regionalism," *Georgetown Law Review* 88 (2000): 1985–2048.

82. David Theo Goldberg has theorized modern racial states as places "where states of being and states of governance meet." "Racial States," in *A Companion to Racial and Ethnic Studies*, ed. David Theo Goldberg and John Solomos (Malden, MA: Blackwell, 2002), 236.

83. James Ferguson and Akhil Gupta, "Spatializing States: Toward an Ethnography of Neoliberal Governmentality," *American Ethnologist* 29, no. 4 (November 2002): 981–1002.

4. DISCURSIVE REGIMES AND EVERYDAY PRACTICES

1. Henri Lefebvre, *The Production of Space*, trans. Donald Nicholson-Smith (Malden, MA: Wiley-Blackwell, 1992).

2. Michel Foucault, *Power/Knowledge: Selected Interviews and Other Writings, 1972–1977*, ed. Colin Gordon, trans. Colin Gordon et al. (New York: Pantheon Books, 1980), 131.

3. Stuart Hall, *The Fateful Triangle: Race, Ethnicity, Nation*, ed. Kobena Mercer (Cambridge, MA: Harvard University Press, 2017), 57.

4. Michel Foucault, *The Archaeology of Knowledge, and the Discourse on Language*, trans. Alan Sheridan Smith (New York: Pantheon, 1982).

5. Foucault, 61.

6. Michael Omi and Howard Winant, *Racial Formation in the United States: From the 1960's to the 1980's* (New York: Routledge, 1995).

7. Hall, *The Fateful Triangle*, 53.

8. P. Khalil Saucier and Tryon P. Woods, "Racial Optimism and the Drag of Thymotics," in *Conceptual Aphasia in Black: Displacing Racial Formation*, ed. P. Khalil Saucier and Tryon P. Woods (Lanham, MD: Lexington Books, 2016), 4.

9. Cedric J. Robinson, *Black Marxism: The Making of the Black Radical Tradition* (Chapel Hill: University of North Carolina Press, 2000).

10. Aihwa Ong, "Cultural Citizenship as Subject Making: Immigrants Negotiate Racial and Cultural boundaries in the United States," in *Race, Identity, Citizenship*, eds. Rodolfo Torres, Louis F. Miron, Jonathan X. Inda (New York: Wiley-Blackwell, 1999).

11. Analysis of transcripts from Missouri Senate Education Committee hearings, public hearings sponsored by the Missouri Department of Elementary and Secondary Education, and Normandy School Board meetings held between July 2013 and March 2014 that were focused on the crisis of the Normandy School District reveals repeated use of the word *urban* in reference to the problems, challenges, and character of the district. The quotation attributing a "ghetto mentality" to Normandy residents is from an interview with an administrator from the Normandy School District in 2009. This attitude, framed by the rhetoric of personal responsibility, was also repeatedly expressed in letters to the editors of local news publications concerning this issue. For example, one writer stated, "The citizens of Normandy need to get off their collective butts and start taking responsibility for educating their children. The reason [other school districts are successful] is because the parents have worked hard, are involved, . . . and follow the American tenet of individual responsibility." Letter to the editor, *St. Louis Post-Dispatch*, February 16, 2014. For information concerning violence and drug activity, see the St. Louis County crime-mapping statistics for 2013, http://maps.stlouisco.com/police.

12. Ty McNichol, district superintendent, statement made at a public hearing of the Missouri Department of Elementary and Secondary Education, November 11, 2013. Persons or families may be classified as functionally homeless if they move often between locations such as the homes of family members or friends, automobiles, or motels. For a discussion of types of housing stability, see Sam Tsemberis et al., "Measuring Homelessness and Residential Stability: The Residential Time-Line Follow-Back Inventory," *Journal of Community Psychology* 35, no. 1 (2007): 29–42.

13. Trymaine Lee, "Missouri School Busing Causes 'Crippling' Fallout," MSNBC, December 9, 2013, http://www.msnbc.com/msnbc/heres-how-not-deal-failing-schools.

14. Stanton Lawrence, "How Missouri Killed the Normandy School District," *Diane Ravitch Blog: A Site to Discuss Better Education for All*, June 22, 2014, https://dianeravitch.net/2014/06/22/stanton-lawrence-how-missouri-killed-the-normandy-school-district/

15. See, for example, Editorial Board, "Editorial: Time to Embrace the Best of the State's Plans for Normandy," *St. Louis Post-Dispatch*, June 20, 2014; Jessica Bock, "Francis Howell Officials Say 'No' to Normandy Students," *St. Louis Post-Dispatch*, June 21, 2014; Elisa Crouch, "Politics and Turmoil Surrounding School Transfers Intensifies," *St. Louis Post-Dispatch*, June 23, 2014; Nikole Hannah-Jones, "School Segregation, the Continuing Tragedy of Ferguson," *ProPublica*, December 19, 2014.

16. For example, views expressed at the Missouri Senate Education Committee hearing on Senate Bills 624 and 516, February 5, 2014.

17. Quoted in John Eligon, "In Missouri, Race Complicates a Transfer to Better Schools," *New York Times*, July 31, 2013.

18. Comments made at Francis Howell School District town hall meeting, attended by author, July 20, 2014. It should be noted that in spite of the many overtly racist statements made by white parents at public hearings, many people in the receiving districts condemned these sentiments, and when Normandy students showed up at Francis Howell schools in August 2013, several groups of students and parents made efforts to welcome them.

19. Missouri Department of Elementary and Secondary Education, District Discipline Incidents, Francis Howell R-III and Normandy, 2013, http://mcds.dese.mo.gov/guidedinquiry/District%20and%20Building%20Student%20Indicators/District%20Discipline%20Incidents.aspx.

20. Comments made at public hearings at the University of Missouri–St. Louis (which sits within the NSD footprint), at which the Department of Elementary and Secondary Education introduced its recommendations for how the state of Missouri should deal with underperforming school districts and heard comments concerning its decision. The author was present at these hearings on November 12, 2013, and February 25, 2014.

21. Public hearings at the University of Missouri–St. Louis.

22. Eligon, "In Missouri, Race Complicates"; "Still Segregated," episode 3 in *The March @ 50*, PBS web series, produced by Shukree Tilghman, September 9, 2013, http://video.pbs.org/video/2365071680.

23. See, for example, Peter Dreier and Todd Swanstrom, "Suburban Ghettos Like Ferguson Are Ticking Time Bombs," *Washington Post*, August 21, 2014; Elizabeth Kneebone, "Ferguson, Mo. Emblematic of Growing Suburban Poverty," *Brookings Institute Blog*, August 15, 2014; Jonathan Rodden, "Is Segregation the Problem in Ferguson?," *Washington Post*, August 18, 2014; Jeff Smith, "In Ferguson, Black Town, White Power," *New York Times*, August 17, 2014.

24. Denver Nicks, "How Ferguson Went from Middle Class to Poor in a Generation," *Time*, August 18, 2014.

25. Judith Butler, *Bodies That Matter: On the Discursive Limits of "Sex"* (New York: Routledge, 1993), 8.

26. Butler.

27. Dianne Harris, *Little White Houses: How the Postwar Home Constructed Race in America* (Minneapolis: University of Minnesota Press, 2013).

28. Margaret Garb, *City of American Dreams: A History of Home Ownership and Housing Reform in Chicago, 1871–1919* (Chicago: University of Chicago Press, 2005), 205.

29. The ghetto, as a stigmatized space of separation and exclusion, can be traced to Venice, where it was adopted in 1516 as a mechanism of Jewish containment and gradually came to represent stigmatized urban space across European cities. In American cities, the Jewish ghetto evolved into a space of ethnic marginalization in the late nineteenth century and eventually became synonymous with African American space. Louis Wirth, *The Ghetto* (Chicago: University of Chicago Press, 1928), including Robert Park's introduction; E. Franklin Frazier, "Negro Harlem: An Ecological Study," *American Journal of Sociology* 43, no. 1 (July 1937): 72–88; St. Clair Drake, "Profiles: Chicago," *Journal of Educational Sociology* 17, no. 5 (January 1944): 261–71; St. Clair Drake and Horace Cayton, *Black Metropolis: A Study of Negro Life in a Northern City* (Chicago: University of Chicago Press, 1945); Robert Weaver, *The Negro Ghetto* (New York: Harcourt, Brace, 1948). Weaver was secretary of the US Department of Housing and Urban Development.

30. The term *suburban ghetto* has been used to refer to poverty and nonwhite ethnicity for at least four decades and has more recently become part of the urban lexicon. For examples, see Richard Koubek, "Wyandanch: A Case Study of Political Impotence in a Black Suburban Ghetto" (master's thesis, Queens College, New York, 1971); Mark Gottdiener, "Politics and Planning: Suburban Case Studies," in *Remaking the City: Social Science Perspectives on Urban Design*, ed. John S. Pipkin, Mark La Gory, and Judith R. Blau (Albany: State University of New York Press, 1983), 310–33; Alexandra K. Murphy, "The Suburban Ghetto: The Legacy of Herbert Gans in Understanding the Experience of Poverty in Recently Impoverished American Suburbs," *City and Community* 6, no. 1 (March 2007): 21–37; Ronald E. Wilson and Derek J. Paulsen, "Foreclosures and Crime: A Geographical Perspective," *Geography & Public Safety* 1, no. 3 (October 2008): 1–2.

31. A review of literature on urban planning and urban history reveals the many ways nonwhite suburbs are qualified, whereas predominantly white suburbs are not qualified as such in sub/urban scholarship.

32. See, for example, Gwendolyn Wright, *Building the Dream: A Social History of Housing in America* (Boston: MIT Press, 1983); Rosalyn Baxandall and Elizabeth Ewen, *Picture Windows: How the Suburbs Happened* (New York: Basic Books, 2000); Setha Low, *Behind the Gates: Life, Security, and the Pursuit of Happiness in Fortress America* (Milton Park, UK: Taylor and Francis, 2003).

33. Mary Jo Wiggins, "Race, Class, and Suburbia: The Modern Black Suburb as a 'Race-Making Situation,'" *University of Michigan Journal of Legal Reform* 35 (2001–2): 749–808.

34. Pertaining to race and urban policy, the term *benign neglect* was coined by Daniel Patrick Moynihan in 1970, to whom the culture-of-poverty thesis is also attributed (although Moynihan borrowed the concept from Oscar Lewis). Within urban policy, the term has come to mean the intentional allowance of physical decay in order to eventually build something new. A version of this idea was reconceptualized by the shrinking cities discourse in urban planning, which argues that abandonment is not necessarily a bad thing.

35. The term *unfavored quarter* makes reference to Sheryll Cashin's conceptualization of the "favored quarter," in "Localism, Self-Interest, and the Tyranny of the Favored Quarter: Addressing the Barriers to New Regionalism," *Georgetown Law Review* 88 (2000): 1985–2048.

36. Edward Said, *Orientalism* (New York: Vintage Books, 1979), 71. George Lipsitz discusses the work of white and Black spatial imaginaries in *How Racism Takes Place* (Philadelphia: Temple University Press, 2011).

37. Said, *Orientalism*, 73.

38. Jodi Melamed, *Represent and Destroy: Rationalizing Violence in the New Racial Capitalism* (Minneapolis: University of Minnesota Press, 2011), 1–2.

39. Interview with an older white resident of Ferguson.

40. This assumption is discussed in detail in chapter 3.

41. Walter Mondale, a cosponsor of the bill that led to the Fair Housing Act, framed many of his arguments for the bill by using the "model Negro citizen" as the example of who would actually escape the ghetto and gain access to desegregated areas. See, for example, Senator Mondale, speaking on the *Fair Housing Act of 1967,* on August 16, 1967, 90th Cong., 1st sess., 113 Congressional Record 113, pt 17:22840-22842.

42. Gregory, "Imaginative Geographies."

43. Bryan Downes, Joan Saunders, and John Collins, *Local Government Intervention in the Face of Mortgage Disinvestment: The Case of Normandy* (report, University of Missouri–St. Louis study, January 1976), box 14, folder 11, archives of the Normandy Municipal Council, Missouri Historical Society Library; Rick Corry and Tom Dyer, University of Missouri–St. Louis report, *Factors in Suburban Blight: A Study of Housing in Northwoods, Pine Lawn, and Hillsdale* (June 1973); Normandy Municipal Council report, *Citizens' GOALS Project,* Don Moschenross, director (November 1973). For example, one of the many fliers at the Missouri History Museum promotes racial zoning in St. Louis city in 1915, stating, "An entire block ruined by negro invasion. Every house marked 'X' now occupied by negroes. ACTUAL PHOTOGRAPH OF 4300 WEST BELLE PLACE." Ta-Nehisi Coates also uses this image in his article "The Racist Housing Policies That Built Ferguson," leading to a number of reader comments stating that the 4300 block of Belle would be better off today had racial zoning stayed in place. *Atlantic*, October 17, 2014, http://www.theatlantic.com/business/archive/2014/10/the-racist-housing-policies-that-built-ferguson/381595/.

44. Rhetoric used by the Federal Housing Authority and Home Owners' Loan Corporation, cited in Colin Gordon, *Mapping Decline: St. Louis and the Fate of the American City* (Philadelphia: University of Philadelphia Press, 2008), 88–92.

45. E. Terrence Jones, "The Municipal Market in the St. Louis Region: 1950–2000," in *St. Louis Metromorphosis: Past Trends and Future Directions*, ed. Brady Baybeck and E. Terrence Jones (St. Louis: University of Missouri Press, 2004).

46. Quoted in Gordon, *Mapping Decline*, 25.

47. As described in chapter 2, Black residents of St. Louis city and county were instrumental in shaping the region and building communities. The history of Kinloch in North St. Louis County is one such example, although there are others: Webster Groves, Rock Hill, and Meacham Park.

48. Interviews with Normandy residents.

49. Five Black mayors in North St. Louis County granted interviews for this research.

50. Interviews with mayors and alderpersons in North St. Louis County municipalities.

51. Interview with Patrick Green, mayor of Normandy, November 30, 2015. Interview conducted by research assistant Daniel Sachs.

52. Over a period of one year, three research assistants and I approached random people in North St. Louis County and asked whether they would be willing to answer a survey with predetermined questions regarding their experiences and perceptions in St. Louis County and St. Louis city. Their names were not documented; however, they were asked to voluntarily provide demographic information such as age, gender, and race. Locations where people were intercepted included grocery stores, farmers markets, bus stops, light rail stations, and city halls.

53. Interviews with North County residents.

54. This paragraph is based on data collected from resident interviews.

55. Based on data collected from resident interviews.

56. Based on data collected from resident interviews.

57. Based on data collected from resident interviews.

58. Based on data collected from resident interviews.

59. See, for example, Michael Brown et al., *Whitewashing Race: The Myth of a Color-Blind Society* (Berkeley: University of California Press, 2003); Howard Winant, *The New Politics of Race: Globalism, Difference, Justice* (Minneapolis: University of Minnesota Press, 2004); Goldberg, *Threat of Race*; Eduardo Bonilla-Silva, *Racism without Racists: Color-Blind Racism and Racial Inequality in Contemporary America*, 3rd ed. (New York: Rowman and Littlefield Press, 2010); Michelle Alexander, *The New Jim Crow: Mass Incarceration in the Age of Colorblindness* (New York: New Press, 2012).

60. See, for example Jones, "Municipal Market in the St. Louis Region."

61. Edward Glaeser and Jacob Vigdor, *The End of the Segregated Century: Racial Separation in America's Neighborhoods, 1890–2010*, Manhattan Institute Civic Report 66 (January 2012).

62. Michel Foucault develops this concept regarding biopower in *Society Must Be Defended: Lectures at the Collège de France, 1975–1976*, ed. Mauro Bertani and Alessandro Fontana, trans. David Macey (New York: Picador, 2003).

63. Rob Nixon conceptualizes slow violence as the processes of structural racisms and the threats that create vulnerable communities, in *Slow Violence and the Environmentalism of the Poor*.

5. POLITICS AND POLICING IN PAGEDALE

1. John A. Wright Sr., *St. Louis: Disappearing Black Communities* (Charleston, SC: Arcadia, 2004), 64.

2. The gates still exist today.

3. Developer's advertising pamphlet, circa 1948, Normandy files, Pagedale folder, Missouri History Museum.

4. Greg Squires discusses the political factors and processes of industrial factories moving from suburban areas in US cities to outer exurbs in *Urban Sprawl: Causes, Consequences, and Policy Response* (Lanham, MD: Rowman and Littlefield, 2002).

5. Interviews with Pagedale residents.

6. See discussion in chapter 2.

7. As told to me in an interview on October 2, 2010, with a former University of Missouri extension employee who facilitated town hall meetings in the Normandy suburbs during this era.

8. Interview with former University of Missouri extension employee.

9. "Legal Aid Society May Challenge Pagedale Occupancy Permit Law," *St. Louis Post-Dispatch*, May 20, 1970.

10. "Legal Aid Society May Challenge."

11. See chapter 2.

12. This observation is based on the number of newspaper articles from this period reporting outbursts by leadership at Pagedale city council meetings.

13. "Race Is Not an Issue, Says All-Black Pagedale Slate," *St Louis Post-Dispatch*, February 28, 1972.

14. "Race Is Not an Issue."

15. George E. Curry, "Police Allege Pagedale Mayor Interfered," *St. Louis Post-Dispatch*, June 6, 1980.

16. Monte Plott, "Pagedale Mayor Is Ousted; City Hall Now All Women," *St. Louis Post-Dispatch*, April 7, 1982.

17. Joe Swickard, "Government Is a Hot Show in a Small Missouri Town," *Detroit Free Press*, July 11, 1982.

18. "Town Run by All Women Now Has Three Police Chiefs Hired," *Chillicothe Tribune*, June 17, 1982.

19. Michael D. Sorkin, "Pagedale Mayor, Her Choice for Police Chief Arrested," *St. Louis Post-Dispatch*, June 17, 1982; Dale Singer and Michael D. Sorkin, "Pagedale Mayor Wants Protection from Chief," *St. Louis Post-Dispatch*, June 20, 1982; Michael D. Sorkin and E. S. Evans, "Injunction Is Issued in Pagedale Dispute," *St. Louis Post-Dispatch*, June 22, 1982.

20. "Injunction Is Issued in Pagedale Dispute."

21. See, for example, Jesse Bogan, "Pagedale Alderman Avoids Felony Charges in Plea Deal," *St. Louis Post-Dispatch*, March 27, 2019.

22. Interviews with North St. Louis County elected officials.

23. Interview with mayor and city alderperson of Pagedale, May 2010.

24. Pagedale resident, interview by author, April 11, 2011.

25. See, for example, the work of Gwendolyn Wright, Barbara Kelly, Alice Hoffman, Stephanie Coontz, Donna Gaines, Rosalyn Baxandall, and Elizabeth Ewen.

26. Roderick A. Ferguson, *Aberrations in Black: Toward a Queer of Color Critique* (Minneapolis: University of Minnesota Press, 2003), 147.

27. Interview with municipal leader.

28. Wendy Cheng, "The Changs Next Door to the Diazes: Suburban Racial Formation in Los Angeles's San Gabriel Valley," *Journal of Urban History* 39, no. 1 (2012): 22.

29. Whitner et al. v. City of Pagedale, Eastern District of MO (U.S.) 4:15-cv-01655-RWS (2016), http://ij.org/wp-content/uploads/2015/11/ECF-1-Complaint-FILE-STAMPED-11.04.15.pdf.

30. Pagedale municipal ordinances (past and present).

31. *Whitner et al.* 4:15-cv-01655-RWS.

32. W. E. B. Du Bois, *The Philadelphia Negro: A Social Study* (Philadelphia: University of Pennsylvania Press, 1996).

33. Interview with Pagedale resident.

34. *Whitner et al.* 4:15-cv-01655-RWS.

35. Interview with Pagedale alderwoman.

36. Interview with Pagedale resident.

37. *Whitner et al.* 4:15-cv-01655-RWS, "Deposition of the Honorable Mary Louise Carter," on behalf of the plaintiffs, July 24, 2017.

38. See table 3.1.

39. The concept of the deserving poor is part of the culture-of-poverty discourse, which sets about to distinguish the working poor and those deemed poor through no fault of their own from groups associated with laziness or a lack of moral and cultural values.

40. Common refrain of Pagedale leaders to the author when working in Pagedale, 2004–10.

41. Interview with Pagedale resident, October 12, 2015.

42. Interview with Pagedale resident, August 11, 2015.

43. This account is based on interviews and interactions with leadership and staff at Beyond Housing, 2004–10. It should be noted that Beyond Housing has had a considerable positive impact on this area, and its leadership is committed to alleviating suffering and improving the lives of residents in North St. Louis County on many levels, including housing, health, education, and economic literacy.

44. Christine Hoehner et al., "Page Avenue HIA: Building on Diverse Partnerships and Evidence to Promote a Healthy Community," *Health and Place* 18, no. 1 (January 2012): 85–95.

45. Jean Bricmont, *Humanitarian Imperialism* (New York: Monthly Review Press, 2006). Many have critiqued humanitarian discourse and practice. See, for example, Mahmood Mamdani, *Saviors and Survivors: Darfur, Politics, and the War on Terror* (New York: Doubleday, 2009); Conor Foley, *The Thin Blue Line: How Humanitarianism Went to War* (New York: Verso, 2010). One example of the critique of early social work organizations and the discourses that accompanied them is Tony Platt, *The Child Savers: The Invention of Delinquency* (Chicago: University of Chicago Press, 1969).

46. Cited in Walter Johnson, "What Do We Mean When We Say, 'Structural Racism'?," *Kalfou* 3, no. 1 (Spring 2016): 58.

47. "24:1 Community, Missouri: 2016 RWJF Culture of Health Prize Winner," Robert Wood Johnson Foundation website, accessed November 27, 2019, https://www.rwjf.org/en/library/features/culture-of-health-prize/2016-winner-24-1-missouri.html.

48. "24:1 Community, Missouri."

49. J. Justin Wilson, "Federal Court Approves Historic Consent Decree Ending 'Policing for Profit' in Pagedale, Mo," Institute for Justice website, May 21, 2018, https://ij.org/press-release/federal-court-approves-historic-consent-decree-ending-policing-for-profit-in-pagedale-mo/.

50. Avery Gordon, *Ghostly Matters: Haunting and the Sociological Imagination* (Minneapolis: University of Minnesota Press, 1997), 4.

51. Gordon, 5.

52. Gordon.

53. Brittany Cooper, *Beyond Respectability: The Intellectual Thought of Race Women* (Urbana: University of Illinois, 2017).

54. For work drawing on Cooper's scholarship, see Hazel V. Carby, "Policing the Black Woman's Body in an Urban Context," *Critical Inquiry* 18, no. 4 (1992): 738–55; Victoria Wolcott, *Remaking Respectability: African American Women in Interwar Detroit* (Chapel Hill: University of North Carolina Press, 2001); Farah Jasmine Griffin, "Black Feminists and Du Bois: Respectability, Protection, and Beyond," *Annals of the American Academy of Political and Social Science* 568, no. 1 (2000): 28–40.

55. Kimberlee Randle-King was arrested in September 2014 by Pagedale police for engaging in a "street fight" with another woman whom she said had jumped her after also threatening her on social media. The other woman was released, but Randle-King was held in jail because of outstanding warrants in other jurisdictions for traffic violations. Randle-King was described by the booking officer as exceedingly distraught over being jailed because she believed she would lose her job and her children. Video cameras reportedly show that within ten minutes of entering the cell Randle-King's body was lifeless, although it would be another fifteen minutes before anyone checked on her. Reports of Randle-King's death led to several days of protest outside the Pagedale jail, which coincided with protests in response to the killing of Michael Brown in Ferguson. The family of Randle-King sued the City of Pagedale for breaching protocol requiring that inmates be monitored at all times. The city settled the lawsuit for $1.2 million in March 2017. See, for example, "Police Identify Woman Who Hanged Herself In Pagedale Jail Cell," *St. Louis Post-Dispatch*, September 22, 2014; Nicholas Phillips, "Why Did This 21-Year-Old Woman Die In the Pagedale Jail?" *Riverfront Times*, July 2, 2015; Nassim Benchaabane, "$1.2M Settlement Reached In death of Woman Who Hanged Herself In Pagedale Jail," *St. Louis Post-Dispatch*, March 31, 2017.

56. Interview with Ferguson protest leader, March 12, 2015.

INTERLUDE

1. *State of Missouri v. Darren Wilson*, "Testimony of Darren Wilson," grand jury transcript, vol. 5, September 16, 2014, 207. https://www.scribd.com/doc/248128351/Darren-Wilson-Testimony#fullscreen&from_embed.

2. This was the most common nontraffic violation residents of North St. Louis County cited when interviewed (N=126).

3. *Mo. v. Wilson*, 212.

4. *Mo. v. Wilson*, 224.

5. *Mo. v. Wilson*, 224–25.

6. *Mo. v. Wilson*, 226.

7. *Mo. v. Wilson*, 229–30.

8. *Mo. v. Wilson*, 236.

9. *Mo. v. Wilson*, 237–38.

10. *Mo. v. Wilson*, 239.

11. This statement is based on interviews with three Canfield Green Apartments residents and two people who arrived after hearing about the shooting. Key-informant interviews with Ferguson residents.

12. Interviews with Ferguson residents.

13. Interviews with Ferguson residents.

14. Quoted in an interview with Sarah Van Gelder and published in "Reverend Sekou on Today's Civil Rights Leaders: I Take My Orders from 23-Year-Old Queer Women," *Yes!*, July 22, 2015, http://www.yesmagazine.org/peace-justice/black-lives-matter-s-favorite-minister-reverend-sekou-young-queer.

15. Interviews with Ferguson residents.

16. See, for example, David Li, "St. Louis Suburbs Erupt in Rioting after Cop Kills Unarmed Man," *New York Post*, August 11, 2014.

17. Li.

6. QUEERING PROTEST

1. Antonio Negri and Michael Hardt, *Commonwealth* (Cambridge, MA: Harvard University Press, 2009), 62–63.

2. These observations are based specifically on interviews with women of the Ferguson Protest Movement between September 2015 and January 2016 and with people involved with the movement between August 2014 and September 2015, as well as on a discourse analysis of several thousand statements made by protesters via Twitter during the same time periods.

3. Katherine McKittrick, ed., *Sylvia Wynter: On Being Human as Praxis* (Durham, NC: Duke University Press, 2015).

4. Saidiya Hartman, *Scenes of Subjection: Terror, Slavery, and Self-Making in Nineteenth-Century America* (New York: Oxford University Press, 1997), 72.

5. Roderick A. Ferguson, *Aberrations in Black: Toward a Queer of Color Critique* (Minneapolis: University of Minnesota Press, 2003), 4.

6. This observation is based on interviews with core organizers of the Ferguson Protest Movement between September 2015 and January 2016.

7. Seyla Benhabib, *Claims of Culture: Equality and Diversity in the Global Era* (Princeton, NJ: Princeton University Press, 2002), 84.

8. Katherine McKittrick, *Demonic Grounds: Black Women and the Cartographies of Struggle* (Minneapolis: University of Minnesota Press, 2006).

9. Nadia Ellis, *Territories of the Soul: Queered Belonging in the Black Diaspora* (Durham, NC: Duke University Press, 2015).

10. Christina Sharpe, *Monstrous Intimacies: Making Post-slavery Subjects* (Durham, NC: Duke University Press, 2009), 4.

11. Interviews with Ferguson protesters.

12. The protesters interviewed for this research were chosen either because they were perceived as leaders within the movement or because they had been consistently present and part of the movement for more than a year following Brown's death. They came from many different backgrounds and experiences that cut across race, age, and gender. The majority of interviews were set up and conducted by Angel Carter, who is also viewed as a leader in the movement and is an accomplished writer and researcher in her own right.

13. Aimé Césaire, *Discourse on Colonialism*, trans. Joan Pinkham (New York: Monthly Review Press, 2000); interviews with Ferguson residents.

14. McKittrick, *Sylvia Wynter*.

15. Cathy J. Cohen, "Punks, Bulldaggers, and Welfare Queens: The Radical Potential of Queer Politics," *GLQ: A Journal of Lesbian & Gay Studies* 3 (1997): 437.

16. Michael Warner, "Fear of a Queer Planet," *Social Text* 29 (1991): 3–17.

17. For example, the Combahee River Collective, a Black feminist organization active in the late 1970s, began its philosophical statement, "The most general statement of our politics at the present time would be that we are actively committed to struggling against racial, sexual, heterosexual, and class oppressions and see as our particular task the development of integrated analysis and practice based upon the fact that the major systems of oppression are interlocking." "The Combahee River Collective Statement," in *Home Girls: A Black Feminist Anthology*, ed. Barbara Smith (New Brunswick, NJ: Rutgers University Press, 1983), 264.

18. Michael Warner, *Publics and Counter Publics* (New York: Zone Books, 2005), 215.

19. José Esteban Muñoz, *Cruising Utopia: The Then and There of Queer Futurity* (New York: New York University Press, 2009), 185.

20. Cohen, "Punks, Bulldaggers, and Welfare Queens," 443.

21. There is a rich literature that explores performativity, eroticism, queered politics, and the Black female body in relationship to resistance. While I engage with several of

these authors, it was not possible to specifically acknowledge the contributions of all this work because of the limited scope of this section. These works include but are not limited to Jaqui M. Alexander, "Danger and Desire: Crossings Are Never Undertaken All at Once or for All," *Small Axe* 24, no. 11 (2007): 154–65; Jafari S. Allen, "*Venceremos? The Erotics of Black Self-Making in Cuba* (Durham, NC: Duke University Press, 2011); Cheryl Clarke, "Lesbianism: An Act of Resistance," in *Feminism and Sexuality: A Reader*, ed. Stevi Jackson and Sue Scott (New York: Columbia University Press, 1996), 155–61; Cathy J. Cohen, "Deviance as Resistance: A New Research Agenda for the Study of Black Politics," *Du Bois Review* 1, no. 1 (2004): 27–45; Brenda Dixon-Gottschild, *The Black Dancing Body: A Geography from Coon to Cool* (New York: Palgrave Macmillan, 2003); Nicole Fleetwood, "The Case of Rihanna: Erotic Violence and Black Female Desire," *African American Review* 45, no. 3 (2012): 419–35; Rosalind C. Morris, "All Made Up: Performance Theory and the New Anthropology of Sex and Gender," *Annual Review of Anthropology* 24, no. 1 (1995): 567–92; Jennifer C. Nash, "Practicing Love: Black Feminism, Love-Politics, and Post-intersectionality," *Meridians* 11, no. 2 (2011): 1–24; Rosemarie A. Roberts, "Dancing with Social Ghosts: Performing Embodiments, Analyzing Critically," *Transforming Anthropology* 21, no. 1 (2013): 4–14.

22. The comments sections following several articles in the *St. Louis Post-Dispatch* that featured Ms. McSpadden in the weeks following Brown's death reflected literally hundreds of heated debates over her culpability and competency as a mother.

23. Interviews with Ferguson protesters.

24. Interview with Diamond Latchison, September 11, 2015.

25. Interviews with Ferguson protesters. *Front line* and *war* are words that protesters and institutional leaders used in describing events following Michael Brown's death. The use of these words differ from the language of war described in chapter 2.

26. Interviews with Ferguson protesters.

27. Audre Lorde, "Uses of the Erotic: The Erotic as Power," in *Sister Outsider: Essays and Speeches by Audre Lorde* (Berkeley, CA: Crossing Press, 2007), 53–59.

28. Lorde, 56.

29. Interviews with Ferguson protesters.

30. Sharon Patricia Holland, *The Erotic Life of Racism* (Durham, NC: Duke University Press, 2012).

31. Sharpe, *Monstrous Intimacies*.

32. Holland, *Erotic Life of Racism*, 46.

33. See the introduction for a discussion of pornotroping.

34. Lorde, "Uses of the Erotic," 58.

35. Nicole Fleetwood, *Troubling Vision: Performance, Visuality, and Blackness* (Chicago: University of Chicago Press, 2011), 6.

36. Fleetwood, 106.

37. Many Black feminist scholars have written about the Jezebel versus Mammy identities conferred on Black women as a means of hypersexualizing and desexualizing Black women's bodies and as a means of control and dehumanization dating back to slavery and continuing into the present. See, for example, Patricia Hill Collins, *Black Feminist Thought* (New York: Routledge, 2008).

38. Aimee Meredith Cox, *Shapeshifters: Black Girls and the Choreography of Citizenship* (Durham, NC: Duke University Press, 2015).

39. Lepecki, "Choreopolice and Choreopolitics: Or, the Task of the Dancer," *The Drama Review* 57, no. 4 (2013):16.

40. Lepecki, 20.

41. Quoted in Lepecki, 20.

42. Quoted in "Nation Horrified By Murder of Kidnapped Chicago Youth," *Jet* 8, no. 19 (September 15, 1955): 8.

43. Frantz Fanon, *Black Skin, White Mask*, trans. Richard Philcox (New York: Grove Press, 2008), 91.

44. Sara Ahmed, *Queer Phenomenology: Orientations, Objects, Others* (Durham, NC: Duke University Press, 2006), 112.

45. Stuart Hall, "What is the 'Black' in Black Popular Culture?," in *Black Popular Culture*, ed. Michelle Wallace and Gina Dent (Seattle: Bay Press, 1992), 21–33.

46. Juana Maria Rodriguez, *Sexual Futures, Queer Gestures, and Other Latina Longings* (New York: New York University Press, 2014), 2.

47. Judith Butler and Athena Athanasiou, *Dispossession: The Performative in the Political* (Cambridge, UK: Polity, 2013), 101.

48. Rodriguez, *Sexual Futures, Queer Gestures*, 5.

49. Lepecki, "Choreopolice and Choreopolitics," 20.

7. ONTOLOGIES OF RESISTANCE

1. Transcript of Al Sharpton's eulogy at the funeral for Michael Brown Jr., in Joe Coscarelli, "Watch Al Sharpton Bring the House Down at Michael Brown's Funeral: 'This is not about you! This is about justice!,'" *New York Intelligencer*, August 25, 2014, http://nymag.com/daily/intelligencer/2014/08/al-sharpton-eulogy-michael-brown-funeral.html.

2. Jamala Rogers, testimony to the Public Safety Committee, St. Louis Board of Aldermen, June 24, 2004.

3. Clarence Lang, "Between Civil Rights and Black Power in the Gateway City: The Action Committee to Improve Opportunities for Negroes (ACTION), 1964–74," *Journal of Social History* 37, no. 3 (March 2004): 725.

4. George Lipsitz documents the culture of opposition in St. Louis in *A Life in the Struggle: Ivory Perry and the Culture of Opposition* (Philadelphia: Temple University Press, 1988).

5. Lang, "Between Civil Rights and Black Power," 725.

6. In May 2015, Ferguson protesters made their feelings known at meetings of both MORE and OBS, claiming that the funds collected through these organizations in the name of Black struggle in Ferguson were not getting to organizers on the ground and that record keeping for funds spent was not comprehensive or transparent. Using the slogan "Cut the Check," people representing various grassroots protest communities formed an organizational board intended to hold people and organizations accountable for how they managed funds brought in through protest activities. A statement was issued through social media demanding that MORE and OBS release records regarding how funds had been distributed. MORE responded by releasing a list of people and organizations that had received money. According to research made public by protest organizers, many people listed had not actually received funds. Furthermore, the executive director of MORE, Jeff Ordower, had personally received over twenty thousand dollars for unspecified expenses incurred during Ferguson October, for which there were no records. In June 2015, MORE released funds to at least seventeen protesters, and Jeff Ordower resigned. For the demands of "Cut the Check" and a discussion regarding its importance, see Angel Carter, "Cut the Check," *Liberated Souls* (blog), accessed March 12, 2018, https://liberatedsouls.org/ferguson-reflections-2/cut-the-check/.

7. Quotations in this paragraph were transcribed from a video clip of Tef Poe and Ashley Yates speaking at the Mass Meeting on Ferguson, October 12, 2014, https://www.youtube.com/watch?v=McT_yie8R1U&t=88s.

8. Video clip of Poe and Yates at the Mass Meeting on Ferguson. The sequence of events described in this paragraph was reiterated by multiple people who were in attendance and were interviewed by the author.

9. Streamed live on STAR67 with Alexis and Brittany, August 3, 2015.

10. Roderick A. Ferguson, *Aberrations in Black: Toward a Queer of Color Critique* (Minneapolis: University of Minnesota Press, 2003), 147–48; William Julius Wilson, *The Truly Disadvantaged: The Inner City, Underclass, and Public Policy* (Chicago: University of Chicago Press, 1987).

11. This observation is based on interviews with core organizers of the Ferguson Protest Movement between September 2015 and January 2016.

12. Interviews with Ferguson protesters.

13. Stuart Hall, "Culture, Identity, and Diaspora," in *Colonial Discourse and Postcolonial Theory: A Reader*, ed. Patrick Williams and Laura Chrisman (New York: Columbia University Press, 1994), 395.

14. Robin D. G. Kelley, *Freedom Dreams: The Black Radical Imagination* (Boston: Beacon Press, 2002), vii.

15. For an insightful discussion on these relationships, see Ferguson, *Aberrations in Black*, introduction.

16. Ferguson, *Aberrations in Black*.

17. Ula Y. Taylor, "Making Waves: The Theory and Practice of Black Feminism," *Black Scholar* 28, no. 2 (Summer 1998): 18–19.

CODA

1. Michel Foucault, "The Ethics of the Concern for Self as a Practice of Freedom," in *Ethics: Subjectivity and Truth*, ed. Paul Rabinow (New York: New Press, 1998), 292.

2. Alexander Weheliye, *Habeas Viscus: Racializing Assemblages, Biopolitics, and Black Feminist Theories of the Human* (Durham, NC: Duke University Press, 2014), 2.

3. Avery Gordon, "Some Thoughts on Haunting and Futurity," *Borderlands* 10, no. 2 (2011): 2.

4. Fred Moten, "Blackness and Nothingness: (Mysticism in the Flesh)," *South Atlantic Quarterly* 112, no. 4 (Fall 2013): 742.

5. See the discussion of choreopolitics in chapter 6, which borrows from André Lepecki's "Choreopolice and Choreopolitics: Or, the Task of the Dancer," *TDR: The Drama Review* 57, no. 4 (Winter 2013): 13–27.

6. Frantz Fanon famously developed the concept of the white gaze, which seals blackness into itself and fixes Black subjectivity, in *Black Skin, White Mask*, trans. Richard Philcox (New York: Grove Press, 2008).

7. Moten, "Blackness and Nothingness," 776.

8. Nadia Ellis, *Territories of the Soul: Queered Belonging in the Black Diaspora* (Durham, NC: Duke University Press, 2015).

9. Gordon, "Some Thoughts on Haunting and Futurity," 2.

10. Moten, "Blackness and Nothingness," 778.

11. Judith Butler theorizes the power of precarity in *Precarious Life: The Powers of Mourning and Violence* (New York: Verso, 2004).

12. Walter Benjamin, "A Critique of Violence," in *Walter Benjamin: Selected Writings Volume 1, 1913–1926*, ed. Marcus Bullock and Michael Jennings (Cambridge, MA: Harvard University Press, 1996), 236–52: 242.

13. Arturo Escobar, *Designs for the Pluriverse: Radical Interdependence, Autonomy, and the Making of Worlds* (Durham, NC: Duke University Press, 2017), 226.

14. Escobar, *Deigns for the Pluriverse*, 208.

Selected Bibliography

The ideas and arguments presented throughout this book rely heavily on the intellectual labor performed by the people included in this selection of work. I am indebted to their contributions.

Agamben, Giorgio. *Homo Sacer: Sovereign Power and Bare Life.* Translated by Daniel Heller-Roazen. Palo Alto, CA: Stanford University Press, 1998.

——. *State of Exception.* Chicago: University of Chicago Press, 2005.

Ahmed, Sara. *Queer Phenomenology: Orientations, Objects, Others.* Durham, NC: Duke University Press, 2006.

Alexander, Jaqui M. "Danger and Desire: Crossings Are Never Undertaken All at Once or for All." *Small Axe* 24, no. 11 (2007): 154–65.

Alexander, Michelle. *The New Jim Crow: Mass Incarceration in the Age of Colorblindness.* New York: New Press, 2012.

Allen, Jafari S. *Venceremos? The Erotics of Black Self-Making in Cuba.* Durham, NC: Duke University Press, 2011.

Allen, Suzanne, Chris Flaherty, and Gretchen Ely. "Throwaway Moms: Maternal Incarceration and the Criminalization of Female Poverty." *Affilia* 25, no. 2 (2010): 160–72.

Anderson, Michelle Wilde. "Cities Inside Out: Race, Poverty, and Exclusion at the Urban Fringe." *UCLA Law Review* 55 (2008): 1095–160.

——. "The New Minimal Cities." *Yale Law Journal* 123 (2014): 1118–227.

Arendt, Hannah. *The Origins of Totalitarianism.* New York: Harcourt, Brace, Jovanovich, 1973.

Arenson, Adam. *The Great Heart of the Republic: St. Louis and the Cultural Civil War.* Cambridge, MA: Harvard University Press, 2011.

August, Emily. "Cadaver Poetics: Surgical Medicine and the Reinvention of the Body in the Nineteenth Century." PhD diss., Vanderbilt University, 2014.

Baker, Lee D. *Anthropology and the Racial Politics of Culture.* Durham, NC: Duke University Press, 2010.

Balibar, Etienne. "Violence and Civility: On the Limits of Political Anthropology." *differences* 20, no. 2/3 (2009): 9–35.

Balibar, Etienne and Immanuel Wallerstein. *Race, Nation, Class: Ambiguous Identities.* Translated by Chris Turner. New York: Verso, 1991.

Ballon, Hilary, and Kenneth T. Jackson, eds. *Robert Moses and the Modern City: The Transformation of New York.* New York: W. W. Norton, 2008.

Banner, Stuart. "Written Law and Unwritten Norms in Colonial St. Louis." *Law and History Review* 14, no. 1 (1996): 33–80.

Barclay, Thomas. *The St. Louis Home Rule Charter of 1876: Its Framing and Adoption.* Columbia: University of Missouri Press, 1962.

Baum, Dan. "Legalize It All: How to Win the War on Drugs." *Harper's Magazine*, April 2016, 1. http://harpers.org/archive/2016/04/legalize-it-all/1/.

Baxandall, Rosalyn, and Elizabeth Ewen. *Picture Windows: How the Suburbs Happened.* New York: Basic Books, 2000.

Benedict, Ruth. *Race: Science and Politics*. New York: Modern Age Books, 1940.
——. *Race and Racism*. London: The Scientific Book Club, 1943.
Benjamin, Walter. "Critique of Violence." In *Walter Benjamin: Selected Writings Volume 1, 1913–1926*, edited by Marcus Bullock and Michael Jennings, 236–52. Cambridge, MA: Harvard University Press, 1996.
Berger, Henry W. *St. Louis and Empire: 250 Years of Imperial Quest and Urban Crisis*. Carbondale: Southern Illinois University Press, 2015.
Bhaba, Homi. *The Location of Culture*. New York: Routledge, 1994.
Bonilla-Silva, Eduardo. "More than Prejudice: Restatement, Reflections, and New Directions in Critical Race Theory." *Sociology of Race and Ethnicity* 1, no. 1 (2015): 75–89.
——. *Racism without Racists: Color-Blind Racism and Racial Inequality in Contemporary America*. 3rd ed. New York: Rowman and Littlefield Press, 2010.
Bourdieu, Pierre. *Outline of a Theory of Practice*. Translated by Richard Nice. Cambridge: Cambridge University Press, 1977.
Brenner, Neil, and Nik Theodore. "Cities and the Geographies of 'Actually Existing Neoliberalism.'" *Antipode* 34, no. 3 (July 2002): 349–79.
Bricmont, Jean. *Humanitarian Imperialism*. New York: Monthly Review Press, 2006.
Briffault, Richard. "Localism and Regionalism." Columbia Law School, Public Law and Legal Theory Working Paper No. 1, http://ssrn.com/abstract=198822.
Bristol, Katharine G. "The Pruitt-Igoe Myth." *Journal of Architectural Education* 44, no. 3 (1991): 163–71.
Brown, Michael, Martin Carnoy, Elliott Currie, Troy Duster, David B. Oppenheimer, Marjorie M. Schultz, and David Wellman. *Whitewashing Race: The Myth of a Color-Blind Society*. Berkeley: University of California Press, 2003.
Brown, Wendy. *States of Injury: Power and Freedom in Late Modernity*. Princeton, NJ: Princeton University Press, 1995.
Brown, William W. *Narrative of William W. Brown, a Fugitive Slave*. Boston: Anti-Slavery Office, 1847.
Buchanan, Richard. "Wicked Problems in Design Thinking." *Design Issues* 8, no. 2 (Spring 1992): 5–21.
Burgess, Ernest W. "The Growth of the City: An Introduction to a Research Project." In Park, Burgess, and McKenzie, *The City*, 47–62.
Butler, Judith. *Bodies That Matter: On the Discursive Limits of "Sex."* New York: Routledge, 1993.
——. *Precarious Life: The Powers of Mourning and Violence*. New York: Verso, 2004.
Butler, Judith, and Athena Athanasiou. *Dispossession: The Performative in the Political*. Malden: Polity Press, 2013.
Byrd, Jodi. *Transits of Empire: Indigenous Critiques of Colonialism*. Minneapolis: University of Minnesota Press, 2011.
Cacho, Lisa Marie. *Social Death: Racialized Rightlessness and the Criminalization of the Unprotected*. New York: New York University Press, 2012.
Camp, Jordan. *Incarcerating the Crisis: Freedom Struggles and the Rise of the Neoliberal State*. Berkeley: University of California Press, 2016.
Carby, Hazel V. "Policing the Black Woman's Body in an Urban Context." *Critical Inquiry* 18, no. 4 (1992): 738–55.
Cashin, Sheryll. "Localism, Self-Interest, and the Tyranny of the Favored Quarter: Addressing the Barriers to New Regionalism." *Georgetown Law Review* 88 (2000): 1985–2048.
——. "Middle-Class Black Suburbs and the State of Integration: A Post-integrationist Vision for Metropolitan America." *Cornell Law Review* 86 (2001): 729–76.

Castells, Manuel. *The Power of Identity*. Oxford: Blackwell Publishers, 1997.

Castells, Manuel, and Alan Sheridan. *The Urban Question: A Marxist Approach*. Oxford: Oxford University Press, 1981.

Césaire, Aimé. *Discourse on Colonialism*. Translated by Joan Pinkham. New York: Monthly Review Press, 2000. First published 1972.

Cheng, Wendy. "The Changs Next Door to the Diazes: Suburban Racial Formation in Los Angeles's San Gabriel Valley." *Journal of Urban History* 39, no. 1 (2012): 15–35.

Christian, Shirley. *Before Lewis and Clark: The Story of the Chouteaus, the French Dynasty That Ruled America's Frontier*. Lincoln: University of Nebraska Press, 2004.

Churchman, C. West. "Wicked Problems." *Management Science* 4, no. 14 (December 1967): B-141–42.

Clamorgan, Cyprian. *The Colored Aristocracy of St. Louis*. Edited by Julie Winch. Columbia: University of Missouri Press, 1999.

Cleary, Patricia. *The World, the Flesh, and the Devil: A History of Colonial St. Louis*. Columbia: University of Missouri Press, 2011.

Coates, Ta-Nehisi. "The Racist Housing Policies That Built Ferguson." *Atlantic*, October 17, 2014. http://www.theatlantic.com/business/archive/2014/10/the-racist-housing-policies-that-built-ferguson/381595/.

Cohen, Cathy J. "Deviance as Resistance: A New Research Agenda for the Study of Black Politics." *Du Bois Review* 1, no. 1 (2004): 27–45.

——. "Punks, Bulldaggers, and Welfare Queens: The Radical Potential of Queer Politics." *GLQ: A Journal of Lesbian & Gay Studies* 3 (1997): 437–65.

Cohn, Robert A. *The History and Growth of St. Louis County*. 6th ed. St. Louis: St. Louis County Office of Public Information, 1974.

Collins, Patricia Hill. *Black Feminist Thought: Knowledge, Consciousness, and the Politics of Empowerment*. Boston: Unwin Hyman, 1990.

Combahee River Collective. "The Combahee River Collective Statement." In *Home Girls: A Black Feminist Anthology*, edited by Barbara Smith, 264–74. New Brunswick, NJ: Rutgers University Press, 1983.

Comerio, Mary C. "Pruitt-Igoe and Other Stories." *Journal of Architectural Education* 34, no. 4 (1981): 26–31.

Cooper, Anna Julia. *A Voice from the South*. Mineola, NY: Dover Publications, 2016. First published 1892.

Cooper, Brittany. *Beyond Respectability: The Intellectual Thought of Race Women*. Urbana: University of Illinois, 2017.

Costa Vargas, João H. *The Denial of Antiblackness: Multiracial Redemption and Black Suffering*. Minneapolis: University of Minnesota Press, 2018.

Cox, Aimee Meredith. *Shapeshifters: Black Girls and the Choreography of Citizenship*. Durham, NC: Duke University Press, 2015.

Cox, Oliver C. *Caste, Class and Race: A Study in Social Dynamics*. New York: Monthly Review Press, 1959.

Crenshaw, Kimberlé. "Color Blindness, History and the Law." In *The House That Race Built*, edited by Wahneema Lubiano, 280–89. New York: Vintage Press, 1998.

Davis, Angela. "Masked Racism: Reflections on the Prison Industrial Complex." *Color Lines*, September 10, 1998.

——. *Women, Race, and Class*. New York: New Vintage Press, 1981.

Davis, Mike. *Beyond Blade Runner: Urban Control and the Ecology of Fear*. Vancouver: Open Media, 1992.

Day, Iyko. *Alien Capital: Asian Racialization and the Logic of Settler Colonial Capital*. Durham, NC: Duke University Press, 2016.

de Certeau, Michel. *The Practice of Everyday Life*. Translated by Steven Rendall. Berkeley: University of California Press, 1984.

Debord, Guy. *Society of the Spectacle*. Detroit, MI: Black and Red, 2010. First published 1967.

Deleuze, Gilles. *Negotiations, 1972–1990*. Translated by Martin Joughin. New York: Columbia University Press, 1995.

Derrida, Jacques. *Of Grammatology*. Translated by Gayatri Chakravorty. Baltimore, MD: Johns Hopkins University Press, 1974.

Dixon-Gottschild, Brenda. *The Black Dancing Body: A Geography from Coon to Cool*. New York: Palgrave Macmillan, 2003.

Drake, St. Clair. "Profiles: Chicago." *Journal of Educational Sociology* 17, no. 5 (January 1944): 261–71.

Drake, St. Clair, and Horace Cayton. *Black Metropolis: A Study of Negro Life in a Northern City*. Chicago: University of Chicago Press, 1945.

Du Bois, W. E. B. "The Concept of Race." In *Dusk of Dawn: An Essay toward an Autobiography of a Race Concept*. New Brunswick, NJ: Transaction, 2011. First published 1940.

——. "The Conservation of the Races." In *Oxford W. E. B. Du Bois Reader*, edited by Eric J. Sundquist, 38–47. Oxford: Oxford University Press, 1996. First published 1897.

——. *The Philadelphia Negro: A Social Study*. Philadelphia: University of Pennsylvania Press, 1996. First published 1899.

——. "The Talented Tenth." In *The Negro Problem: A Series of Articles by Representative American Negroes of To-day*, 33–75. New York: J. Pott, 1903.

Ellis, Nadia. *Territories of the Soul: Queered Belonging in the Black Diaspora*. Durham, NC: Duke University Press, 2015.

Escobar, Arturo. *Designs for the Pluriverse: Radical Interdependence, Autonomy, and the Making of Worlds*. Durham, NC: Duke University Press, 2017.

Esmonde, Jackie. "Criminalizing Poverty: The Criminal Law Power and the Safe Streets Act." *Journal of Law and Social Policy* 17 (2002): 63–86.

Essed, Philomena. "Everyday Racism." In *Race Critical Theories*, edited by Philomena Essed and David Theo Goldberg, 460–68. Oxford: Blackwell, 2000.

Eze, Emmanuel Chukwudi, ed. *Race and the Enlightenment: A Reader*. Malden, MA: Blackwell, 1999.

Fanon, Frantz. *Black Skin, White Mask*. Translated by Richard Philcox. New York: Grove Press, 2008. First published 1952.

——. *The Wretched of the Earth*. Translated by C. Farrington. New York: Grove Weidenfeld Press, 1991. First published 1961.

Fausz, J. Frederick. *Founding St. Louis: First City of the New West*. Charleston, SC: History Press, 2011.

Feagin, Joe, and Sean Elias. "Rethinking Racial Formation Theory: A Systemic Racism Critique." *Ethnic and Racial Studies* 36, no. 6 (2013): 931–60.

Ferguson, James, and Akhil Gupta. "Spatializing States: Toward an Ethnography of Neoliberal Governmentality." *American Ethnologist* 29, no. 4 (November 2002): 981–1002.

Ferguson, Roderick. *Aberrations in Black: Toward a Queer of Color Critique*. Minneapolis: University of Minnesota Press, 2003.

Ferriss, Lucy. *Unveiling the Prophet*. Columbia: University of Missouri Press, 2005.

Fleetwood, Nicole. "The Case of Rihanna: Erotic Violence and Black Female Desire." *African American Review* 45, no. 3 (2012): 419–35.

——. *Troubling Vision: Performance, Visuality, and Blackness*. Chicago: University of Chicago Press, 2011.

Foley, William E. "Slave Freedom Suits before Dred Scott: The Case of Marie Jean Scypion's Descendants." *Missouri Historical Review* 79, no. 1 (October 1984): 1–23.

Fornet-Betancourt, Raúl, Helmut Becker, Alfredo Gomez-Müller, and J. D. Gauthier. "The Ethic of Care for the Self as a Practice of Freedom: An Interview with Michel Foucault on January 20, 1984." *Philosophy & Social Criticism* 12, no. 2–3 (July 1987): 112–31.

Foucault, Michel. *The Archaeology of Knowledge, and the Discourse on Language*. Translated by Alan Sheridan Smith. New York: Pantheon, 1982.

——. *Discipline and Punish: The Birth of the Prison*. Translated by Alan Sheridan. New York: Vintage Press, 1995.

——. "The Ethics of the Concern for Self as a Practice of Freedom." *Ethics: Subjectivity and Truth*. Edited by Paul Rabinow. New York: New Press, 1998.

——. *Power/Knowledge: Selected Interviews and Other Writings, 1972–1977*. Edited by Colin Gordon. Translated by Colin Gordon, Leo Marshall, John Mepham, and Kate Soper. New York: Pantheon Books, 1980.

——. *The Punitive Society: Lectures at the Collège de France, 1972–73*. Edited by Bernard E. Harcourt. Translated by Graham Burchell. New York: Palgrave MacMillan, 2015.

——. *Society Must Be Defended: Lectures at the Collège de France, 1975–1976*. Edited by Mauro Bertani and Alessandro Fontana. Translated by David Macey. New York: Picador, 2003.

Frazier, E. Franklin. *The Negro Family in the United States*. Notre Dame, IN: University of Notre Dame, 1939.

——. "Negro Harlem: An Ecological Study." *American Journal of Sociology* 43, no. 1 (1937): 72–88.

Frazier, Harriet C. *Lynchings in Missouri, 1803–1981*. Jefferson, NC: McFarland, 2009.

——. *Slavery and Crime in Missouri, 1773–1865*. Jefferson, NC: McFarland, 2001.

Friesema, H. Paul. "Black Control of Central Cities: The Hollow Prize." *American Institute of Planners Journal* 35 (March 1969): 75–79.

Frug, Gerald, and David J. Barron. *City Bound: How States Stifle Urban Innovation*. Ithaca, NY: Cornell University Press, 2013.

Gans, Herbert. *The Levittowners*. New York: Columbia University Press, 1967.

Garb, Margaret. *City of American Dreams: A History of Home Ownership and Housing Reform in Chicago, 1871–1919*. Chicago: University of Chicago Press, 2005.

Gerteis, Louis S. *Civil War St. Louis*. Lawrence: University of Kansas Press, 2001.

Gill, McCune. *The St. Louis Story*. St. Louis: Historical Record Association, 1952.

Gilmore, Ruth Wilson. "Fatal Couplings of Power and Difference: Notes on Racism and Geography." *Professional Geographer* 54, no. 1 (February 2002): 15–24.

——. *Golden Gulag: Prisons, Surplus, Crisis, and Opposition in Globalizing California*. Berkeley: University of California Press, 2007.

Gilroy, Paul. *Darker than Blue: On the Moral Economies of Black Atlantic Culture*. London: Belknap Press, 2011.

——. *There Ain't No Black in the Union Jack: The Cultural Politics of Race and Nation*. Chicago: University of Chicago Press, 1987.

Goldberg, David Theo. "Racial States." In *A Companion to Racial and Ethnic Studies*, edited by David Theo Goldberg and John Solomos, 233–58. Malden, MA: Blackwell, 2002.

——. *The Threat of Race: Reflections on Racial Neoliberalism*. Oxford: Wiley-Blackwell, 2009.

Gordon, Avery. *Ghostly Matters: Haunting and the Sociological Imagination*. Minneapolis: University of Minnesota Press, 1997.

——. "Some Thoughts on Haunting and Futurity." *Borderlands* 10, no. 2 (2011): 1–21.

Gordon, Colin. *Mapping Decline: St. Louis and the Fate of the American City*. Philadelphia: University of Philadelphia Press, 2008.

Gotham, Kevin Fox. "Separate and Unequal: The Housing Act of 1968 and the Section 235 Program." *Sociological Forum* 15, no. 1 (2000): 13–37.

Gottdiener, Mark. "Politics and Planning: Suburban Case Studies." In *Remaking the City: Social Science Perspectives on Urban Design*, edited by John S. Pipkin, Mark La Gory, and Judith R. Blau, 310–33. Albany: State University of New York Press, 1983.

Gregory, Derek. *Geographical Imaginations*. Cambridge, MA: Wiley-Blackwell, 1994.

——. "Imaginative Geographies." *Progress in Human Geography* 19, no. 4 (1995): 447–85.

Gregory, Steven. *Black Corona: Race and the Politics of Place in an Urban Community*. Princeton, NJ: Princeton University Press, 1999.

Griffin, Farah Jasmine. "Black Feminists and Du Bois: Respectability, Protection, and Beyond." *Annals of the American Academy of Political and Social Science* 568, no. 1 (2000): 28–40.

Gustafson, Kaaryn. "The Criminalization of Poverty." *Journal of Criminal Law and Criminology* 99, no. 3 (2009): 643–716.

Habermas, Jürgen. *The Structural Transformation of the Public Sphere: An Inquiry into a Category of Bourgeois Society*. Translated by Thomas Burger with the assistance of Frederick Lawrence. Cambridge, MA: MIT Press, 1995.

Hall, Stuart. "Culture, Identity, and Diaspora." In *Colonial Discourse and Postcolonial Theory: A Reader*, edited by Patrick Williams and Laura Chrisman, 392–403. New York: Columbia University Press, 1994.

——. *The Fateful Triangle: Race, Ethnicity, Nation*. Edited by Kobena Mercer. Cambridge, MA: Harvard University Press, 2017.

——. "Representation, Meaning, and Language." In *Representation: Cultural Representations and Signifying Practices*, edited by Stuart Hall, Jessica Evans, and Sean Nixon, 15–64. Thousand Oaks, CA: Sage, 1997.

——. "Race, Articulation, and Societies Structured in Dominance." In *Sociological Theories: Race and Colonialism*, edited by M. O'Callaghan, 305–45. Paris: UNESCO, 1980.

Hall, Stuart, Chas Critcher, Tony Jefferson, John Clarke, and Brian Roberts. *Policing the Crisis: Mugging, the State and Law and Order*. London: Palgrave Macmillan, 2013. First published in 1978.

Hancock, Ange-Marie. *The Politics of Disgust: The Public Identity of the Welfare Queen*. New York: New York University Press, 2004.

Hanhardt, Christina. *Safe Space: Gay Neighborhood History and the Politics of Violence*. Durham, NC: Duke University Press, 2013.

Hardt, Michael, and Antonio Negri. *Commonwealth*. Cambridge, MA: Harvard University Press, 2009.

——. *Labor of Dionysus: A Critique of the State-Form*. Minneapolis: University of Minnesota Press, 1994.

Harney, Stephano and Fred Moton. *The Undercommons: Fugitive Planning & Black Study*. Brooklyn, NY: Autonomedia, 2013.

Harris, Cheryl. "Whiteness as Property." *Harvard Law Review* 106, no. 8 (1993): 1707–91.

Harris, Dianne. *Little White Houses: How the Postwar Home Constructed Race in America*. Minneapolis: University of Minnesota Press, 2013.

Harris, Nini. *A Most Unsettled State: First-Person Accounts of St. Louis During the Civil War*. St. Louis: Reedy Press, 2013.

Harrison, Faye. "The Persistent Power of 'Race' in the Cultural and Political Economy of Racism." *Annual Review of Anthropology* 24 (1995): 47–74.

Hartman, Saidiya. *Lose Your Mother: A Journey along the Atlantic Slave Route*. New York: Farrar, Straus and Giroux, 2008.

——. *Scenes of Subjection: Terror, Slavery, and Self-Making in Nineteenth-Century America*. New York: Oxford University Press, 1997.

——. *Venus in Two Acts*. Bloomington: Indiana University Press, 2008.

Harvey, David. *A Brief History of Neoliberalism*. Oxford: Oxford University Press, 2007.

——. "From Managerialism to Entrepreneurialism: The Transformation in Urban Governance in Late Capitalism." *Human Geography* 71, no. 1 (1989): 3–17.

——. *Justice, Nature and the Geography of Difference*. Malden, MA: Blackwell, 1996.

——. *Social Justice and the City*. London: Edward Arnold, 1973.

Haynes, Bruce. *Red Lines, Black Space: The Politics of Race and Space in a Black Middle-Class Suburb*. New Haven, CT: Yale University Press, 2006.

Hegel, Georg Wilhelm Friedrich. *The Philosophy of History*. Mineola, NY: Dover Publications, 1899.

Hernandez, Jesus. "Race, Market Constraints, and the Housing Crisis: A Problem of Embeddedness." *Kalfou: A Journal of Comparative and Relational Ethnic Studies* 1, no. 2 (2014): 29–58.

Hesse, Barnor. "Im/Plausible Deniability: Racism's Conceptual Double Bind." *Social Identities* 10, no. 1 (2004): 9–29.

Hillier, Amy. "Redlining and the Homeowners' Loan Corporation." *Journal of Urban History* 29, no. 4 (2003): 394–420.

Hinton, Elizabeth. *From the War on Poverty to the War on Crime: The Making of Mass Incarceration in America*. Cambridge, MA: Harvard University Press, 2016.

Hoehner, Christine, J. Rios, C. Garmendia, S. Baldwin, C. M. Kelly, D. M. Knights, C. Lesorogol, G. G. McClendon, and M. Tranel. "Page Avenue HIA: Building on Diverse Partnerships and Evidence to Promote a Healthy Community." *Health and Place* 18, no. 1 (January 2012): 85–95.

Holland, Sharon Patricia. *The Erotic Life of Racism*. Durham, NC: Duke University Press, 2012.

——. *Raising the Dead: Readings of Death and (Black) Subjectivity*. Durham, NC: Duke University Press, 2000.

hooks, bell. *Ain't I A Woman: Black Women and Feminism*. Boston: South End Press, 1981.

Hurston, Zora Neale. *I Love Myself When I'm Laughing and Then Again When I'm Looking Mean and Impressive*. New York: The Feminist Press at CUNY, 1979.

Irigaray, Luce. *An Ethics of Sexual Difference*. Ithaca, NY: Cornell University Press, 1993.

Jackson, Kenneth. *Crabgrass Frontier*. Oxford: Oxford University Press, 1987.

Jackson, Shona. "Risk, Blackness, and Postcolonial Studies: An Introduction." *Callaloo* 37, no. 1 (Winter 2014): 63–68.

James, David. "The Racial Ghetto as a Race-Making Situation: The Effects of Residential Segregation on Racial Inequalities and Racial Identity." *Law & Social Inquiry* 19, no. 2 (1994): 407–32.

Jameson, Fredric. *Postmodernism, or, The Cultural Logic of Late Capitalism*. Durham, NC: Duke University Press, 1992.

Johnson, E. Patrick. *Appropriating Blackness: Performance and the Politics of Authenticity*. Durham, NC: Duke University Press, 2003.

Johnson, Walter. "Ferguson's Fortune 500 Company," *Atlantic*, April 25, 2015.

——. *River of Dark Dreams: Slavery and Empire in the Cotton Kingdom*. Cambridge, MA: Harvard University Press, 2013.

——. "What Do We Mean When We Say, 'Structural Racism'?" *Kalfou: A Journal of Comparative and Relational Ethnic Studies* 3, no. 1 (2016): 36–62.

Jones, E. Terrence. *Fragmented by Design: Why St. Louis Has So Many Governments*. St. Louis: Palmerston and Reed, 2000.

——. "The Municipal Market in the St. Louis Region: 1950–2000." In *St. Louis Metromorphosis: Past Trends and Future Directions*, edited by B. Baybeck and E. T. Jones 275–92. St. Louis: Missouri Historical Society Press, 2004.

Jones, J. Christopher. *Design Methods: Seeds of Human Futures*. New York: John Wiley & Sons, 1981. First published 1970.

Keckley, Elizabeth. *Behind the Scenes: Or, Thirty Years a Slave and Four Years in the White House*. Rockville, MD: Wildside Press, 2015. First published 1868.

Keith, Michael. *After the Cosmopolitan?: Multicultural Cities and the Future of Racism*. New York: Routledge, 2005.

Kelley, Robin D. G. *Freedom Dreams: The Black Radical Imagination*. Boston: Beacon Press, 2002.

Kelling, George, and James Q. Wilson. "Broken Windows: The Police and Neighborhood Safety." *Atlantic*, March 1982, 29–38.

King, Tiffany Lethabo. "Humans Involved: Lurking in the Lines of Posthumanist Flight." *Critical Ethnic Studies* 3, no. 1 (2017): 162–85.

——. "One Strike Evictions, State Space and the Production of Abject Black Female Bodies," *Critical Sociology* 36, no. 1 (2010): 45–64.

Kremer, Gary R. *Race and Meaning: The African American Experience in Missouri*. Columbia: University of Missouri Press, 2014.

Lang, Clarence. "Between Civil Rights and Black Power in the Gateway City: The Action Committee to Improve Opportunities for Negroes (ACTION), 1964–74." *Journal of Social History* 37, no. 3 (March 2004): 725–54.

——. *Grassroots at the Gateway: Class Politics and Black Freedom Struggle in St. Louis 1936–1975*. Ann Arbor: University of Michigan Press, 2009. Lassiter, Matthew, and Christopher Niedt. "Suburban Diversity in Postwar America." Introduction to special issue, *Journal of Urban History* 39, no. 1 (2013): 3–14.

Latour, Bruno. *Reassembling the Social: An Introduction to Actor-Network-Theory*. Oxford: Oxford University Press, 2007.

Lauer, T. E. "Prolegomenon to Municipal Court Reform in Missouri." *Missouri Law Review* 31, no. 1 (Winter 1966): 69–97.

Lefebvre, Henri. *The Production of Space*. Translated by Donald Nicholson-Smith. Malden, MA: Wiley-Blackwell, 1992.

Lepecki, André. "Choreopolice and Choreopolitics: Or, the Task of the Dancer." *TDR: The Drama Review* 57, no. 4 (Winter 2013): 13–27.

Lewis, Tyson E. "But I'm Not a Racist! Phenomenology, Racism, and the Body Schema in White, Pre-service Teacher Education." *Race, Ethnicity and Education* 29 (June 2016): 1–14.

Lipsitz, George. *How Racism Takes Place*. Philadelphia: Temple University Press, 2011.

——. *A Life in the Struggle: Ivory Perry and the Culture of Opposition*. Philadelphia: Temple University Press, 1988.

———. *The Possessive Investment in Whiteness: How White People Benefit from Identity Politics*. Philadelphia: Temple University Press, 2006.

———. *The Sidewalks of St. Louis: Places, People, and Politics in an American City*. Columbia: University of Missouri, 1991.

Logan, John R., and Harvey L. Molotch. *Urban Fortunes: The Political Economy of Place*. Berkeley: University of California Press, 1987.

Lorde, Audre. *Sister Outsider: Essays and Speeches by Audre Lorde*. Berkeley, CA: Crossing Press, 2007.

———. "The Master's Tools Will Never Dismantle the Master's House." In *This Bridge Called My Back: Writings by Radical Women of Color*, edited by Cherríe Moraga and Gloria Anzaldúa 94–103. New York: Kitchen Table, 1983.

Louridas, Panagiotis. "Design as Bricolage: Anthropology Meets Design Thinking." *Design Studies* 20, no. 6 (October 1999): 517–35.

Low, Setha. *Behind the Gates: Life, Security, and the Pursuit of Happiness in Fortress America*. Milton Park, UK: Taylor and Francis, 2003.

Lumpkins, Charles. *American Pogrom: The East St. Louis Race Riot and Black Politics*. Athens: Ohio University Press, 2008.

Mamdani, Mahmood. *Saviors and Survivors: Darfur, Politics, and the War on Terror*. New York: Doubleday, 2009.

Massey, Douglas S., Jacob S. Rugh, Justin P. Steil, and Len Albright. "Riding the Stagecoach to Hell: A Qualitative Analysis of Racial Discrimination in Mortgage Lending." *City & Community* 15, no. 2 (June 2016): 118–36.

Massey, Douglas S. and Nancy A. Dentin. *American Apartheid: Segregation and the Making of the Underclass*. Cambridge, MA: Harvard University Press, 1998.

Mbembe, Achille. *Critique of Black Reason*. Translated by Laurent Dubois. Durham, NC: Duke University Press, 2017.

———. "Necropolitics." Translated by Libby Meintjes. *Public Culture* 15, no. 1 (2003): 11–40.

———. "Provisional Notes on the Postcolony." *Journal of the International African Institute* 62, no. 1 (1992): 3–37.

McClintock, Anne. *Imperial Leather: Race, Gender, and Sexuality in the Colonial Contest*. New York: Routledge, 1995.

McDermott, John Francis. "The Myth of the 'Imbecile Governor': Captain Fernando de Leyba and the Defense of St. Louis in 1780." In McDermott, *The Spanish in the Mississippi Valley*, 314–405.

———, ed. *The Spanish in the Mississippi Valley, 1762–1804*. Edwardsville: Southern Illinois University Press, 1974.

McKittrick, Katherine. *Demonic Grounds: Black Women and the Cartographies of Struggle*. Minneapolis: University of Minnesota Press, 2006.

———, ed. *Sylvia Wynter: On Being Human as Praxis*. Durham, NC: Duke University Press, 2015.

Melamed, Jodi. *Represent and Destroy: Rationalizing Violence in the New Racial Capitalism*. Minneapolis: University of Minnesota Press, 2011.

Merleau-Ponty, Maurice. *Phenomenology of Perception*. Translated by Colin Smith. New York: Routledge, 2002.

Mirzoeff, Nicholas. *The Right to Look: A Counterhistory of Visuality*. Durham, NC: Duke University Press, 2011.

Moore, Donald S. *Suffering for Territory: Race, Place, and Power in Zimbabwe*. Durham, NC: Duke University Press, 2005.

Morris, Rosalind C. "All Made Up: Performance Theory and the New Anthropology of Sex and Gender." *Annual Review of Anthropology* 24, no. 1 (1995): 567–92.

Moten, Fred. "Blackness and Nothingness: (Mysticism in the Flesh)." *South Atlantic Quarterly* 112, no. 4 (Fall 2013): 737–80.

Mumford, Lewis. "What Is a City?" In *The City Reader*, edited by Richard T. LeGates and Frederick Stout, 183–96. New York: Routledge, 1996. First published 1937.

Muñoz, José Esteban. *Cruising Utopia: The Then and There of Queer Futurity*. New York: New York University Press, 2009.

Murakawa, Naomi. *The First Civil Right: How Liberals Built Prison America*. Oxford: Oxford University Press, 2016.

Murphy, Alexandra K. "The Suburban Ghetto: The Legacy of Herbert Gans in Understanding the Experience of Poverty in Recently Impoverished American Suburbs." *City & Community* 6, no. 1 (March 2007): 21–37.

Nash, Jennifer C. "Practicing Love: Black Feminism, Love-Politics, and Post-intersectionality." *Meridians* 11, no. 2 (2011): 1–24.

Nixon, Rob. *Slow Violence and the Environmentalism of the Poor*. Cambridge, MA: Harvard University Press, 2011.

Nopper, Tamara K. "Strangers to the Economy: Black Work and the Wages of Non-blackness." In Saucier and Woods, *Conceptual Aphasia in Black*, 87–102.

Norwood, Kimberly Jade. "Minnie Liddell's Forty-Year Quest for Quality Public Education Remains a Dream Deferred." *Washington University Journal of Law and Policy* 40 (2012): 1–66.

Ocen, Priscilla A. "The New Racially Restrictive Covenant: Race, Welfare, and the Policing of Black Women in Subsidized Housing." *UCLA Law Review* 59 (2012): 1540–82.

Omi, Michael, and Howard Winant. *Racial Formation in the United States: From the 1960's to the 1980's*. New York: Routledge, 1995.

Ong, Aihwa. "Cultural Citizenship as Subject Making: Immigrants Negotiate Racial and Cultural Boundaries in the United States." In *Race, Identity, and Citizenship: A Reader*, edited by Rodolfo Torres, Louis F. Miron, and Jonathan X. Inda. Malden, MA: Wiley-Blackwell, 1999.

Orff, Annie L. Y. "From City to Suburb: A Glimpse of the Beautiful Spot in the Shadow of St. Louis." *Chaperone Magazine* (1893): 69–71.

Park, Robert E., Ernest W. Burgess, and Roderick D. McKenzie. *The City: Suggestions for Investigation of Human Behavior in the Urban Environment*. Chicago: Chicago University Press, 1925.

Patterson, Orlando. *Slavery and Social Death: A Comparative Study*. Cambridge, MA: Harvard University Press, 1982.

Peterson, Charles E. *Colonial St. Louis: Building a Creole Capital*. Tucson, AZ: Patrice Press, 1993.

Platt, Anthony M. *E. Franklin Frazier Reconsidered*. New Brunswick, NJ: Rutgers University Press, 1991.

Ranciére, Jacques. *The Politics of Aesthetics: The Distribution of the Sensible*. Translated by Gabriel Rockhill. London: Continuum, 2004.

Reddy, Chandan. *Freedom with Violence: Race, Sexuality, and the US State*. Durham, NC: Duke University Press, 2011.

Rios, Jodi. "Everyday Racialization: Contesting Space and Identity in Suburban St. Louis." In *Making Suburbia: New Histories of Everyday America*, edited by John Archer, Paul J. P. Sandul, and Katherine Solomonson, 185–207. Ann Arbor: University of Michigan Press, 2015.

——. "Flesh in the Street." *Kalfou* 3, no. 1 (2016): 63–78.

——. "Reconsidering the Margin: Relationships of Difference and Transformative Education." In *Service-Learning in Design and Planning: Educating at the*

Boundaries, edited by Tom Agnotti, Cheryl Doble, and Paula Horrigan, 39–54. Oakland, CA: New Village Press, 2011.

Roberts, Rosemarie A. "Dancing with Social Ghosts: Performing Embodiments, Analyzing Critically." *Transforming Anthropology* 21, no. 1 (2013): 4–14.

Robinson, Cedric J. *Black Marxism: The Making of the Black Radical Tradition*. Chapel Hill: University of North Carolina Press, 2000. First published 1983.

Rodriguez, Juana Maria. *Sexual Futures, Queer Gestures, and Other Latina Longings*. New York: New York University Press, 2014.

Roediger, David. *The Wages of Whiteness: Race and the Making of the American Working Class*. New York: Verso, 1991.

——. *Working toward Whiteness: How America's Immigrants Became White*. New York: Basic Books, 2006.

Rose, Harold M. "The All-Negro Town: Its Evolution and Function." In *Black America: Geographic Perspectives*, edited by Robert Ernst and Lawrence Hugg, 352–67. Garden City, NY: Anchor Press, 1976.

Rylander, Anne. "Design Thinking as Knowledge Work: Epistemological Foundations and Practical Implications." *Design Management Journal* 4, no. 1 (Fall 2009): 7–19.

Said, Edward. *Orientalism*. New York: Vintage Books, 1979.

Salsich, Peter W., Jr., and Samantha Caluori. "Can St. Louis City and County Get Back Together? (Do Municipal Boundaries Matter Today?)." *St. Louis University Public Law Review* 34, no. 13 (2014): 13–50.

Sandweiss, Eric. *St. Louis: The Evolution of an American Urban Landscape*. Philadelphia: Temple University Press, 2001.

Sandweiss, Lee Ann, ed. *Seeking St. Louis: Voices from a River City, 1670–2000*. St. Louis: Missouri Historical Society Press, 2000.

Saucier, P. Khalil, and Tryon P. Woods. *Conceptual Aphasia in Black: Displacing Racial Formation*. Lanham, MD: Lexington Books, 2016.

——. "Racial Optimism and the Drag of Thymotics." In Saucier and Woods, *Conceptual Aphasia in Black*, 1–34.

Schmandt, Henry J. "Municipal Home Rule in Missouri." *Washington University Law Quarterly* 4 (1953): 385–412.

Scott, David. *Conscripts of Modernity*. Durham, NC: Duke University Press, 2004.

Seematter, Mary E. "Trials and Confessions: Race and Justice in Antebellum St. Louis." *Gateway Heritage* 12 (1991): 36–47.

Self, Robert O. *American Babylon: Race and the Struggle for Postwar Oakland*. Princeton, NJ: Princeton University Press, 2003.

Sexton, Jared. *Antiblackness and the Critique of Multiracialism*. Minneapolis: University of Minnesota Press, 2008.

——. "The Vel of Slavery: Tracking the Figure of the Unsovereign." *Critical Sociology* 42, nos. 4–5 (2014): 583–97.

Shabazz, Rashad. *Spatializing Blackness: Architectures of Confinement and Black Masculinity in Chicago*. Urbana: University of Illinois Press, 2015.

Sharpe, Christina. *Monstrous Intimacies: Making Post-slavery Subjects*. Durham, NC: Duke University Press, 2009.

——. *In the Wake: On Blackness and Being*. Durham, NC: Duke University Press, 2016.

Simone, AbdouMaliq. *For the City Yet to Come: Changing African Life in Four Cities*. Durham, NC: Duke University Press, 2004.

Smith, Neil. *The Urban Frontier: Gentrification and the Revanchist City*. New York: Routledge, 1996.

Soja, Edward. *Postmodern Geographies: The Reassertion of Space in Critical Social Theory*. London: Verso Press, 1989.

Spillers, Hortense. "Mama's Baby, Papa's Maybe: An American Grammar Book." *Diacritics* 17, no. 2 (Summer 1987): 65–81.

Spivak, Gayatri. *In Other Worlds: Essays in Cultural Politics*. York, UK: Methuen Books, 1987.

Stoddard, Amos. *Sketches of Louisiana: Historical and Descriptive*. Carlisle, MA: Applewood Books, 2010. First published 1812.

Stuart, Guy. *Discriminating Risk: The U.S. Mortgage Lending Industry in the 20th Century*. Ithaca, NY: Cornell University Press, 2003.

Sutker, Solomon, and Sara Smith Sutker. *Racial Transition in the Inner Suburb: Studies of the St. Louis Area*. New York: Praeger Press, 1974.

Taylor, Ula Y. "Making Waves: The Theory and Practice of Black Feminism." *Black Scholar* 28, no. 2 (Summer 1998): 18–28.

——. *The Veiled Garvey: The Life and Times of Amy Jacques Garvey*. Chapel Hill: University of North Carolina Press, 2003.

Thiong'o, Ngũgĩ wa. *Decolonizing the Mind: The Politics of Language in African Literature*. Portsmouth, NH: Heinemann Press, 1987.

Thomas, Deborah. *Modern Blackness: Nationalism, Globalization, and the Politics of Culture in Jamaica*. Durham, NC: Duke University Press, 2004.

Thomas, James. "Affect and the Sociology of Race: A Program for Critical Inquiry." *Ethnicities* 14, no. 1 (February 2014): 72–90.

Thomas, William L. *The History of St. Louis County Missouri: The Story Told 100 Years Ago*. Clayton, MO: County Living, 2011. First published 1812.

Thompson, Edgar T. "The Plantation as a Race-Making Situation." In *Plantation Societies, Race Relations, and the South: The Regimentation of Populations. Selected Papers of Edgar T. Thompson*. Durham, NC: Duke University Press, 1975.

Thompson, Heather Ann. *Whose Detroit?: Politics, Labor, and Race in a Modern American City*. Ithaca, NY: Cornell University Press, 2004.

Tiebout, Charles. "A Pure Theory of Local Expenditures." *Journal of Political Economy* 64, no. 5 (October 1956): 416–24.

Trogdon, Jo Ann. *The Unknown Travels and Dubious Pursuits of William Clark*. Columbia: University of Missouri, 2015.

Tuck, Eve, and Christine Ree. "A Glossary of Haunting." In *Handbook of Autoethnography*, edited by Stacy Holman Jones, Tony E. Adams, and Carolyn Ellis, 639–58. Walnut Creek, CA: Left Coast, 2013.

Tuttle, Brad. "Suburban Ghetto: Poverty Rates Soar in the Suburbs." *Time*, September 26, 2011.

US Department of Justice, Civil Rights Division. *The Ferguson Report: Department of Justice Investigation of the Ferguson Police Department*. New York: New Press, 2015.

Wacquant, Loïc. "A Janus-Faced Institution of Ethnoracial Closure: A Sociological Specification of the Ghetto." In *The Ghetto: Contemporary Global Issues and Controversies*, edited by Ray Hutchison and Bruce D. Haynes, 1–32. Boulder, CO: Westview Press, 2012.

Ware, Vron. *Beyond the Pale: White Women, Racism, and History*. New York, Verso, 1992.

Warner, Michael. "Fear of a Queer Planet." *Social Text* 29 (1991): 3–17.

——. *Publics and Counter Publics*. New York: Zone Books, 2005.

Weaver, Robert. *The Negro Ghetto*. New York: Harcourt, Brace, 1948.

Weheliye, Alex. *Habeas Viscus: Racializing Assemblages, Biopolitics, and Black Feminist Theories of the Human*. Durham, NC: Duke University Press, 2014.

Wiese, Andrew. *Places of Their Own: African American Suburbanization in the Twentieth Century*. Chicago: University of Chicago Press, 2005.

Wiggins, Mary Jo. "Race, Class, and Suburbia: The Modern Black Suburb as a 'Race-Making Situation.'" *University of Michigan Journal of Legal Reform* 35 (2001–2): 749–808.

Wilderson, Frank B., III. "The Prison Slave as Hegemony's (Silent) Scandal." *Social Justice* 30, no. 2 (2003): 18–27.

Williams, Patricia J. *The Alchemy of Race and Rights*. Cambridge, MA: Harvard University Press, 1992.

Wilson, Bobby M. *America's Johannesburg: Industrialization and Racial Transformation in Birmingham*. Athens: University of Georgia Press, 2019. First published 2000.

Wilson, William Julius. *The Truly Disadvantaged: The Inner City, Underclass, and Public Policy*. Chicago: University of Chicago Press, 1987.

Winch, Julie. *The Clamorgans: One Family's History of Race in America*. New York: Hill and Wang, 2011.

Wirth, Louis. *The Ghetto*. Chicago: University of Chicago Press, 1928.

——. "Urbanism as a Way of Life." *American Journal of Sociology* 44, no. 1 (1938): 1–24.

Wolcott, Victoria. *Remaking Respectability: African American Women in Interwar Detroit*. Chapel Hill: University of North Carolina Press, 2001.

Wright, Gwendolyn. *Building the Dream: A Social History of Housing in America*. Boston: MIT Press, 1983.

Wright, John A., Sr. *Kinloch: Missouri's First Black City*. Charleston, SC: Arcadia, 2000.

——. *St. Louis: Disappearing Black Communities*. Charleston, SC: Arcadia, 2004.

Wynter, Sylvia. "Unsettling the Coloniality of Being/Power/Truth/Freedom: Towards the Human, after Man, Its Overrepresentation—an Argument." *CR: The New Centennial Review* 3, no. 3 (2003): 257–337.

Index

Page numbers in italic refer to figures and tables.